FORGOTTEN COVENANT

R.L. WATSON

Ark House Press
PO Box 1722, Port Orchard, WA 98366 USA
PO Box 1321, Mona Vale NSW 1660 Australia
PO Box 318 334, West Harbour, Auckland 0661 New Zealand
arkhousepress.com

© R.L. Watson 2021

Unless otherwise stated, all Scripture quotations are from the ESV® Bible (The Holy Bible, English Standard Version®), copyright © 2001 by Crossway, a publishing ministry of Good News Publishers. Used by permission. All rights reserved.

Cataloguing in Publication Data:
Title: Forgotten Covenant
ISBN: 978-0-6451417-9-5 (pbk)
Subjects: Biblical Resource; Bible Commentary; Bible Study: Covenant;
Other Authors/Contributors: Watson, R.L

Design by initiateagency.com

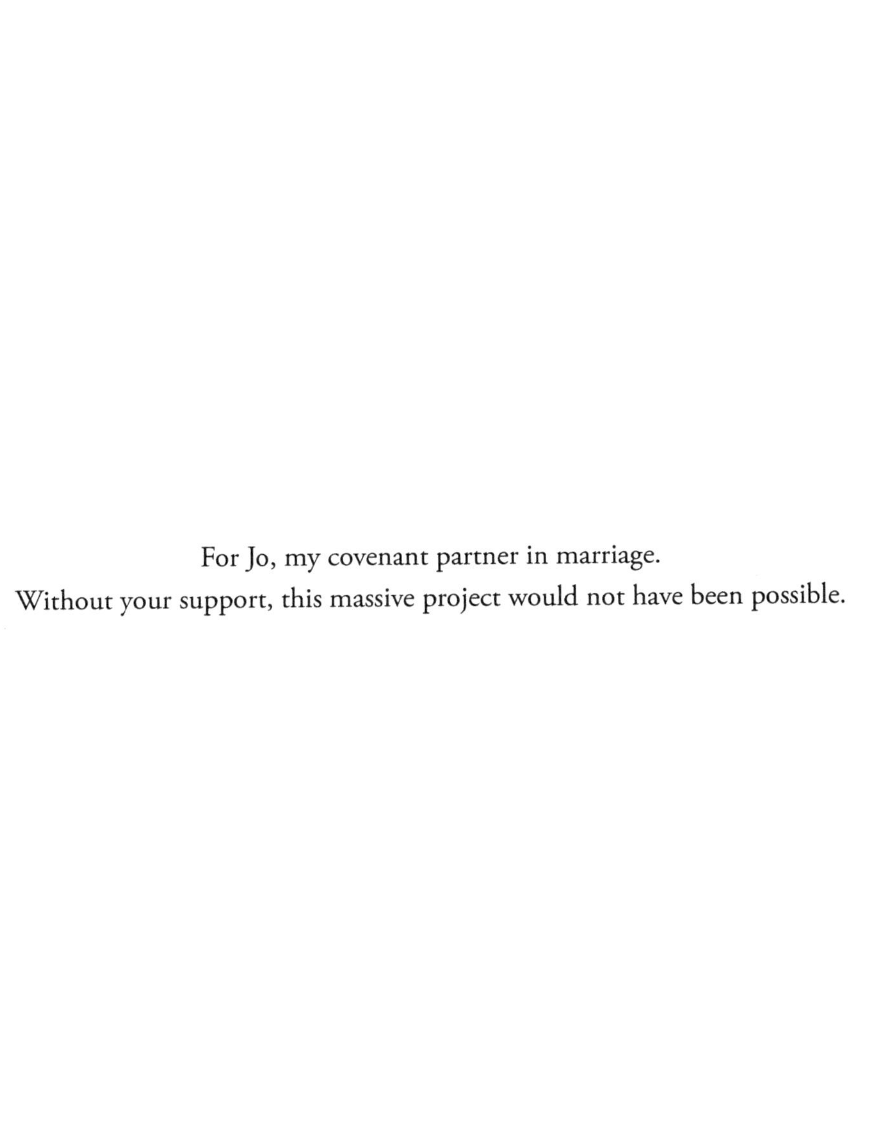

For Jo, my covenant partner in marriage.

Without your support, this massive project would not have been possible.

CONTENTS

Part II – THE TANAKH

Part III – THE MESSIAH

Part IV – THE CONCLUSION

INTRODUCTION

"Reality is not a function of the event as event, but of the relationship of that event to past, and future, events"[1]

No historical event occurs in a vacuum. No king will reign, no war will rage, and no cultural shift will transpire independent of the forces of the surrounding context. Past events, emerging attitudes and beliefs, natural disasters, political edicts, and economic changes are all intertwined.

Consider how much the world changed on 9/11. For the modern Western world, September 11, 2001, is the new 0AD, the dividing point of modern history. From that time, there was a notable change in the themes and content of our entertainment. And no, I am not simply referring to having to re-film the New York skyline for establishing shots. In the months following the attack, there was a focus on producing more family-friendly films. But soon after, there was an emergence of somewhat more historical, patriotic films with the themes of war that demonstrate the 'American

1 Warren, R. *All the King's Men.* p.578

Spirit', such as *Blackhawk Down* (2001) and *We Were Soldiers* (2002), and films that address the anxiety of personal security like *Panic Room* (2002).[2]

Religious attitudes also began to change and become more polarised. Alongside a revived seeking after God, there was also a growth in negative attitudes towards religion that were being promoted, somewhat successfully, by 'leaders' of the New Atheist movement such as Dawkins and Hitchens. Their message was 'religion is the cause of all the world's problems'. This triggered, I believe, the decline of the "mushy middle."[3] The ongoing wars in Afghanistan and Iraq continue to shape economics through investment in warfare and the impact of displaced people. And the emphasis on and development of stringent security measures in airports, boat terminals, and government buildings is still experienced by travellers today. For a time, there was a deepened trust in conservative politics in the US. But now, because of how the Bush administration responded to the attack with the controversial war in Iraq, many have become disillusioned.

Rewind 500 years and consider how the changing world made the Reformation possible: the emergence of nationalism and the middle class, developments in technology such as the printing press, and the growing corruption of the Roman Catholic Church. All these factors are what made the Reformation possible and successful. In historiographic terms, these connections are referred to as cause and effect. And considering the historical reality of Christianity, we can apply this concept when understanding and interpreting parts of the Bible. In fact, it was the discovery of how intertwining contexts brought about different events and attitudes in Scripture that inspired my love of history.

---

2 Markovitz, J. "Reel Terror Post 9/11." *Film and Television after 9/11*. p.215-221

3 Nominal Christians who would identify as Christians and come to church sporadically. (Keller, T. "Dr. Timothy Keller at the March 2013 Faith Angle Forum.")

I caught the 'history bug' while studying my Master of Arts in Theology when I took a course called 'The New Testament in Context', led predominantly by author Bruce Winter. In it, we examined the historical context of the events and details of the New Testament. For example, how the *parousia*[4] was a reference to the visiting Caesar, and how the practice of reciprocation and patronage explains why Paul refused to be paid by the Corinthians.[5] There was something in these discoveries and connections that excited me, and I just had to learn more. More than that, it gave me the tools and skills to better understand and interpret the Bible and to make sense of and recognise idiomatic phrases and customs of the day.

The words of Scripture sit in a tension between divine and human authorship. Although they are universally true and divinely inspired, they are also a product of the culture in which they were written. More than that, since the Bible tells a historical narrative, the events of any one part have been influenced and shaped by what has come before. Consequently, it is important that we remember that the Bible was not birthed with the writing of the Gospel of Matthew. Jesus was a true historical figure, and therefore his emergence, identity, and ministry did not pop into existence in a vacuum. For millennia, God was preparing the world for the one promised in Genesis 3 who would 'crush the serpent's head.' He was revealing His character, nature, and purposes to humanity long before the angel appeared to Mary and Joseph. Rather than the beginning, the birth of Christ can be best labelled as what in literary terms is referred to as the *climax*, or *turning point,* of the one singular narrative that is The Bible. And if we are to understand this point in the story, and the goals and purposes of our protagonist, God, who entered the world in human flesh, we need

4 The second coming of Christ

5 2Cor 11:9

to consider what has come before. When reading *The Outsiders* by S.E Hinton, we can't just jump to the moment of the big brawl between the Greasers and the Socs and expect to understand why they're fighting or who Ponyboy is. Nor can someone commence reading *Wuthering Heights* at chapter 34 and expect to understand Heathcliff's state of mind. Thus, the Old Testament is crucial for understanding the New Testament and we do both a disservice by separating them from one another.

Unfortunately, the connotations behind the designators of *old* and *new* suggest a stronger division in the story than there really is, and this is the view of a number of followers of Christ. For some, the Old Testament is irrelevant and unnecessary for Christians, something we need to 'unhitch' from. This position is a clear departure from Paul's words in 2 Timothy 3:16-17 that "all scripture is… profitable for… training in righteousness, that the man of God may be complete…" And Scripture, in the minds of believers in Paul's day most certainly included, if not exclusively, the Old Testament. The people who hold to this view are those who read their bibles as though the blank page between the Old and the New Testament is a thick piece of lead to make sure the division is clear and to prevent any accidental contamination. They acknowledge its divine authorship, but it is nothing more than a helpful prequel to the New Testament. As N.T Wright aptly describes, for them the Old Testament and the story of Israel exists and functions merely as some allegorical, figurative backdrop to the New Testament narrative, serving no greater purpose than providing proof-texts and 'shadows' of Jesus.[6] Although many people, deeds, and institutions within the Old Testament do serve as foreshadows that point the reader to Christ, it does so in a real and concrete way. Real promises and real prophesies were made in real history to real people in the Law, Prophets,

6 Wright, N.T, *Justification: God's Plan and Paul's Vision.* loc 156.

and Writings - or as the Jews refer to their scriptures, the *Tanakh*[7] – that were really fulfilled in the real person of Christ. More than that, these writings contain God's actual outworking of His divine plan. It wasn't as though God made a promise and waited thousands of years to do anything about it. Rather, through their fulfilment, God had begun to make His will and character known to humanity, making the Tanakh more than a mere ancient "*Where's Jesus?*" book for us to find Christ hiding behind every rock and priest on every page. And if the Old Testament had no doctrinal compatibility or relevance to the New Testament, then why did its authors use it so often to define and describe their theology? For this reason, it is clear that a real continuity between 'the Old' and 'the New' exists, and thus making these designators flawed titles.

That the designators Old and New Testament as a division of scripture is misleading can also be seen in the way that they were created after the writing of the New Testament. The earliest recorded mention of a collection of books of scripture being called the Old Testament is from Melito of Sardis, who lived at the end of the second century.[8] Although it appears that the term was in use before the writing of his letter to Onesimus, the absence of usage prior to this suggests it was a recent creation.

This division of old and new seems to have begun with a conflation between covenants and canon. The word 'testament' comes from the Latin *testamentum,* which was a written, legal agreement, most commonly taking the form of wills.[9] This comes from the word *testor,* which means 'I invoke as witness, solemnly declare', and *instrumentum*, or instruction. Thus, in a sense, testaments were a kind of covenant. So, when Jerome translated the Bible into Latin in the fourth century and called the divisions old and new

---

7 A contraction of *Torah* (Law), *Nevi'im* (prophets), and *Ketuvim* (writings).

8 Eus. *Ecc Hist.* 4.26.13-14

9 Jones, P. *Quid Pro Quo: What the Romans really gave the English Language.* p.94-95

testament, he was effectively saying that the first was the 'Old Covenant' and the second is the 'New Covenant.' This is also reflected in Melito's writing as the Greek he used for Testament, is the same as the Greek for covenant.[10]

To say that the 'Old Testament' is the Old Covenant is flawed for a number of reasons. Firstly, what we know as the Old Testament actually contains multiple covenants,[11] so which one are they referring to? Secondly, the words 'old' and 'new' had become loaded terms by this time. For Clement of Alexandria, who wrote around the time of Melito, the old is for the Jews who do not know God properly and worship Him in inferior ways, but the new is for 'us', the Gentiles, who worship in the new, true and better ways.[12] Moreover, the growing animosity towards the Jews during this period and a desire for Gentile Christians to separate themselves from anything that appears 'Jewish'[13], meant that this designation of the first 39 books of the Bible as The Old Covenant is to effectively say 'those books are for those terrible Jews' and thus declare them irrelevant and inferior. And thirdly, a covenant is not a collection of books, nor is it a period of time; it is an eternal and unchangeable promise of God. As Martin Luther explains in his commentary on Galatians, "The word testament[14] is another name for the promise that God made unto Abraham... A testament is not a law, but an inheritance."[15] Although the Old Testament, as noted earlier, contains the record of multiple covenants, and the New Testament contains the events that established the New Covenant and are faithful testimonies of those

---

10 Gk: *diatheke*. E.g. Lk 22:20

11 Covenants were made with Adam, Noah, Abraham, Moses, David.

12 Clem. *Strom.* 6.5

13 E.g. Justin Martyr, *Dialogue with Trypho.* 18

14 The word for covenant Luther would be familiar with from the Latin Vulgate in Galatians 3:15

15 Luther, M. *Commentary on the Epistle to the Galatians.* p.86

promises, the books themselves are not the covenants. They are an account of His faithfulness to His promises.

So, considering the meaning of Testament, the definition of a covenant, and the time in which these titles appeared, the designators Old and New Testament are anachronistic and arbitrary designators that reinforce an unnecessary division, and not biblical categories. Thus, it is more accurate to refer to the Old as the Tanakh, and the New as the Apostolic Scriptures. Therefore, if the books of Genesis through to Malachi aren't a covenant, and if they contain promises that are fulfilled between Matthew and Revelation,[16] it doesn't make sense to separate them and call the first redundant and old. In fact, it makes more sense to say that they are quite interrelated.

Consider a story of a hero who vows to seek vengeance against an enemy, much like Beowulf and the monster Grendel. Would we call those first few chapters irrelevant to the conclusion of the story when the enemy is defeated? Can one say, 'all we need is the final chapters of the book'? Surely not. No one would read a book or watch a film or play and make such a definitive division between oath and fulfilment. On the contrary, the beginning makes the story more meaningful because it shows the hero has the qualities required to achieve their goals and purposes. We would consider the outcome and promise as two sides of the same coin. Although they could be divided, any division would be superficial. How much more should we consider the promises made by God in the Tanakh, and their fulfilment in the person and work of Jesus as recorded in the Apostolic Scriptures, as two parts of the same story. The implication of this is that since we participate in that story, all the events recorded in Scripture leading

16 The outworking of many promises does begin in the Tanakh, however to a more significant extent in the Apostolic Scriptures, albeit not completely until the consummation of creation.

up to the fulfilment of God's promises in the person of Christ, are as much a part of *our* history and heritage as they were for those who experienced them.

There are some Christians today who might see the origins of their entrance into God's story as happening almost *ex nihilo*[17] in the first century. As though Jesus merely popped into history and by his death saved sinners, and by their faith in Him are able to join God's family. Such an understanding strips the person and work of Christ from its theological background and historical context which was the approximate four millennia that preceded Him. Although, if asked, they would still affirm the significance of the Tanakh to understanding the coming of the promised Messiah, they would just not see it as having much relevance to them. Nonetheless, this approach still means that the historical context has been isolated. They might be aware of their redemption as a fulfilment of the promise made to the woman in Genesis 3 as deliverance from the fall, and other various prophecies made throughout Scripture. However, a number may not see their faith, forgiveness, and adoption as a fulfilment of the promise made to Abraham. If they do, it is in an abstract and figurative sense. For example, Abraham had a promised son and Jesus was a promised son. But as I hinted at above, and as I will argue in this book, we enter into God's story as a fulfilment of the Abrahamic covenant in a very real way.

The purpose of the calling of Abraham was not to simply give a typological foreshadowing, or even a good moralistic example, of faith, nor was it a means-to-an-end to merely to create an Israel from which Jesus was to be born. The calling of Abraham was to establish a people of faith, who would become known as Israel, of whom Christ would be the head, and by our faith in Christ, we would join this 'family' and covenant. This is the

17 Latin: Out of nothing.

narrative that unites the 'old' and the 'new'. This is the forgotten covenant. Consider the significant time given in Scripture to the story of Abraham and the use of repetition throughout the Bible to emphasise the importance and significance of the promise made to him by God. Think about how the ongoing narrative is shaped by the way God acts in faithfulness towards Abraham's descendants based on this promise. And this is not merely from Genesis to Malachi, but also, as the authors of the Apostolic Scriptures often state, right through the emergence and ministry of Christ, and the going out of the Gospel to the nations. As Lasor explains: "The salvation promised Abraham will ultimately embrace all humankind… This promise stands as a key to understanding all of scripture."[18] For this reason, as followers of Christ, it is important that we know more about this forgotten covenant.

In this book, I want to examine this Abrahamic narrative and covenant more deeply. I want us to look at the details of the promises made to Abraham in Genesis 12 to 17, its partial fulfilment in the emergence of Israel in the Exodus and their ongoing history, and consider how the Apostles understood these promises in the light of the coming of Christ, both in the Gospels and the Epistles. I want us to grasp beyond the superficial and immaterial explanations of what it means for Christ to be the fulfilment of the promises made to Abraham, and what they mean for us as His followers. This is something, I believe, Christians need to comprehend because if Jesus is the climax of the narrative of God fulfilling his promises to Abraham, and we are united in Christ, then the details of this covenant will have big implications for not only how we see the Apostolic Scripture's relationship with the Tanakh, but also for our identity and what it means for us to belong to the redeemed people of God.

---

18 Lasor, W, Hubbard, D, and Bush, F. *Old Testament Survey*. p.47

Part I
ABRAHAM

THE PROMISE

[Abraham] grew strong in his faith as he gave glory to God, fully convinced that God was able to do what he had promised."[19]

I don't have a lot of time for word games. I believe people should say what they mean and mean what they say. On a number of occasions, I have been caught out and ended up looking foolish because I, perhaps naively, took people at their literal word. For example, there were a couple of times when job interviewers, perhaps wanting to help me relax, said they 'just wanted to catch up for a chat.' And so, I behaved and spoke like a person catching up for a chat. And because of this, I didn't demonstrate the passion, energy, and conviction they were after. There have also been times when people have said things they didn't really mean because they were just being polite. "We should catch up…", "Let me know if you want to do some kind of ministry activity together.", "I owe you a…" The ironic thing about doing this is that although they are trying to preserve feelings, when one realises they didn't really mean it, feelings become even more

[19] Rom 4:20-21

hurt because they thought they had a friend, but it turned out they merely had a polite acquaintance.

Fortunately for us, when God promises to deliver, He's not just being polite; He will actually do it. He always intends to see things through. God's faithfulness is an essential element of who He is - but then again, all aspects of His identity are – and this reality is crucial for our walk with Christ. This quality means that we can trust what He says and have confidence in His promises, which is the foundation of our faith: taking God at His word that He will do all that He has promised to do. We see this even in the etymology of the word confidence, which derives from the two Greek words *com* and *fides*, meaning 'with faith.' And with this confidence in God comes a number of implications.

Firstly, if we are to be imitators of Christ, and He is not faithful, then what reason is there to expect faithfulness from us? Why should I be faithful to my friends, family, wife, or God Himself? Secondly, the faithfulness of God, which is the foundation for our faith in His promises, gives His people hope and endurance in times of difficulty. Knowing that He has promised to give us an eternal, glorious inheritance makes the worst horrors of this life seem nothing more than a bad dream.[20] If we take away God's faithfulness, not merely in intention but also ability, for there are many who make promises to do things they are unable to do, then this hope is nothing more than wishful thinking. If we cannot be certain of God's oath, we will either delude ourselves with naivety or give up because who would suffer for the faith now only to be left with nothing later. This is what Paul meant when he wrote:

> ...if the dead are not raised, not even Christ has been raised. And if Christ has not been raised, your faith is futile and

[20] Rom 8:18, 2Cor 4:17

> you are still in your sins. Then those also who have fallen asleep in Christ have perished. If in Christ we have hope in this life only, we are of all people most to be pitied.[21]

If this were the case, then God's moral character would need to be questioned. The faithfulness of God, therefore, makes our faith, our hope, and our commitment meaningful.

It also provides the foundation for the reliability and authority of Scripture. God's faithfulness is what provides meaning to the Scriptures, not simply so that we can have confidence that God will deliver on the promises recorded therein, but it is what helps drive the narrative forward. The Bible's narrative is essentially the story of God acting on and fulfilling His promise to undo the effects of sin through the 'seed of the woman' from Genesis 3. Without His faithfulness, the Bible becomes driven by an unreliable narrator and author since there are inconsistencies between the words of the storyteller and the events of the "diegetic world". And if the reader cannot rely on the words of Scripture as an accurate representation of the thoughts, emotions, motives, will, and values of our creator, then it becomes meaningfulness. Consequently, its function as authoritative, divine revelation falls apart and our faith, the requirement for justification, collapses. This is why identifying, understanding, and following the promises in Scripture are important, not just to know what you're getting, but to find encouragement as we recognise the faithful and trustworthy character of God.

Despite not having scripture in the form that we do, Abram quite possibly had some knowledge of the promises made and fulfilled by God prior to his calling. Although the Bible is silent on this, it's not unreasonable to consider so. For instance, according to the genealogies of Genesis 9 and 11,

---

21 1Cor 15:16-19

Noah and Shem were still alive for a significant portion of Abram's life. In fact, Noah was alive for Abram's first 58 years and Shem actually outlived Abram. And because of this, it is very likely Abram would have known that God fulfilled his promise to Noah and his family that He would get them through the flood. And, as we will consider later in this book, the Apostolic Scriptures reveal that Abram was aware of the promised deliverer and knew of the promise made to the woman in the garden. It is because the Lord had already demonstrated Himself as faithful, that Abram was able to trust God when He made his promises to him.

God's Covenant Promises

The Abrahamic promises are explained and elaborated on primarily in Genesis 12, 15 and 17, and progressively fulfilled through the remainder of the Tanakh. These three chapters of Genesis, as part of the Abrahamic narrative, will be the focus of the first section of this book.

Three key promises were made to Abram, forming the foundation of God's covenant with him. We find the giving of these promises in Genesis 12:1-3:

> Now the Lord said to Abram, "Go from your country and your kindred and your father's house to the land that I will show you. And I will make of you a great nation, and I will bless you and make your name great, so that you will be a blessing. I will bless those who bless you, and him who dishonors you I will curse, and in you all the families of the earth shall be blessed."

These promises form what is known as the 'Abrahamic covenant.' A covenant is a relationship based on a promise, or promises, with consequences for each party that fails to uphold their obligations. It was a relational bond, connecting people together from all walks of life, based on immutable oaths. Some examples of ancient covenants include marriage, peace treaties, and a King giving his representative gifts in return for loyalty and faithfulness. When God establishes covenants with people in the Bible, it is more like the last example, with the image of a king functioning as a relational metaphor, whereby God "in sovereign fashion dispenses His grace to men and fulfils His promises to them."[22] And although all of God's covenants take different forms with different promises, their goal can be all be ultimately boiled down to the fulfilment of his purposes and plans that "will ultimately heal the breach that sin has placed between God and the world."[23] As we will see, this is what He has done with Abraham.

Abram's Land Grant.

The first promise is that of land. In the giving of this promise, God is telling Abraham (or Abram, as he was still known), to depart the land he was living in, and go to the new land that He would give him. In so doing, God is symbolically calling Abram to depart from his old life, his traditions, customs, rulers and gods, (since there was a belief in territorial deities) and enter into a new life with Him according to His ways, His rule, committed to the sole worship of Him. This giving of land was significant, not merely on a symbolic level of a change of lifestyle, but for what the gift represented. In the ancient world, gifts had value not simply in and of themselves, although some gifts no doubt had inherent wealth value. Rather, the real value of the gift was determined by who was giving it and

---

22 Thompson, J. "Covenant (OT)" *ISB Encyclopedia, Vol. 1.* p.792

23 Lasor, Hubbard, Bush. *Old Testament Survey.* p.33

why. Because of this, a towel from a king to commemorate a new treaty was more valuable than a diamond ring given by some peasant merchant because they needed to get rid of it. So, for Abram to be told that he and his descendants would inherit a large portion of land from the King of Kings as part of a covenantal relationship makes it a significantly valuable gift. This practice in the ancient world was known as a Land Grant. A Land Grant was when a great King would, as a gracious gift, give a loyal vassal or servant a portion of land in perpetuity to his descendants. Even in spite of 'sins', the land would remain the property of that family, although the unfaithful one may be removed from that land. This covenant with Abraham, as we will see, definitely falls under the category of a Land Grant.

Later in Genesis 15, when Abram is actually in the land, the author reports that "On that day the Lord made a covenant with Abram, saying, 'To your offspring I give this land, from the river of Egypt to the great river, the river Euphrates…'"[24] This wording, with the detailing of land boundaries, reflects the legal language of the Land Grants. An example of this was found in the agreement made by Abba-El, a Syrian King, to Yarinlim: "On that day, Abba El… gave the city…" By using this contractual vocabulary, the author of Genesis is reflecting the sincerity and certainty of the gift and promise. We also find parallels in the conditions of the gift. In the 'Treaty of Hattusilis', written by a Hittite King for an Ulmi-Tesup, the author promises:

> After you, your son and grandson will possess it, nobody will take it away from them… from the descendent of Ulmi-Tesup, either his house or his land in order to give it to a descendent of somebody else.

[24] Gen 15:18

This perpetual gift of land is reflected in God's words to Abram in the following chapter after entering the Promised Land:

> Lift up your eyes and look from the place where you are, northward and southward and eastward and westward, for all the land that you see I will give to you and to your offspring *forever.*[25]

Not only do the Abrahamic promises reflect the perpetual nature of the ancient Land Grants, but also the faithfulness of the one being blessed. In the grant of Ashurtanipal to Bulta, we find the following:

> Bulta… whose heart is devoted to his master, served me with truthfulness, acted perfectly in my palace, grew up with a good name and kept the charge of my kingship.

The language of this prologue is echoed in the words of the Lord to Isaac when He established His covenant with him:

> I will multiply your offspring as the stars of heaven and will give to your offspring all these lands. And in your offspring all the nations of the earth shall be blessed, because *Abraham obeyed my voice and kept my charge, my commandments, my statutes, and my laws.*[26]

Moreover, God's warnings to Israel in Deuteronomy about exile as punishment for sins is reflective of the somewhat conditional nature of the ancient Land Grants. Conditional, at least in the sense that Israel needed

---

25 Gen 13:14-15
26 Gen 26:4-5

to maintain their covenant obligations in order to continue experiencing its blessings.

Promise of Descendants.

For the recipient, this giving of land was a way to guarantee the continuity of their descendants, which is described as the giving of a 'house', or family.[27] This connects the first promise of God to Abram with the second: the promise of descendants. By receiving the land, the descendants of Abram who were to grow into a great nation had a place to flourish and thrive. The difference between the natural and divine Land Grants is that while the grant of lineage by a King was somewhat passive and consequential, the sovereign power of the creator was much more direct, as seen in the miraculous conception of Isaac. And within these grants, as part of the master's obligation to their servant, were curses upon those who violated the vassal's, or their descendants' rights.[28]

This obligation is connected to the third promise in the covenant: the promise of blessing. And this promise, indeed the entire covenant, reveals that Abraham had significant favour with God. But we, the reader, are not exactly told why. We know nothing of the first seventy-odd years of his life: how he came to know and worship the one true God in a land of false gods, his socioeconomic status, nor his obedience prior to his calling. It appears that from this silence one could conclude that God's decision to make this covenant with Abraham is purely a gracious and unmerited act. That God simply chose to. Not because of anything Abram did, his status, or as some reward for coming around to the truth, but simply because the Lord chose

27 The term 'house' will be used in this sense of family line and dynasty from here on.

28 Weinfeld, M. "Covenant of Grant in the Old Testament", *AOS*, p.185

to for his salvific purposes. And while Abram's obedience and faithfulness were in this unique occasion required for God's promise to be realised to him, the calling and invitation were unconditional.

This calling and setting apart is what is known as election: the choice of God to select individuals, means, objects, etc... above others. What might be perceived as a negative rejection and judgement of the 'non-elect', is actually a choice based on God's perfect character and plan. We find this concept reflected in the words of Ephesians:

> Blessed be the God and Father of our Lord Jesus Christ, who has blessed us in Christ with every spiritual blessing in the heavenly places, even as *he chose us* in him before the foundation of the world, that we should be holy and blameless before him. In love he predestined us for adoption to himself as sons through Jesus Christ, according to the purpose of his will, to the praise of his glorious grace, with which he has blessed us in the Beloved.[29]

Election, despite its common usage today, is not always salvific in nature. God's election of Shem over his three siblings, for instance, was not His decision to 'save' one and 'damn' the other. He chose Shem to be the one through whom the promise would continue and eventuate in the arrival of the messiah. Other examples of non-salvific election include the geo-political nation of Israel as God's witnesses, Aaron, and his family as High Priests, and the city of Jerusalem as the place where His glory would reside. Abram's election as the one whom God would bless was also non-salvific. The existence of the likes of Melchizedek as a priest to God Most High tells us Abram was not the only follower of Yahweh. The other

---

29 Eph 1:3-6

thing they have in common is that their election was not merely for any personal benefit. The election of Aaron was to serve the people on God's behalf, the election of David as king was to righteously lead Israel, and the election of Noah was to preserve humanity. And when we look at the final part of the three-fold promise, we see that this blessing of land and lineage was not merely for Abram's benefit, nor for his bloodline, but in some way for the whole world.

Promise of Blessing

The Lord said to Abram, "I will bless those who bless you… and in you all the families of the earth shall be blessed." What's interesting is that in some translations such as the NIV, we find this verse rendered as "all peoples on earth will be blessed *through* you…" The connotations of this phrasing in English suggests that there is a disconnect between Abram, and the worldwide beneficiaries his blessings, experiencing them through some secondary influence. But the more accurate rendering is 'in you' as when the authors of the Greek translation of the Tanakh, the Septuagint (or LXX) uses the preposition *en*. In doing so, they are saying that the promise will come by means of Abram as an effective cause in a more immediate way, rather than a passive conduit. This is further supported by the use of the Greek grammar behind the pronoun 'you'[30], highlighting the connection between Abram and those being blessed. What this means is that in order to participate in these blessings, there needs to be some kind of union with Abram. As we read on through Genesis, we find this principle repeated when the foundation of God establishing this covenant with Abraham's

30 Dative: a case that emphasises a personal relationship and connection. E.g. "If you…know how to give good gifts to *your* children" (Lk 11:13).

descendants - Isaac, Jacob, and ultimately the twelve tribes - was due to their relationship to the patriarch. Thus, by means of Abram, we are blessed by virtue of a relationship with him.

To help us understand the nature of this promise, we need to consider the biblical meaning of blessing. The term blessing is often equated with 'doing good things' for someone. By somehow making their lives nicer and easier, which does reflect the word's meaning of granting physical and spiritual benefits of well-being and protection. However, there's more to blessing than merely getting something. In Genesis 1:22 it says, "And God blessed them. And God said to them, 'Be fruitful and multiply and fill the earth and subdue it…'" This declaration seems to be an example of the Lord, by the power of his word which he had just used to bring all things into existence, supernaturally empowering and equipping Adam and Eve to fulfil their intended purpose as image-bearers of their creator. Thus, by blessing Abram – and those who bless him – God was making possible the achievement of His purposes in Abram's life. In fact, the LXX translates 'bless' in Genesis 12:3 with the word *eulogeo,* which literally means 'good word.' This is the etymological root of our English word eulogy and means to speak well of someone. The Apostolic Scriptures use this word in passages such as Matthew 5:44 which reads, "Love your enemies and pray for (*eulogeo*) those who persecute you." And because of His power, when God speaks a good word over us, He is bringing that thing into existence. And this is what happened with Abraham when he was blessed. But what were these blessings?

On one level, the blessing promised to Abram was material in nature, which we see as the Abrahamic narrative plays out. He was blessed with the provision of wealth in the form of livestock, silver, and gold;[31] he was

[31] Gen 13:2

blessed with protection and victory in battle;[32] and he was, in accordance with the second promise, blessed with children.[33] In fact, towards the end of his life, we read that the Lord had blessed Abram 'in every way.'[34]

But these blessings experienced by Abram were not limited to the material, and by no means should they be seen as the main and central blessing. As wonderful as those gifts are, since all gifts from God are good and perfect, the primary blessing of this covenant is God Himself. At the heart of the covenant's promise of blessing was a relationship with the Lord. And along with this covenantal relationship came the revelation of the character and will of their creator. Given that this promise of blessing was intended to extend to all the families of the earth, it becomes apparent that this promise in Genesis 12:3 was the foundation for Israel's commission to be a light to the Gentiles.[35] John Walton in his commentary on Genesis elaborates on this by saying that the Israelites, and ultimately the nations, were "blessed as they were shown what God was like and as the means were provided for them to become justified, reconciled to God, and forgiven of their sins."[36] The blessing, therefore, was the making possible the fulfilment of the promise of the restoration of the relationship between humanity and God that was broken by sin. And that the Lord had this end in mind is evident in the original wording of the second promise.

When revealing to Abram that he would become a great *nation*, the word *goy* instead of *am* is used. Often in the Tanakh, Israel is referred to as a people (*am*)[37] which is a group of closely connected people. The *goyim,* are political nations based on shared geographical boundaries and culture

32 Gen 14:14-20
33 Gen 16:15, 21:2-7
34 Gen 24:1
35 Isa 49:1-6; Jer 1:5; Rom 3:2
36 Walton, J. *The NIV Application Commentary: Genesis*. p.402
37 E.g. Ex 8:20, Ruth 1:16, 2Sam 5:2

and are typically those people groups in the world who are not Israelites.[38] William Dumbrell suggests that this is because the use of *am* may not have been a sufficient descriptor, especially since the Bible's redemptive narrative culminates in Revelation 21-22 with the redeemed society in the New Jerusalem, ruled and governed perfectly by the Lord for eternity, as the eternal *goy*.[39] Therefore, the promises made to Abraham must have an eschatological goal in mind.

The means by which this end would be achieved were in some way revealed within the covenant promises. We see this in the way that Jesus' declaration to the Jews that "Your father Abraham rejoiced that he would see my day. He saw it and was glad"[40] was an explanation that "Abraham did indeed understand, however imperfectly, that the covenant promise that in him all the nations of the earth would be blessed… involved God's provision of a redeemer."[41] We will look at this in greater detail later in the book, however for now it should suffice to say that the Abrahamic covenant was not simply a Jewish thing or something to fill in time until Moses. It was the significant beginning of God working in the world to rescue all humanity from the effects of the fall, which commenced with the unmerited election of the man Abram through these three promises of land, house, and blessing.

Understanding the Promises Corporately

Writing about this covenant, Keith Essex explains that although the promises can be categorised into the three groups of descendants, land, and

38 E.g. Num 24:8, Deut 15:6, Ps 59:8, Isa 42:6
39 Dumbrell, W. *Covenant and Creation.* Paternoster, Crownhill (2013). p.72-73
40 Jn 8:56
41 Kostenberger, A. "John." *CNTUOT.* p.458-459

blessing, a more natural way of classifying them is to see the promises as national, personal and universal. Firstly, God promised to make Abram into a *nation*, and these descendants would inherit the land of Canaan. Second, He promised to bless Abram *personally*, which we see fulfilled materially and spiritually in the ongoing narrative. And thirdly, God promised that these blessings would be experienced *universally* by all nations through him. That's not to say that everyone without exception will enjoy them, which is the common understanding of universalism, but rather that no one because of their nationality will be excluded. The epiphany made by food critic Anton Ego at the end of the film *Ratatouille* helps illustrates this principle:

> In the past, I have made no secret of my disdain for Chef Gusteau's famous motto, "Anyone can cook." But I realize, only now do I truly understand what he meant. Not everyone can become a great artist; but a great artist *can* come from *anywhere*. (emphasis added).

In the same way, not everyone will experience the full Abrahamic blessing, but the one who does can come from anywhere.

The benefit of understanding the promises in these categories is that it better reflects the corporate experience of the covenantal blessings. While the things being promised to Abram are important, and their fulfilment needs to be recognised throughout Scripture, it's more important that we recognise that the emphasis is upon God's relationship with the people He is blessing.

This calling and covenant made with Abram is the significant driving force of the biblical narrative. Although the promise in Genesis 3 is a foreshadowing of God's solution to sin, it can be considered a part of the prologue[42] that sets up the calling of Abram which builds on that promise. Perhaps we could liken it to *The Lord of Rings*. In the beginning, it is revealed as a kind of subtle narrative promise that the ring of evil can be destroyed in the fires of Mount Doom, with the remainder of the narrative headed towards that resolution. Following that revelation, we are given some history on how the ring ended up in the hands of Bilbo, and then Frodo who was 'called' to go with the fellowship to the mountain and destroy it. The remainder of Tolkien's story is about the fulfilment of this calling, just as the rest of Scripture describes the fulfilment of the promises made to Abraham as the 'road map' set out to fulfil that initial goal. Unfortunately, some authors break their narrative promises. For instance, when David, the cyborg in Spielberg's 2001 film *A.I.*, spends most of the two-and-a-half-hour movie hunting for the Blue Fairy, with the expectation that he will get his wish to become a real boy, only to discover she was just a statue making the 146-minute film a waste of time. Fortunately, the divine author and narrator of the Scriptures is able and faithful to deliver on his promises, as the remainder of the biblical narrative reveals.

42 Genesis 1-11, also known as the prehistory period.

CUTTING A COVENANT

For when God made a promise to Abraham, since he had no one greater by whom to swear, he swore by himself...[43]

Waiting is an enduring test that seeks to build patience in us. As parents, we try to teach our children the concept of delayed gratification. As a teacher, I need to encourage my students to demonstrate patience by enduring through the full lesson and waiting until being instructed to pack up and get ready to leave. These lessons are important because the reality of life - particularly in a world of fast food, instant messaging, and next-day delivery guarantees - is that we need to wait for things. Even Homer Simpson has to wait 40 seconds to deep-fry a buffalo in Moe's super deep-fryer, despite wanting it now. Apart from practical reasons, the Bible tells us in many places that as Christians, we need to be patient in this life as we await the return of Christ and to not give up hope in the midst of trial and tribulation.[44] Therefore patience, if we are to raise our children to endure in the faith, is a very important lesson.

43 Heb 6:13

44 Rom 12:12, 2Cor 1:6, 2Tim 2:24, Js 5:7-8

But let's be honest: waiting sucks. When we wait for too long, we can get anxious and even uncertain. There have been times where I've been over early for meetings or a catch-up with someone, and the thought enters my mind: 'are you sure it was today?' Then I get out my phone and check my calendar and text messages to confirm the details. And when I realise that I was right, I get bored waiting and worried that I look weird sitting by myself. The feeling of longing that comes with waiting isn't much fun either. You really want something that you know will be good, enjoyable, and will bring life satisfaction, but you can't have it yet. It's one thing to know when you're going to expect it because it helps to build certainty. But when someone vaguely says, 'I will do something', and you spend so much time wondering, 'is it today?', making the waiting even worse. This is what Abram had to endure after God had made his promises to him.

Hope Challenged

After a journey through the land God promised him, a trip into Egypt and a battle or two, Abram and Sara were still waiting. They experienced the blessing of God's protection and provision, but the more long-term promises seemed so far off. About ten years passed during this time and Sara and Abram are probably scratching their heads wondering when they're going to fall pregnant, and how it will happen so that God's promises can be fulfilled. Perhaps, after experiencing warfare, Abram has had to confront the reality of his own mortality and felt that time was running out. To become a great house, and then a great nation, they need to start with at least one child. And this child didn't seem to be coming. And so, they most likely began to think that the promise would continue not through bloodline, but via other means. These questions, doubts, and concerns are at the heart of Genesis 15, which in comparison to the action-packed events of the previous two chapters is quite dull. But whatever is lacking in narrative tension, is compensated for by theological significance. As Charles Swindoll explains, this chapter "records a quiet conversation between two close friends. It would be dull reading if one of the friends didn't happen to be the almighty creator of the universe…"[45]

When we begin reading Genesis 15, we find that the Lord has come to reaffirm his promises to Abram. This is just one of a number of promise-reaffirmation speeches made by God, each of which is a response to some threat to the promises of land and offspring being fulfilled. For instance, the separation of Lot from Abram that left him without a potential heir, and Abram's journey into Egypt after the famine threatening the possibility of his descendants inheriting the Land, is followed up with a reaffirmation of the covenant in Genesis 13:14. And this is the case for Genesis 15 as well, especially with regards to the problem of not yet having a descendant or heir from which to build His great nation.

Divine Reassurance

Appearing to Abram in a vision, God declares to him that He has much to give him. Abram, therefore, begins to ask about 'the big gift.' He inquires:

> O Lord God, what will you give me, for I continue childless, and the heir of my house is Eliezer of Damascus? …Behold, you have given me no offspring, and a member of my household will be my heir.[46]

45 Swindoll, C. *Abraham*. p54
46 Gen 15:2-3

From this, it seems that Abram and Sara had begun to make plans to adopt Eliezer of Damascus, who was likely one of their most loyal servants, and make him their heir. In that time and culture, this was a common practice and custom. However, the Lord says in response, "This man shall not be your heir; your very own son shall be your heir…", which means that God's promise will come not merely by way of some human legal transaction, but through the miraculous conception that will come to this childless and aging couple.

God, wanting to show off his glory and power to Abram, and us the reader, says 'I'm going to do more than simply give you a child.' He does this by getting Abram to do a little star gazing. After calling him out of his tent, the Lord says: "Look toward heaven, and number the stars, if you are able to number them… So shall your offspring be."[47] Here, God was reminding Abram of the initial promise, and the scale on which He would deliver it. That He has big things He wants to achieve through Abram's line, and that these purposes and plans will span a period of time long enough to build Abram's family to that size. It is possible that God was referring to the exact number of visible lights in the night sky, but the impossible challenge of counting the vast number of stars, especially in a time and place with no light pollution suggests a form of hyperbole. It could have been easy for Abram to think back in Genesis 12, 'Yeah, I'll have some descendants and we might become a large tribe.' But here God was showing him that He's going to do so much more. I believe that through this experience, He was reassuring Abram of His promise by saying: 'Look, I made billions of stars with a word, surely I can do what I promised you and give you a child.' But there is another angle to this experience that, mostly because of artistic interpretations, is not usually recognised. It was recently at the time of writ-

47 Gen 15:5, c.f. Rev 7:9

ing that I had it pointed out to me that based on the timeline details, this vision seems to have actually happened during the daytime, not at night. We find that in this chapter, we are given an account of the divine meeting, Abram's responsive actions which would have taken a bit of time, and it was not until *then* in verse twelve that Moses records that the sun started to set. Perhaps this is the difficulty Abram had in counting the stars. Knowing that this conversation took place in the daytime, I think, speaks more to Abram's faith than the reassurance of a beautiful night sky. Abram knew the stars were there, he just couldn't see them. This means that the Lord was effectively telling Abram:

> 'Just as you cannot see the stars, neither can you see your vast line of descendants. But just as you have confidence that the stars are there, even though you cannot see them, you can be assured that I will give you what I promised.'

What an amazing image of faith: confidence in the existence of the unseen. And it was in response to the strengthening of Abram's faith through this experience that we are given the line of text that defines the attitude and posture that God desires from humanity and the foundational principle of entering a covenant with our creator. The narrator tells us that after this experience, Abram "believed the Lord, and he counted it to him as righteousness."[48] While this statement might be well known by many Christians, since Paul makes much of this verse in arguing for justification by faith, I think it is worth unpacking what exactly is meant in this statement.

First, note that Abram did not merely believe that the promise would come true as though God was letting him know about what would happen

---

[48] Gen 15:6

to him. The object of Abram's faith was not the promise, because from a human perspective, what was being promised was impossible. What Abram believed was that God is more than capable of delivering his promise, not simply a confidence that God would try really hard to do His best. This is reflected in the way that the word used here for 'believe', *v'he'emin*, also carries a sense of reliance along with this trust. Indeed, Abram did need to rely on the Lord to make it happen. Thus, this belief is theological in nature as it presupposes two facets of God's character. One, that God is all-powerful; the one who can bring into existence that which does not exist. And two, that God is faithful; the one who always delivers on His promises.

Second, the narrator highlights that this theology is relational and that there are relational consequences of this faith. This is true of any relationship since without trust, even at a basic level, a relationship cannot happen, at least not a healthy one. While this does appear to be saying that it was at this moment that Abram believed God, the declaration seems to be more general. This comes through in two key ways. One is that earlier, we see Abram exercising faith in his response to God's direction to "Go from your country and your kindred and your father's house to the land that I will show you."[49] After receiving the instruction and the promises, we read: "So Abram went, as the Lord had told him."[50] This account shows that 'to believe' is an active verb, and thus, for Abram to believe God requires him to act on that belief. The other is that the Hebrew uses what is called the perfect tense which describes a completed action that could be another past act. For example, when we read in Genesis, "God saw everything *he had made...*" the *making* is in the perfect tense. This is also reflected in the Greek translation of the Tanakh, the Septuagint, by using the aorist[51]

49 Gen 12:1

50 Gen 12:4

51 A completed action. E.g. They *built* the tower in 1960

tense for believe. Although the wider text and grammar show that Abram's faith did not come into existence at this encounter, we can say that it was a significant moment where his faith was solidified and reinforced further.

And thirdly, the outcome of this faith and confidence in God is that it is counted to Abram as righteousness. Now righteousness is one of those 'Christianese' words that gets thrown around a bit, but the nuance of the concept gets a bit lost sometimes. Righteousness is generally understood as pertaining to goodness and morality, as opposed to wrong and sinful behaviour, which to a point is true. However, at the heart of righteousness is the idea of what is the appropriate conduct of people *within a covenant towards each other*. For example, love, respect, and loyalty would be considered 'righteous' actions. A sovereign king defending his vassal state that he promised to protect would likewise be considered righteous. Here, it appears as though this faith, this reliance, this confidence, and trust is declared to be a righteous act, and in a manner of speaking it is. However, the term 'reckon' is used here with the sense of giving Abram a quality, or status that does not inherently belong to him. Thus, "Abraham's relationship with God is established as an act of God's grace in response to Abraham's faith."[52] Therefore, we learn here that faith is not only the right response to the declarations and promises of our faithful creator but the foundational prerequisite of humanity's covenantal relationship with Him. As defined earlier, a covenant is a relationship based on promises with obligations on both parties. And what this encounter teaches us is that at a foundational level, the obligation of the Lord is to come through with His promises, and the obligation of humanity is to believe that God is who He says He is and will do all that He Has promised to do. And as

---

52 Moo, D. *The Epistle to the Romans*, p.262

the second half of Genesis 15 will further reveal, God's covenants are quite unilateral in nature.

Divine Responsibility

Although Abram had faith that he would receive a son, when the Lord affirmed the promise of land, he still had questions. This promise was such a big thing that it seemed impossible. Not only were there many inhabitants in the land, but the war he was involved in years earlier suggested to him that defending his inheritance would be a full-time task. Thus, God's encouragement that He is Abram's shield and reward in verse one was a logical reassurance after the war of the five kings and waiving the reward from the King of Sodom.[53] Moreover, that the timescale of the fulfilment of this promise was beyond his lifetime would have also added to his anxiety. In light of this, Abram asks, "O Lord God, how am I to know that I shall possess it?"[54] The tone of this question is not one of doubtful accusation, nor was it an ungrateful testing of the Lord that demands something of Him to somehow prove Himself. The kind of which Abram's descendants would be guilty of in Exodus 17 and forbidden in Deuteronomy 6:16, "You shall not put the Lord your God to the test." It is not the sceptical kid in the playground responding to another child's far-fetched claim with 'prove it.' It seems that Abram needed a sign, something to hold onto when doubts arose. Like all people who call on the name of the Lord, he believed God, but His belief was not perfect. And not unlike Gideon and his fleece,[55] or the father who required help from Jesus with his unbelief,[56] Abram needed

---

53 Gen 14:21-24
54 Gen 15:8
55 Jg. 6:36-40
56 Mark 9:24

further reassurance. Spurgeon in his commentary on Genesis puts it this way:

> What! Abraham, is not God's promise sufficient for thee? O father of the faithful, though thou dost believe, and art counted as righteous through believing, dost thou still ask, "Whereby shall I know?" Ah, beloved! Faith is often marred by a measure of unbelief; or, if not quite unbelief, yet there is a desire to have some token, some sign, beyond the bare promise of God.[57]

The fact that God expressed no anger, frustration, or rebuke at this question further shows the righteous spirit behind his inquiry. We could perhaps say that the question was being asked out of faith. His faith knew that God was capable of all things, but his knowledge gap created curiosity as well as the potential for doubt. And so, in faith, he was confident of receiving a sign. We could elaborate on Abraham's question by wording it like this:

> I know that nothing is impossible for you and that you can and will deliver on this promise, but I'm not sure how. But I know that if you give me a sign, just as you gave us the sign of the rainbow, then I can be reassured of this great and gracious gift you have promised me. So please Lord, how can I know that I will inherit this land?

Expounding on this verse, Timothy Keller describes a similar concept, albeit from a different angle. Drawing from Hebrews 6:19, he explains that faith and confidence in the promises of God is an anchor for the soul,

---

[57] Spurgeon, CH. *Commentary on Genesis 15:4.*np

connected to a sure foundation to ground us on the tumultuous waters of life. And Abram, in the face of these big promises says, 'okay, but how can I know?' Almost as though he has lowered his anchor of faith, but it's still floating in the water. And with what follows, God answers with, 'let me help you get the anchor down.'[58]

The Ceremony

To deepen Abram's faith, God responds to his honest and humble inquiry by granting his request in a manner that modern readers would find not only bizarre, but also unexpected. We might expect some kind of supernatural phenomena such as fire or lightning from the heavens, or the materialisation of a deed out of clay written by the finger of God, or some stranger walking by saying, 'Here, have this land.' Or maybe rearranging the trees to say: 'Property of Abram.' But instead, the Lord instructs Abram:

> Bring me a heifer three years old, a female goat three years old, a ram three years old, a turtledove, and a young pigeon." And he brought him all these, cut them in half, and laid each half over against the other. But he did not cut the birds in half.[59]

For us, this instruction would be met with confusion. But Abram knew exactly what was happening. This was the way people in the Ancient Near East established and formalised covenants. If faith is the foundational premise upon which the covenant is sanctioned, this ceremony was its formal ratification and establishment. To draw on the analogy of a more

58 Keller, *Abraham and the Torch.*

59 Gen 15:9-10

familiar covenant, marriage: the calling of Abram is the engagement where the promise of covenant is made, Abram's faith is the love, trust, and trustworthiness that forms the foundation of a relationship, and this ritual is the wedding day that officially formally establishes the covenant. During the ceremony, various oaths and promises are made between the bride and groom, typically as expressions of commitment, loyalty, and demonstrations of love. Afterwards, they sign on the dotted line as a way of saying 'this is how you know my word is true.' When we sign our name to a promise, we are held to it, and there are consequences for failure to uphold our commitment. Ancient Near Eastern covenants follow a similar process, although the consequences are more ominous, and the 'signing' much more dramatic, than modern contracts. This is what God did with Abram.

As described in verses nine to ten, animals were cut in half as a sacrificial and solemn act, which reflects the origin of the Hebrew phrase, 'to *cut* a covenant.' In Genesis 15:18 it reads, "On that day the Lord made a covenant with Abram…", and the word translated as 'made' is *karath*, which literally means to cut, or cut off. For instance, when David was in the cave with Saul, he *karath* the corner of Saul's robe.[60] This word is the one often used throughout the Tanakh to refer to the initiation or creation of a covenant with his people. Thus, with this ceremony, God was 'cutting a covenant' with Abram.

At sunset, after Abram had arranged the animals, God gave him a rundown of the 'future history' of his descendants, outlining their future captivity in Egypt and the subsequent exodus and entrance into the land four generations later. He also explained that He is waiting to use Abram's descendants as an instrument of judgement upon the Amalekites once their iniquity is complete. This would certainly have helped Abram trust God

60 1Sam 24:5

more and remove some of his doubt. I know for myself when I expect something will happen, but not when or how, or there is a risk it might not work out, it can result in stress. Uncertainty is the birthplace of anxiety, but information can bring peace, and this is the message the Lord was giving to Abram: 'This is what's going happen, and this is what I'm going to do. I'm just waiting for the right time.'

After this declaration, came the ceremony. But the way God handled this ceremony was unique and different to the ancient custom, and no doubt surprised Abram. Once it was dark, Abram looked, and "a smoking fire pot and a flaming torch passed between these pieces." This was the Lord, represented symbolically as a smoking fire pot and a flaming torch which were traditionally carried in this ceremony, passing between the pieces. But this ceremony was different for a couple of reasons. Firstly, instead of having family members as witnesses, who live for a time and die, the stars of the night sky and the surrounding land were witnesses. This idea of calling 'heaven and earth' as witnesses, which are established until the end of this age, was a way of reflecting the eternal nature of this covenant. As described often through the Tanakh, heaven and earth are considered permanent elements of reality. For example, as David proclaims in his song of thanksgiving: "Worship the Lord in the splendour of holiness; tremble before him, all the earth; yes, the world is established; it shall never be moved."[61] That these witnesses would be called upon became common in God's covenants.

The second difference was that traditionally, either both the greater and lesser party would walk through together, or sometimes the subordinate by themselves, and declare an oath in order to ratify the covenant. Although in modern English 'vow' and 'oath' can be used interchangeably, there is a dif-

61 1 Chro 16:30; Ps 96:10, 104:5

ference in the biblical use of these terms. Vows were promises made exclusively by people to do something such as offer an animal sacrifice or a declaration of praise in the temple, typically in response to God's intervention during difficult times, and carried the conditional 'if... then...' formula. Oaths, on the other hand, were a solemn declaration to fulfil a promise, and the most common type of oaths found in Scripture are unconditional. There are a few conditional oaths that are mentioned, however, these are made between people in situations where carrying out their promises might be beyond their control. For example, Abraham exempted his servant from his oath to find Isaac a wife if she was unwilling to come with him. In the Ancient Near East, these oaths in covenantal contexts typically involved some divine invocation that went along the lines of 'as the Lord lives', or 'by the life of the god...', which is the equivalent of the modern phrase 'I swear to God.' This demonstrated to the other party the weight of the sincerity of their oath as it was believed that the god, in order to maintain their honour, would punish the one who did not uphold their oath. Therefore, within an oath is a conditional curse should they fail to keep their word. And in the context of this ceremony, the symbolic act of walking between the pieces makes explicit the implicit self-curse that declares to their god, the witnesses, and the other parties of the covenant: 'if I don't fulfil my promises, may I be cut down and left to die like these animals.' This concept is expressed in the treaty document between Ashurnirari V and Matilu that describes this cutting ceremony by stating:

> This ram was not taken from its flock for sacrifice...if Matiliu (shall violate) the covenant and oath to the gods, then, as this ram, which was taken from its flock and to its head will not return... so Matilu with his sons... shall be taken from their city, and to his city he will not return...

> as the head of this ram shall be struck off so shall his head be struck off.[62]

This is reflected in other places in Scripture as well. In Jeremiah, the Lord declares: "the men who transgressed my covenant and did not keep the terms of the covenant that they made before me, I will make them like the calf that they cut in two and passed between its parts…"[63] As we can see, walking between the pieces and cutting covenants was a big deal. Traditionally, the consequences were a little one-sided as the greater was often the one declaring the punishment, and the lesser had little to no power when it came to enforcing the consequence should the greater fail to uphold their end. But what God did with Abram was unique as it was He, the superior party, who walked through the pieces alone. God was taking full responsibility for this covenant, declaring: *Should I fail to give you offspring, land, or use your house to bless the nations, may I be cut down like these animals. May my blood be shed and may I be divided like these animals.*

Can you imagine if our political leaders took their promises so seriously? Can you suppose that before coming into office, they made an oath declaring that they will do everything they said they would. And if they didn't deliver, not only would they have to resign from their position, but they would do time in prison, or even face execution? Economist Robin Hanson, offering an idea with a less costly consequence, suggests that if politicians wanted to communicate that they are committed to their promises, they should post bonds to their property that are forfeited if they break a promise.[64] Not only would these pledges demonstrate the reliability of our leaders, but would ensure they work their hardest to deliver on what

62 In Weinfeld, M. *Covenant of Grant in the Old Testament*, p.198

63 Jer 34:18

64 Hanson, R. "Yes, Tax Lax Ideas." *Overcomingbias.com*

the people voted for. The reality though, is that no political leader ever fulfils every promise. A study on the fulfilment of campaign promises from the past 40 years in North America and Europe found that on average, parties keep only 67% of their promises.[65] This is because, as author Chris Berg suggests:

> Parties don't see election promises as promises in the plain English meaning of the word. Instead, promises are signals designed to express a deeper character of the political party. When [Australian Prime Minister Tony] Abbott promised not to change the pension and not to cut public broadcasters he was trying to signal that his would not be a radical government; that he was firmly targeting the median voter.[66]

Thus, politicians expect voters to see election promises more like proverbs than covenantal declarations. However, this is not the only explanation. Sometimes they try to do things, but they get blocked in parliament. Other times, situations change, or as they research a problem more, they realise that their prior promise is not the best solution. But the sceptic in me thinks this is a smaller portion of that 33 per cent. The point here is not to create a political book, that is something beyond my scope of knowledge. Rather, it is to highlight that in this oath we see that where human leaders fail in wisdom, faithfulness, and capacity to deliver, God is infinitely capable and committed to fulfilling his promises.

As incredible as this declaration of obligation to His side of the covenant was, it was only half the story.

---

65 Pétry F., Collette B. "Measuring How Political Parties Keep Their Promises". p.65
66 Berg, C. "Election promises are there for the breaking." *ABC News*.

This act of walking through the pieces alone was not merely God taking responsibility for *His* faithfulness to the covenant, God was taking responsibility for Abram and his descendants' faithfulness too. By replacing Abram in his role of walking between the pieces, the Lord was declaring: 'if you, or those who belong to you, fail to remain faithful to me, then may I be cut down like these animals as instead.' This was monumental and unheard of in the ancient world; a King taking total responsibility for a covenant, let alone the mighty creator of the universe, willing to lay down His life should He, or Abram, or his descendants, become unfaithful to the covenant. If Abram needed assurance, this was it. The Lord was communicating to Abram in this moment that He would use His sovereign power and will to ensure the blessings promised to Abram would come. Hence, this event reveals some significant elements of God's sovereignty. As we will consider in greater detail later, God's sovereignty will most definitely be needed to bring about these promises as various forces seek to come against God's purposes being worked out in creation. Wayne Grudem defines the sovereignty of God as "his exercise of rule (as 'sovereign' or 'king') over his creation"[67] and that this rule is infinite. That the Lord swore that his promises would most certainly be carried out on pain of death is a declaration that His exercise of power would overrule anything that would come against the giving of house, land, and blessing to Abram and his descendants. It also shows that God's unlimited sovereignty is, in a strange sense, limited. Not that there are external forces that could constrain God's will, or that there is a degree of impotence that would stop Him. On the contrary, as the Lord would say to Sara a number of years later when He visits their tent: "Is anything too hard for the Lord?" But rather, God's sovereignty and omnipotence are constrained by His character and will. As He would

67 Grudem, W. *Systematic Theology*. p.217

later reveal through Balaam: "God is not man, that he should lie, or a son of man, that he should change his mind. Has he said, and will he not do it? Or has he spoken, and will he not fulfill it?"[68] The author of Hebrews would later pick up on this when they wrote concerning the certainty of the promises made to Abraham:

> For when God made a promise to Abraham, since he had no one greater by whom to swear, he swore by himself, saying, 'Surely I will bless you and multiply you.' … For people swear by something greater than themselves, and in all their disputes an oath is final for confirmation. So when God desired to show more convincingly to the heirs of the promise the unchangeable character of his purpose, he guaranteed it with an oath, so that by two unchangeable things, in which it is impossible for God to lie, we who have fled for refuge might have strong encouragement to hold fast to the hope set before us.[69]

By making an oath, especially in the manner he did in Genesis 15, God is constraining His will and His future sovereign actions to ensure the deliverance of these promises. In fact, in a subtle way, God's walk through the pieces was kind of a hint to Abram that if He doesn't deliver, and consequently prove Himself unfaithful and a liar, He would cease to exist as God. This is the reason why God's promises are so meaningful. They describe our infinite creator, the self-existent and sufficient one who has no one to answer to, binding Himself to ensure His promises of blessing are worked out in our lives.

---

[68] Num 23:19

[69] Heb 6:13-18

Servant Leadership

When I was at Bible College and completing my undergraduate degree in Christian Ministry, I remember a big concept that the lecturers kept highlighting and emphasising to us was that of servant leadership. This concept, we were told, is explained most explicitly in Jesus' teaching recorded in Matthew and Mark's gospels in response to James' and John's request to sit at His left and right hand:

> You know that those who are considered rulers of the Gentiles lord it over them, and their great ones exercise authority over them. But it shall not be so among you. But whoever would be great among you must be your servant, and whoever would be first among you must be slave of all. For even the Son of Man came not to be served but to serve, and to give his life as a ransom for many.[70]

Thus, servant leadership is best understood as someone using their authority, power, and position of influence to the benefit of others, rather than fulfilling their own sense of feeling important as they get others to work for their personal advancement in life. And in this teaching, Jesus reveals that this is at the heart of His incarnation and ministry; coming in the form of a servant[71] to bring salvation for the world at the cost of His own life. This servant leadership is an expression of God's character demonstrated not only in the cross, but also in the ceremonial oath He has made to Abram, and that He would use His sovereignty to bring about the promises made to him. An attitude, we have seen, is different from the rulers of the world.

---

70 Mk 10:42-45

71 Phil 2:7

Mind you, this devotion does not mean that our wants and needs supersede and overtake God's goal of His glorification. In fact, quite the opposite is true. God fulfils His promises to bless us as the blessings we enjoy are given primarily for His glory. The conclusion to the 'hymn of Christ' - or *Carmen Christi* as it is sometimes referred to - from Philippians 2 that describes the incarnation demonstrates this concept well. It states that Jesus humbled himself and died for our sins on the Cross, and that the Father raised and exalted him *to the glory of God the Father*. The ultimate purpose of Jesus serving us in His ministry was to glorify God. This is the essence of what the reformers called *Soli Deo Gloria*: Glory to God alone, a doctrine reflected in several other places in Scripture:

> I acted for the sake of my name, that it should not be profaned in the sight of the nations in whose sight I had brought them out.[72]

> For my name's sake I defer my anger, for the sake of my praise I restrain it… for my own sake I do it, for how should my name be profaned? My glory I will not give to another.[73]

> In love he predestined us for adoption to himself as sons through Jesus Christ, according to the purpose of his will, to the praise of his glorious grace, with which he has blessed us in the Beloved…[74]

And this was the case for Abram too. Although he would benefit from the blessings of the promises made to him, their fulfilment would ulti-

---

72 Ez 20:14
73 Isa 48:9-11
74 Eph 1:4-6

mately be to the glory of God as a demonstration of His sovereignty and His faithfulness. And therefore, we see in God's total participation in this ceremony of the pieces that these two intertwined attributes are dependent upon each other. For God to be faithful to His promises, He needs to be sovereign over all forces which would work against his purposes. Moreover, His sovereignty needs to be bound by his faithfulness so that when He acts in history, each action is working towards the fulfilment of His promises.

A Lesson on Faith

This bizarre, alien, and extravagant encounter between Abram and the creator of the heavens and earth teaches us not only something about the complicated nature of the sovereignty of God. It also reveals a few things about what it means to have faith in God.

What stands out to me in this story is that faith is not blind. Well, not completely blind. When Abram believed God would fulfil His promises, it wasn't because he simply thought, 'Well, this sounds great. I hope it all comes true.' Rather, through his experiences and interactions with God, he came to grow in his certainty of God's faithfulness. Identifying the foundation of this confidence is difficult since the first account we have of God interacting with Abram is His three-fold promise and calling him to leave his family and go into the promised land. And Abram responded to this call with faith, but faith founded on what? Abram didn't have the record of Scripture we have today. Hebrews 11, however, may help us to unravel this question, although applying this to Abram requires some speculation since Scripture is silent. Nevertheless, the conclusions would not be entirely unreasonable. Hebrews 11:3 suggests to us that believing the Lord created all things out of nothing is a foundational act of faith, which is something that Abram would have come to a realisation of in one way or another. According to Romans 1, rebel sinners suppress this fact,[75] however, Abram had clearly come to acknowledge it. Most likely as God revealed his character and nature to Abram, he would have had some awareness of the greatness, majesty, and authority of God which would be true of one who could and did create *ex nihilo*. This is an act of faith since he wasn't there, but he believed it because he recognised that God's nature affirms it. And in response to this revelation, as a demonstration of faith, Abram worshipped in some form or another. Most likely through sacrifice and building an altar which we find him doing often throughout the Abrahamic narrative.[76] And just as Abel was commended for his righteous sacrifice which was made by faith,[77] Abram would have experienced a supernatural commendation too. As Hebrews 11:2 tells us: "For by [faith] the people of old received their commendation." Moreover, as the author explains in verse six, "… whoever would draw near to God must believe that he exists and that he rewards those who seek him." And therefore, through this ongoing interaction between Abram and God over the years leading up to Genesis 12, came the foundation for Abram's faith, which became more entrenched as he continued to follow the Lord. It was not that Abram did reckless things, overly hopeful that God would protect him, and call it faith; it was a confidence that God's promises would come to pass. Nonetheless, as we looked at earlier, this faith was stretched when it came to trusting that the Lord would give him a child. But rather than saying, 'just trust me', God makes a meaningful and extravagant oath upon which Abram can anchor his faith to. Therefore, faith is not blind - although it does require us to hope for things that are unseen - it is a trusting response to God's revelation in history. Faith isn't some spiritual optimism that crosses its fingers and hopes

75 Rom 1:18-20
76 Gen 12:7-8, 13:4, 18
77 Heb 11:4

for the best. Nor is it an invitation that asks us to abandon our common sense and believe in the absurd. Faith, rather, requires reasoned confidence in God and his promises.

From this ceremony, we also learn that faith is something that is built by God. Abram was struggling to trust in God and his promises, and instead of being expected to convince himself, Abram's request for God to help his unbelief was met with a tangible demonstration and declaration of an oath. In the same way for us, faith is not some force that we need to try really hard to grow by gritting our teeth and embracing naivety. God has provided for us in Scripture a revelation of His faithfulness to His promises to help build our faith. And these words, being grounded in the historical facts of God's interaction with humanity, are not some mythological legend that happened in the 'time before time'. This fact makes them verifiable and reliable, allowing us to intellectually bolster our faith. But more significantly, I believe genuine faith comes about primarily by the supernatural empowerment of God. As Jesus said in response to Peter's declaration that He is the Messiah, which would have been deducible by observing His teachings and actions: "Blessed are you, Simon Bar-Jonah! For flesh and blood has not revealed this to you, but my Father who is in heaven."[78] Indeed, many of the Jews saw all that Jesus did, yet they did not have faith.[79] It is almost as though when we encounter the facts and details, the Lord empowers the faith for us to trust in them. And therefore, our faith is built by God, not only by initiating the revelation for us to respond to, but also through the supernatural ability to trust Him.

The most theologically significant aspect of this encounter is the relationship between faith and righteousness, especially in the way that this is

---

78 Matt 16:17

79 Jn 10:24-26

the first occurrence in Scripture that connects the two concepts. Both the declaration that Abram's faith resulted in God counting him as righteous, and the lengths the Lord went to in order to build that faith, highlights that faith is the prerequisite of a right relationship (righteousness) with God. This is because "without faith it is impossible to please him."[80] The belief that commended Abram was not just faith that God would make him into a great nation, but also the faith that through him by the hand of God would come blessings to the whole world. In fact, implicit in this revelation is the expectation that, because of the connection between Abram's faith that credits righteousness and the Abrahamic promises, God's plan to bless the nations through him would involve a righteousness that comes through faith.

There are two key reasons why faith is so important. One is that if we cannot trust the declarations of our King and creator, we are denigrating His perfect character. To say, 'your word isn't true' is to say, 'I know better.' And to say a finite human's speech is greater and more reliable than that of an infinite creator is nothing short of blasphemy. The other is that faith keeps God first and foremost in the relationship. As Paul explains, if a right relationship with God were based on what we do and how good we are, then we would have reason to boast in ourselves[81] instead of boasting in God and His goodness and faithfulness. And this principle of faith as a vital element of a relationship with God is not a new development. It was not as though God got to Abram and said, 'Okay, I'm now going to start this faith-righteousness thing with you.' As we look in Hebrews 11, we find Noah and Enoch and Abel listed as righteous people commended by God and in a relationship with Him because of their faith. The hermeneutical

---

80 Heb 11:6

81 Rom 3:27; 4:2-5

principle that this highlights is that although a theological principle may not yet be explicitly mentioned, or extensively spelt out in the preceding revelation, doesn't mean it wasn't necessarily there. Nonetheless, one must venture cautiously beyond the plain text as the descent into error is a steep one. Therefore, it is in Genesis 15 that we can point most clearly to the universal principle and truth that a right relationship with God, and the deliverance of His promises, are dependent on the divinely inspired and empowered faith of humanity.

This ceremonial ritual and oath are not only greatly significant theologically because it reinforces such an amazing truth about God's faithfulness and commitment to His promises. It is narratively significant as well. If God has so adamantly sworn that He will come through with the giving of a child, nationhood, and worldwide blessing, then the story demands that we can expect to see this being fulfilled. It is this oath, as we will explore later, that continues to drive the Bible's narrative, anchoring the ongoing plot to this Abrahamic covenant which is fleshed out over the remaining chapters of Genesis and beyond. Failure to do so would not only result in theological and cosmological consequences (i.e. God ceases to exist and the universe caves in on itself) but also narrative consequences.

Imagine if after meeting Obi-Wan, Luke decides to not begin training and returns home to live with Owen and Beru. Or what if Neo chose the blue pill? Imagine that Bruce Wayne decided to allow Gotham's justice system to take care of crime. What a disappointing and short story. The same could be said of the biblical narrative. Imagine if the story ended at the conclusion of Genesis. God would have given Abram descendants who could eventually take the land of Canaan, and because of Joseph, nations were blessed during the famine. But we know that the outcome of the millennia-long narrative is much better than that. That when this covenant with Abram came into effect, we see that the intention and fulfilment of the promises are greater than this anti-climactic ending. Before we map out the ongoing narrative, we need to look at the concept of the sign of the covenant, and what it teaches us about God and His promises.

DON'T JUMP AHEAD

But the son of the slave was born according to the flesh, while the son of the free woman was born through promise....[82]

Impatience, nervousness, and heat are not good for the brain. In a spark of genius, my wife and I decided that we should have our wedding in early December. We did this so that I wouldn't be away on exercise with the Army on our anniversary - an experience I had heard of from married defence members. This just happened to fall on one of the hottest summers in Brisbane. In fact, NASA stated that that year was the hottest to date since the late 1800s.[83] But apart from sweating myself into oblivion wearing a three-piece suit, it was a wonderful day and the joy and excitement of marrying the woman I loved, along with seeing how beautiful she looked, overshadowed my discomfort. However, it was not without its subtle embarrassment (subtle in the sense that not many people knew), as the heat, as well as the excitement of the day, meant I couldn't think very clearly. My wife, unbeknownst to me in preparation for the exchanging of

82 Gal 4:23

83 https://www.nasa.gov/vision/earth/environment/2005_warmest.html

rings, had put her engagement ring on her right hand since, apparently, the wedding ring goes behind the engagement ring. And after I had said my vows and put the ring on her finger, I panicked as I saw the engagement ring on the other hand. Without saying anything, I quickly tried to fix it up by attempting to take the ring off her finger and put it on what I thought was the correct hand. The details of what happened next over the following few seconds aren't perfectly clear in my mind, but I do remember the embarrassment of realising the mistake I had made and my rush to correct it. I took the sign of our covenant seriously, and I wanted to make sure it was done properly. But I rushed in according to my limited knowledge. I should have trusted the silence of our pastor who did not correct me, as an indication that all was well. The same could be said of the silence of my wife.

The following chapters of the Abrahamic narrative likewise sees an intersection of rushing ahead and covenantal signs, although in a more dramatic and significant way.

The Promises Unpacked

Even though the reader has only advanced five chapters, twenty-five years had passed for Abram since leaving his family and entering the land. And it was at this point, at the age of ninety-nine, that the Lord comes for the fourth time to reaffirm His covenant and calling with Abram. On this occasion, as well as repeating the promises, the Lord elaborates on them by explaining what He intends to do through Abram. The inclusion of extra details does not make this another covenant, nor does it require a repetition of the ceremony. Rather, God was unpacking what was 'hidden' within those promises and explaining further how they will ultimately be fulfilled. It is kind of like the part of the story where the hero, or some other leading character, lays out the plan. The audience knows it is coming, but now they get a glimpse into how it will play out. Like when General Dodonna explained the mission on how to destroy the Death Star. Or when someone describes how that diegetic world works, such as in *Inception* when Cobb, Eames, and Yusuf tell Ariadne about the compressed relativity of time within a dream. In Scripture, this further unveiling is known as 'progressive revelation': the principle that God's divine revelation of His identity, plans, and purposes were not given all at once. Rather, it was given over time in stages.

When it comes to progressive revelation, for the most part, what we are given is elaboration and unpacking over time of something that was revealed earlier in 'seed form.' Thus, when understanding how progressive revelation builds on the biblical narrative and develops theological themes and doctrines, it is important to remember that "later revelation builds on earlier revelation, complementing and supplementing," [84] rather than evolving, nullifying, or contradicting the original. Moreover, these new details can be considered the result of elaboration rather than anything separate and new. This faulty understanding of progressive revelation is used by groups such as Mormons and Jehovah's Witnesses to try to explain those passages that contradict their doctrines, claiming that they have 'new light.' Genuine progressive revelation, however, is always consistent with what has gone before.

Possibly, the best illustration I can think of is an example from photography. A key principle that most photographers use or manipulate is that of depth-of-field: the distance between the nearest and furthest objects in focus. If a friend in front of you is clear and the beach just behind them is blurry, then you have a short depth of field. This is common with portrait

---

84 Erickson, M. *Christian Theology*. p.222-223

photography. If the cow in the paddock and the mountains in the background are both in focus, then you have a deep depth of field, which is common in landscape photography. The role of progressive revelation is to lengthen the depth of field of what God has revealed in Scripture. Just as the focussing of the blurred mass in the background brings out its shape and texture to reveal a park filled with children, so too does the progressive revelation of God bring out the details and workings of the plans and purposes of the Lord.

In a sense, my students encounter progressive revelation in my classroom. When I take my English class through any unit of study, I start by giving them an introduction and overview of the term's content, and a general description of the assessment tasks they will need to complete. Then, over the following lessons, the students progressively discover the details of what content they will focus on, the activities that will help them learn, the skills they will practice, and how they all fit together to allow them to reach their goal: completing their assessment as a demonstration of learning. And even though they will be learning about things like the historical context of Shakespeare one week, reading a story the next, and writing their assessment in the closing weeks of the term, it is not as though they have changed units or subjects. Rather, the details of the plan towards achieving the unit's goal, which was given in a brief summarised version at the beginning, are progressively unveiled. The same applies to progressive revelation in Scripture.

There are numerous examples of this process in Scripture. For example, in Genesis 1, it says that as the pinnacle of creation God created man and woman in His image. Then in Genesis 2, we discover the actual process of how that happened. Another example is seen in the Law. Having given the Ten Commandments through Moses, God fleshes out their application in cultic and daily life as kinds of case law over the expanse of the remainder of the Torah. Other examples cover wider amounts of text, often spanning the entire canon of Scripture. For instance, when it comes to the doctrine of the afterlife, we don't encounter anything specific regarding judgement or the resurrection until Daniel 12. Then later in the Apostolic Scriptures, its authors elaborate on it more completely, culminating in the description of the new heavens and earth in Revelation 21. The most significant example of progressive revelation, however, is God's plan of redemption. Throughout the Tanakh, hints and markers of this plan are laid out, sometimes explicitly, but more often they are subtle and at times hidden. These signposts culminate in the person and work of Christ and are explained by the teachings of Jesus and the Apostles. The most famous is the Emmaus road experience when Jesus, "beginning with Moses and all the Prophets… interpreted to them in all the Scriptures the things concerning himself."[85] The author of Hebrews picks up on this when they describe Jesus as the culmination of God's self-revelation.[86] And Peter, on Pentecost, under the influence of the Holy Spirit, reveals how within Psalm 16 was a prophetic revelation of the resurrection as a sign that Jesus was the promised Messianic King.[87] Interestingly, we find little in the Gospels by way of instruction or evidence for justification by faith in the death and resurrection of Christ. The closest we come is the words of John 3:16, "For God so loved the world, that he gave his only Son, that whoever believes in him should not perish but have eternal life…" which is itself still a little vague, and "the Son of Man came not to be served but to serve, and to give his life as a ransom for many."[88] Beyond that, one must consult the sermons in Acts and the Epistles to gain a clearer understanding of that doctrine. It was as though

---

85 Lk 24:27
86 Heb 1:1-2
87 Acts 2:24-33
88 Mk 10:45

the Tanakh's messianic revelations were pregnant with the meaning and significance that were only realised and recognised after the crucifixion and resurrection of Christ. And rather than creating new spiritualised meanings, or explaining Jesus as an alternate plan, the Apostles, empowered by the Holy Spirit, were able to faithfully deliver the truth hidden within, and proclaim it in their teaching. It was according to this pattern of progressive revelation that God was explaining the details of His promises to Abram.

It is as though back in Genesis 12 God showed Abram a box labelled 'promises' and then proceeded to pull out another from inside it labelled: land, descendants, and blessing to the nations. In Genesis 15, God began to open this second box and begin to show in greater detail how the land will be occupied. Here in chapter 17, God is continuing to unpack this second box to reveal how the land and Abram's descendants will bring about the blessing to the nations.

We see this first in the way that the Lord declares that He will 'make His covenant with Abram.'[89] Although it sounds like the Lord is either making a new covenant or is confused and forgot that He has already made this covenant, the language suggests something else. The word for make, *natan*, in this context, suggests that He is about to set into motion the covenant that was ratified in Genesis 15:8. Thus, in this conversation, God is explaining how the promises of 15:8, which are based on 12:1-3, will work themselves out.[90] The Lord does this to demonstrate to Abram that is He in control of the story He is writing and that He has everything planned out to the very end. But more than that, He is also challenging Abram to think even bigger about what He intends to do through him and his descendants.

---

89 Gen 17:2

90 Dumbrel, W. *Covenant and Creation.* p.101-102

Father of Nations

The first elaboration we encounter is that Abram would become 'the father of a multitude of nations.'[91] To commemorate and reflect this new identity, the Lord changed his name from Abram (exalted father) to Abraham (father of a multitude). God had previously told him that he would have innumerable descendants and that in him all nations would be blessed, but now God reveals a closer connection between the two. Consequently, the second elaboration is that "kings shall come from you." Indeed, Abram would become the father of nations besides Israel primarily through Ishmael and Esau, and those nations would have kings. However, as the biblical narrative unfolds, it is revealed that numerous kings of Israel would play a role in the fulfilment of God's promise to Abraham. However, as we see in the continued elaborations of the Lord's promises, as well as the ongoing Abrahamic narrative, we find that just like the nature of the promise of blessing, there is more to this declaration than 'as your family grows, they will become different nations who have kings.'

The first hint of this greater picture is found in how God tells Abraham:

> I will establish my covenant between me and you and your offspring after you throughout their generations for an everlasting covenant, to be God to you and to your offspring after you.[92]

This too is a significant elaboration as it reveals further details about the Abrahamic promises. One is that it reinforces the perpetual nature of the covenant the Lord made with Abram since his descendants after him would experience the ongoing fulfilment of the promises of the everlasting

---

91 Gen 17:4
92 Gen 17:7

covenant. Another is that it makes explicit the heart of the promise of blessing discussed in the first chapter, namely, that 'He will be their God.' This combination of the relational and perpetual nature of the covenant reveals the depths of its corporate and communal reality. It wasn't some kind of divine 'trickle-down economics' where Abraham would be blessed, and his descendants would share in the overflow of God's provision. God would establish His covenant with each of Abraham's descendants and they would be united in a common bond with the creator of the universe. This promise of relationship, which has its roots in the *protoevangelium* of Genesis 3, would become a significant goal for the remainder of the biblical narrative. As George Ladd explains, the declaration that

> God will be God to his people is the central element of God's covenant with his people throughout the entire course of redemptive history... in the covenant made with Abraham... with Moses [Ex 6:7]... and with David (2Sam 7:24f).[93]

This desire to be God to Abraham's descendants was repeated by the Lord through prophets like Jeremiah and Hosea, as He sought a reconciled relationship with the people who had strayed from him into idolatry. The repetition of this invitation over many generations after Abraham shows us that God was indeed faithful to this promise and that His plans and intentions never changed. Thus, the combination of the promise of Abraham's fatherhood and God's divine headship is a foreshadowing that the people Abraham would be the father of were those of whom the Lord, Yahweh, is their God and that they would come from a multitude of different nations.

---

93 Ladd, G. *A Theology of the New Testament.* p.682

Despite the large potential scope of the Abrahamic promises, when God revealed to Abraham that Ishmael was not to be His intended heir, we find a narrowing of the covenant's beneficiaries taking place. For thirteen years, Abraham was no doubt convinced that the boy Ishmael had arrived as the child of promise. But God told Abraham that He was also changing Sarai's name to Sarah, meaning princess, and that He was going to bless her too. He declared, "I will give you a son by her. I will bless her, and she shall become nations; kings of peoples shall come from her."[94] Prior to this conversation, the reader has only heard that it was from Abraham that the promised lineage would come. But now Abraham and the reader discover that Sarah was to be involved as well. Upon hearing that it was through her that the nations and kings would come, Abraham realised that the promise was not for Ishmael. He desired that the Lord would continue His covenant through Ishmael, so he begged God, "Oh that Ishmael might live before you!" But God said 'no', and explained that Sarah would have a son, and they were to name him Isaac, and the Lord would establish His covenant with *him*.[95] Therefore, despite being the offspring of Abraham, and later receiving the sign of circumcision, Ishmael was not to be in the line of the covenant.

This revelation lays the foundation for the principle that not all the descendants of Abraham would belong to the covenant of promise. To participate in the blessings of the covenant, and to be in a relationship with the creator as their God, is not according to blood lines, but rather something more substantial: the faith of Abraham. And this concept is reflected in the meaning of the covenant sign of circumcision.

---

94 Gen 17:16

95 Gen 17:18-21

Sign of the Covenant

In the midst of God's conversation with Abraham, as He was reaffirming his covenant with him, He gave him the following instruction:

> This is my covenant, which you shall keep, between me and you and your offspring after you: Every male among you shall be circumcised. You shall be circumcised in the flesh of your foreskins, and it shall be a sign of the covenant between me and you. He who is eight days old among you shall be circumcised. Every male throughout your generations, whether born in your house or bought with your money from any foreigner who is not of your offspring, both he who is born in your house and he who is bought with your money, shall surely be circumcised. So shall my covenant be in your flesh an everlasting covenant.[96]

It is here, in telling Abraham that he and all his descendants are to be circumcised, that the Lord is instituting circumcision as a sign of the covenant.

Within any language, nouns provide a vital role in communication as they indicate the what of the sentence. There are different types of nouns. One key distinction between nouns is their ontological differences, expressed in the categories of concrete and abstract nouns. Concrete nouns are the things we can see, touch and taste like building, chicken, and phone. Abstract nouns are things that cannot be experienced by the senses such as love, peace, and fear. What has this got to do with circumcision? Well, signs provide a concrete demonstration of abstract realities. In other words, a

[96] Gen 17:10-13

sign functions as a physical and visual reminder that points to something else more abstract. In a sense, some of the deities of the Ancient Greeks and Romans such as Nike and Fortune worked in a similar way as they were personifications of abstract concepts like victory and fate, except a sign was much more substantial and concrete. A significant covenantal sign in today's society is the wedding ring. Although its history is a little vague, the wedding ring is generally considered to have originated in Ancient Egypt as a symbol of never-ending love, as represented by the endless circle that is its shape. For the Romans, it functioned more as a sign of ownership, and the iron it was made from symbolised strength and permanence. Thus, the nature of a concrete sign helps us to understand something of the abstract reality being symbolised and pointed to. In poetry, we call this a metaphor. Today, the original understanding of the ring as a symbol of the pledge of lifelong love that forms the foundation of a marriage is most common. Circumcision functions in a similar way as it is a physical symbol of the spiritual and theological realities of the covenant.

There is a range of understandings and interpretations among Christians when it comes to making sense of what circumcision was about. The opinions of those writing in the early centuries of the church are particularly interesting. For instance, in the apocryphal Gospel of Thomas, the author - influenced by their gnostic dismissal of the material world - expresses a rejection of circumcision, saying that the practice is meaningless and unhelpful. They do this by putting the following words into the mouth of Jesus:

> If [circumcision] helped, people's fathers would beget them from their mothers already circumcised. But true circumcision in spirit has become very profitable.[97]

[97] *Gospel of Thomas*, Saying 53

Justin Martyr in his Dialogue with Trypho puts an anti-Semitic twist on his argument against circumcision, arguing that it served as a sign of God's displeasure and a marker for judgement:

> For the circumcision according to the flesh, which is from Abraham, was given for a sign; that you may be separated from other nations, and from us; and that you alone may suffer that which you now justly suffer; and that your land may be desolate, and your cities burned with fire; and that strangers may eat your fruit in your presence, and not one of you may go up to Jerusalem.[98]

Fortunately, the church has moved on from anti-Semitic polemics, although some passive supercessionist attitudes still exist in a few circles. I have often heard it claimed that circumcision was the old way of 'getting saved' and the Jew's assurance of their adoption. And when reading Paul's polemics in the New Testament about the matter at face value, it is an easy conclusion to draw. Others, connecting it with the Mosaic Law consider it a part of the 'legalistic bondage' that Jesus liberated us from. Still others, because of the teachings of the Reformers, see Baptism as having replaced circumcision as a sign of the covenant. Calvin, for instance, explains that "there is no difference in the internal meaning [between circumcision and baptism]... Hence, we may conclude that everything applicable to circumcision applies also to baptism."[99] And no doubt, there are still some believers who understand it as some rite the Jews had to go through, but not sure why or what it's about.

---

98 Justin Martyr. *Trypho*. 16

99 Calvin, *Institutes*. 4.16.4

But what exactly is circumcision and what did it mean for the Abrahamic covenant? If it is a sign, then what specifically was it pointing to?

But first, it is important to realise that in this moment God was not inventing circumcision. It was not as though God was asking Abraham to do something radically new. Rather, he was taking a well-known, pre-existing practice, and redefining its meaning for His purposes. There are numerous anthropological theories as to why and when circumcision began, and no doubt different societies had different interpretations of the practice. Some hypothesise that it served as an initiation rite into adulthood which may have simultaneously carried with it a symbol of social status. Others suggest it was a ritual to promote fertility. And there are those who believe that it was some kind of sacrificial gift to the gods in return for a good harvest. The reality is we cannot know for certain, and perhaps there's some truth in all of them depending on the society. The point is that God was contextualising this practice, just as he did with the ceremony in Genesis 15. The exact meaning of circumcision in a biblical, covenantal setting is never explicitly explained. Nonetheless, by considering what preceded this conversation between Abraham and God, and other instances of circumcision through Scripture, we can draw some conclusions about what it means.

The key to the interpretation of the sign is in the events that had come before. In the previous chapter of Genesis, time was ticking on for Abram and Sarai. They had been in the land for ten years, yet they remained childless and landless. And after that huge ceremony, they no doubt believed that the promised child was at arm's length; but still nothing. And because their inheritance appeared to be delayed, Sarai concluded "the Lord has prevented me from bearing children..."[100] We may look back and deride

[100] Gen 16:2a

her for her lack of faith, but we need to remember that a significant amount of time had passed. I doubt many Christians today who believe they have been called to do something, and after pursuing it for ten years with no success would conclude much differently. We also need to realise that, as I explained earlier, it wasn't until several years after the ceremony that they learned explicitly that the child of promise was to come through Sarai as well. From a rational level, this seemed like a fair conclusion. Thus, because the Lord was taking a long time, they decided to do something. Pursuing what was considered a common custom for barren wives in that society and culture, Sarai tells Abram: 'Go in to my servant; it may be that I shall obtain children by her.'[101] What is worth noting is that there was no consultation with the Lord. Neither Abram nor Sarai ever called on God and asked Him, 'is this the way the promise is to come?' And perhaps, this is the reason why the Lord never gave Abram all the information. Maybe this was a way to test his dependence on God's wisdom and encourage him to seek Him. Nonetheless, this failure to wait on the Lord for his guidance and direction is where they went wrong. And what made their error so serious was the significance of what the Lord was wanting to achieve and reveal about Himself and His purposes through Abram. Thus, by seeking to fulfil the promise of Yahweh by means of human customs, traditions, and wisdom, they were jumping ahead without thinking. They weren't paying attention to the silence of the Lord who said nothing about conceiving through Hagar. And by doing this, they were demonstrating a lack of faith in God.

Although the consequences were much greater for Abram and his family, this was similar to what happened to me at my wedding in the story I mentioned earlier. Abraham and I were acting without thinking in an

[101] Gen 16:2b

attempt to bring about and preserve a good thing in an unnecessary way. The other side of this act with Hagar that made it wrong was that it was denying God the possibility of being glorified for bringing about what He had promised. If I had told my wife that I wanted to get her a nice gift to show her I love her and make her feel special, and she goes out and gets it before I can, I'd be quite annoyed. I would have wanted to be the one who gave her something special, but that joy and privilege has been robbed from me. And while it may be prideful for me to want to demonstrate how good a husband I could be, it would not be prideful for God to show off how powerful He is. God wants to demonstrate His power and glory for the benefit of Abram, Sarai, and those of the families of the earth who would be blessed through them. And this is most likely the reason why He took such a long to deliver the promise of descendants. Just like Jesus left Lazarus in the tomb for four days, the Lord was allowing enough time to pass so that any procreation between Abraham and Sarah could only be a work of God. And by miraculously achieving the impossible, God would be glorified. To allow the oath to be fulfilled by human effort, would corrupt the essence of the promise of blessing that was to come by faith, and not by works, and hinder the demonstration of God's omnipotence and faithfulness.

It is this context and understanding of Abram and Hagar that serves as the background for circumcision. The symbolic act of cutting the flesh from the male reproductive organ serves as a reminder that the promised seed of Abraham, and the blessings that come through him, will be delivered not by human efforts. And the one that bears the sign does so as a demonstration of their faith that the fulness of the Abrahamic promises will be fulfilled purely by the sovereign hand of God.

In his article on circumcision, Hector Avalos proposes the theory that since branding and marking of the body served as a sign of slavery,[102] and that the Lord was a slave owner of the Israelites he redeemed from Egypt,[103] circumcision, therefore, functioned as a symbol of submission to the divine will.[104] Despite the scantiness of any historical evidence of circumcision as a sign of slavery, that Egyptian nobility including the pharaoh was circumcised, and that this sign was established long before the exodus, the logic of the metaphor still works. The act of circumcision demonstrated submission to the sovereignty of God in order to fulfil His promises. This reflects not only the Lord's declaration to Abraham that He would be God to his descendants but also the way slaves needed to follow the leading of their master so that their lord's purposes can be worked out through them. This submission is nothing less than a declaration of faith. Thus, circumcision is a sign of the bearer's faith in Yahweh's commitment and ability to deliver on his covenant promises. Moreover, it is a perpetual reminder and declaration that God's restoration of all things will be achieved by the child who will come by a sovereign act of God through the line of Abram. It was never intended as a means of salvation. As Martin Luther in his commentary on Galatians explains, "The fathers were not justified by circumcision. It was to them a sign and seal of righteousness. They looked upon circumcision as a confession of their faith."[105]

Writing on the significance of circumcision, John Goldingay elaborates on this idea by highlighting that whenever we come across a significant act of circumcision in Scripture - such as Abraham, Moses and Zipporah,[106]

---

102 Ex 21:5-6

103 Lev 25:39-42

104 Avalos, Hector. "Circumcision as a Slave Mark", *Perspectives in Religious Studies.* p.261

105 Luther, M. *Galatians.* p.29 – Writing on Gal 2:3.

106 Ex 4:24-26

and the people of Israel at Gilgal[107] - it is in the context of God being about to deliver His promises that He made to Abraham. In the above cases, it was in preparation for the giving of descendants and the deliverance from Egypt to bring them into the Land. Interestingly, in each of these instances, they had previously taken some action that could potentially communicate that their actions will bring about God's promise: Abram's begetting of a child through Hagar, Moses killing an Egyptian, and Joshua and the Israelites crossing the Jordan River. When we consider each event and how the imminent fulfilment of God's promises - the begetting of Isaac, the victory over the Pharaoh, the conquest of Jericho - are impossible, we can see how the cutting back of the flesh with its potency demonstrates the subordinating of human strength to the divine plan.[108]

Considering the wider narrative of these significant major circumcision passages, and the dependence on the Lord to bring about His impossible covenant promises, we see that the practice of circumcision is no spiritually meaningless, legalistic work of the flesh about group identity. Although by the Hellenistic era this had become the case, it was never the original intended meaning. Rather, it is a sign of the faith of its bearer in the commitment and capacity of the Lord to deliver on His impossible promises.

Covenant Obligations

Another interesting development in the Abrahamic covenant that is apparent in the inclusion of the demand for circumcision is that law has now become a part of the agreement. This, however, is not the first time the Lord placed obligations on Abraham. He is told to "Go from your country

[107] Josh 5:2-9

[108] Goldingay, J. "The Significance of Circumcision." *JSOT.* p.13-14

and your kindred and your father's in house" in 12:1, to walk to-and-fro through the land in 13:17, and to "walk before me, and be blameless" here in Genesis 17:1. Based on the grammar of the sentence, it appears that the instruction to 'walk before me', which, based on the Hebrew grammar, is to be a continuous action (or, 'walk, and keep walking') that would result in his blamelessness.

The Hebrew word used here for blameless, *tamiym*, when referring to people does not mean to live without sin, for that is impossible. In fact, Noah, Job, Elizabeth, and Zechariah among others were described as blameless, however, they could not have possibly been without sin. The question that follows, therefore, is how are we to understand blamelessness? Blamelessness is more about internal character rather than external conformity, although the two are related. It means to have integrity and a fear of the Lord. When someone is blameless, they hate sin and seek a life of obedience. Moreover, their love of the Lord and faith in him are genuine. They don't harbour sin in their heart and pretend God isn't watching. Rather, when they do sin, because of their integrity, love for God and His ways, and pursuit of righteousness, they confess their sin in accordance with God's word. In the case of Elizabeth and Zechariah, or anyone else living in the time of the Tabernacle or either Temple, they would have brought the appropriate sacrifice accompanied by a contrite heart as a part of their reconciliation in accordance with God's Law. For Abraham, blamelessness meant a persevering faith, as well as a pursuit of living according to God's ways, with confession and sacrifice forming a part of this.

With the introduction of law and the call to be blameless, does this then mean that the Abrahamic covenant has become a conditional covenant? Connected with each of the above instructions to Abraham was some declaration that obedience allows God to fulfil His promises. Indeed, Abraham is told that by his compliance, he is 'keeping the covenant.' This language is repeated often throughout Scripture, in particular when Israel was told by God: '*obey* my voice and *keep* my covenant.'[109] And later in Jeremiah, the prophet explains that it was because of their disobedience that the Israelites failed to keep the covenant.[110] The term, keep, or *shamar*, means to guard, protect, and preserve. This word is also used in Genesis 2:15 when "The Lord God took the man and put him in the Garden of Eden to work it and *keep* it." To keep a covenant, therefore, means in essence to be diligent to fulfil one's required covenantal obligations in order to preserve a positive and good-natured connection, which is similar to the relationship between parents and children. When our are kids disobedient, the essence and substance of the relationship changes to a posture of anger, displeasure, and discipline, yet love, compassion, and commitment remain. And when they are obedient, the parent's posture is happy, pleased, and celebratory. As discussed previously, since the ultimate blessing of the Abrahamic promises is the restored relationship with the Lord that was broken by sin, keeping the covenant is what allows one to experience the fullness of the blessings of that divine relationship. And this is what we see in the case of Abraham. For example, in the following chapter, the Lord said to the 'men'[111] accompanying Him:

> I have chosen [Abraham], that he may command his children and his household after him to keep the way of the Lord by doing righteousness and justice, *so that* the Lord may bring to Abraham what he has promised him.[112]

---

109 Ex 19:5

110 Jer 34:18

111 The Genesis narrative at this point refers to them as men, however the two men are most certainly the angels who rescue Lot from Sodom.

112 Gen 18:19. Emphasis added. See also Gen 22:18.

What makes the question more confusing is that these conditional statements are juxtaposed with indications of unconditional promises. Not just in the symbolism of the ceremony in Genesis 15, but also in the way the perpetual nature of the covenant requires God's sovereignty long after Abraham had died in order for it to be fulfilled.[113] How, then, are we to make sense of this? If, as we have seen repeatedly through the Abrahamic narrative, the promises are unconditional – a fact Paul makes much of in his letters – why do we have phrases such as '*so that*' wedged between obedience and the fulfilment of promises? The answer may be found in looking at the big picture of the Abrahamic promises.

Walter Kaiser argues that "the conditionality was not attached to the promise but only to the participants who would benefit from those promises."[114] In other words, God will fulfil his promises, but only those who walk blamelessly before him will experience them. Does this mean that one must live in perfect obedience to benefit from the blessings of the covenant? Not at all. Rather, by walking blamelessly (as defined earlier) in the pursuit of a close relationship with the Lord, one is demonstrating the genuineness of their faith, which is required to become true covenant members. Thus, the blessings of the covenant are contingent on faith, of which obedience is a necessary fruit. Therefore, circumcision and blameless living flows out of and derives from, rather than being a prerequisite for, the covenant relationship. Speaking on this, John Piper[115] explains that because of these conditional statements, one might suggest that the promises are not certain of fulfilment, for what if Abraham did not walk blamelessly before God? "But that is not true," he responds.

---

113 Essex, K. "The Abrahamic Covenant." *TMSJ* 10/2 (1999). p. 209

114 Kaiser, W. *Toward an Old Testament Theology*. p.94

115 Piper, J. *The Covenant of Abraham*. np

> It is a false assumption based squarely on the conviction that man is autonomous and self-determining. But if, as Ezekiel 36:27 says, God puts his Spirit in man and causes him to walk in his statutes (and thus fulfill the conditions of the covenant), then a promise can be both conditional and certain of fulfillment.

In other words, God's work of sanctification in Abraham as a righteous covenant member as a result of his faith meant that his blamelessness is a sign and proof of the certainty of his relational status. As James explains in his letter, "Was not Abraham our father justified by works when he offered up his son Isaac on the altar?"[116] It is important to note that the Greek word for justified used here, *dikaioo*, can mean to justify in the sense to make righteous (such as in Romans 3:26 and Galatians 3:11), but can also mean to vindicate or demonstrate one's righteousness. For example, in Luke 7:35 Jesus said, "...wisdom is justified [*dikaioo*] by all her children." The immediate context of James' letter and Paul's teaching in Romans 4 that Abraham was not justified by works shows that the second definition is James' meaning here in 2:21. The necessity, therefore, for Abraham to bear the sign of the covenant of circumcision, and to walk blamelessly before the Lord, in order for the promises to be fulfilled can be compared to going swimming. For someone to get into the pool, they must become wet. This doesn't mean that they needed to drench themselves before getting in the pool, but by jumping in they will definitely get wet. And their soggy state and dripping water on the floor is evidence of having gone swimming. And this is why the uncircumcised was to be cut off from His people. Not because they failed to qualify, or that their election was somehow based on their works. But rather, by not being circumcised, they are failing to

---

[116] Js 2:21

identify themselves as belonging to the people of God who were within the sphere of his blessing and were thus in effect denying God's ability to fulfil His promises. In other words, their lack of faith was what actually cut them off.

On the other side of this coin, one's circumcision was no guarantee that they were genuine covenant members either. To extend the previous metaphor, it's easy for someone to wet themselves with a bucket or hose without getting in the pool. Because of this, it's difficult to say that Ishmael was in genuine covenant with God. For not only is the Bible is silent on this matter, but also the fact that he was circumcised despite the Lord telling Abram that he wasn't going to continue his promises through Ishmael. Perhaps God was simply saying that Ishmael wasn't the child of promise through whom the covenant line would be fulfilled and continued, but was nonetheless still invited to believe in the promised one to come. We aren't told about the faith of Ishmael, even though the covenant God made with him was material and merely by virtue of his connection to Abraham. It is possible that his circumcision was a representation of his genuine faith, but the silence of Scripture means we cannot be certain. What is evident here is there seems to be the emergence of material aspects of the covenant that would point the covenant member to the spiritual realities. The material was experienced by virtue of their connection with Abraham, the spiritual by their Abraham-like faith.

Another aspect of the relationship between obedience and the fulfilment of covenant promises is evident in its effect. For Abraham to bear the sign of circumcision to experience the fruit of the promises was not merely for his own benefit. In fact, Abraham would see very little of the fullness of what the Lord had sworn to him in his life. As the narrative in the *Torah* develops, it becomes evident that the obedience of Abraham and his descendants, and the faithfulness of God to deliver his promises, are primarily for the Lord's glory. And this glorification was to be a witness to the nations so that they might turn to God and receive the blessings of God's global restoration. An intention that was in focus with the inauguration of the Abrahamic covenant.

What we have considered about the obligational nature of the covenant, expressed in blamelessness and circumcision functioning as law, has great implications for our understanding of the nature of the Law. Some, such as George Ladd, would argue that "Circumcision… in its true significance does not belong to the Law, but is a sign and seal of justifying faith."[117] This interpretation suggests a cold and legalistic perception of the law. This view is misguided since, whenever moral obligations are placed on people, it is within the context and by-product of a covenantal, faith-based relationship – a concept emphasised by the way the author of Hebrews equates obedience with faith.[118] Perhaps a more accurate wording of Ladd's evaluation would be that 'Circumcision in its true significance is a sign and seal of justifying faith, as is the Law.'

The significance of this encounter in Genesis 17 is not so much the introduction of new principles and promises, but rather an explanation of how those existing principles would affect the delivery of the Lord's promises. We see that not everyone who is a descendant of Abraham will experience the true and ultimate blessings of the covenant, although there are temporal blessings for all his children for the sake of His promise to Abraham. Instead, it is those who have the genuine faith that brings one into a true relationship with God, and diligent to demonstrate that faith that will experience the fullness of those blessings. Moreover, at the heart of the Abrahamic covenant is a reminder of the miraculous nature of the

---

117 Ladd, *New Testament Theology*. p.550
118 Heb 4:2

fulfilment of God's promises and the necessity of His sovereignty, apart from the efforts of humanity, to bring about the restoration of creation. These two seemingly separate realities, God's divine and sovereign intervention to bring about His purposes and people's obligation to the covenant, come together in the sign of circumcision. It is almost as though the apparent paradox is resolved in this one symbolic act of cutting.

Summary of the Covenant

From our consideration of the Abrahamic narrative thus far, we have learned the essential elements of the Abrahamic covenant that play out through the remainder of the biblical story: that God graciously elected Abram so that through him He would do two things. One was to miraculously give him a child who would become a great nation that would inherit what was then known as the land of Caanan. The other was that this promise made within the context of a relationship, for which God took ultimate responsibility, would culminate in the restoration of creation that was damaged by sin. For God had also promised that He would invite Abram's 'descendants' into a relationship with Him to be their God. And the way that one entered this covenant, as the foundation of a relationship with the Lord, was by faith. However, obligations were made for Abraham and those covenant members who would come after him, as a demonstration of their faith in the one who made these promises.

The Abrahamic narrative continues over the following eight chapters of Genesis, which spans another seventy-six years as the promises made decades earlier begin to play out. The following year at the age of 100,

Abraham received the son of promise born to Sarah and was named Isaac. Later, God would test Abraham's faith and commitment. Eventually, Sarah dies and is buried in a plot of land that Abraham acquired from a Hittite. Sometime after, Isaac was married to Rebekah, and they, like his parents, experienced difficulty conceiving a child, having to wait forty years until the age of sixty before Jacob and Esau were born. This was the extent that Abraham got to enjoy the fulfilment of God's promises to him. He got to see the birth of not only his own descendent but also his grandchildren, Jacob and Esau, at the age of 160; a far cry from the innumerable children from many nations. And the most territory he actually inherited was the plot of land where Sarah and he were buried. But the story does not end there. As we continue to read through the remainder of Genesis, God, true to his word establishes and reaffirms the Abrahamic covenant with Isaac and Jacob, who, like Abraham, purchases a plot of land.[119] However, unlike Abraham, the land was intended for living upon, and not for the dead. And while the narrative's promised outcome has begun to be worked out, there is still some way to go. Through the book of Exodus and the Mosaic narrative, and right through the history of the nation of Israel, we can see how God's covenant with Abraham and its promises are fulfilled as they drive the narrative through the remainder of the Tanakh. This will be the focus of Part II.

[119] Gen 33:19

Part II
THE TANAKH

ABRAHAM AND MOSES

For the Lord your God is a merciful God. He will not leave you or destroy you or forget the covenant with your fathers that he swore to them.[120]

A sequel can either improve a movie franchise or bring shame and disappointment to its fans. Consider the embarrassing incident of the fourth Indiana Jones film. What was so detrimental to the success of *The Crystal Skull*, apart from the cringe-worthy monkey man scene, is that it had departed from the film series' theme of the religious, supernatural, and spiritual to the scientific. In short, the franchise had shifted its genre from fantasy to science-fiction. Curtin University lecturer Andrew Cameron explains that the previous

> three films reinforce the importance of mythology and religious tradition... In these films, Indy takes the role of guardian, protecting [religious] artefacts from abuse and misappropriation... Indy upholds and defends our oldest beliefs.

---

120 Deut 4:31

> The Crystal Skull does not follow the same formula. It is a distinctly science-fictional story, with the crystal skulls revealed to have an extraterrestrial origin… It should also be mentioned that crystal skulls, which are often depicted as pre-Columbian Mesoamerican artifacts containing mystical powers, are actually products of the nineteenth and twentieth centuries. They are basically elaborate hoaxes… The film is therefore not based in an established religious tradition, but one that is more akin to recent pseudoscience.[121]

In short, fans were disappointed because it was, essentially an Indiana Jones film in name only. Other sequels like *Terminator 3*, although remaining true to the genre, failed because of poor writing and lack of creativity. For example, the writers — who apparently dislike the original films and took on the role purely to buy a new house — got John Connor's age wrong, the enemy T-X and its mission were poorly designed, and the use of humour didn't work. This sometimes happens in 'unplanned' sequels. In fact, most sequels are unplanned. Consider that *The Empire Strikes Back*, *Shrek 2*, and *Back to the Future II*, all very successful sequels, were developed because of the success of the original film. What makes for a successful sequel is continuity. These films, and others such as *Aliens*, pick up where the last story left off. The characters, plot, and themes are consistent, and the effort that goes into writing it shows that they aren't sequels for the sake of money. When this happens repeatedly, especially with plot continuity, you end up with a successful saga.

The classic type of saga is the three-part variety, best represented in the aforementioned *Star Wars*, *Back to the Future*, *The Lord of the Rings*, and

[121] Cameron, A. *Learning Lessons from Indiana Jones 4.* (sic)

Christopher Nolan's Batman trilogy. What is common across these saga narratives, whether film or novel, is that in the first text we are introduced to the central characters, their initial goals and obstacles, and the overarching problem that needs to be resolved. By the end of the first narrative, there's been a small, albeit significant, victory, but the overarching problem is still there. Then, when we enter the second story, although the rules are unchanged, the stakes are a little higher. Moreover, the diegetic world often expands as it allows the audience to discover more about it. In *The Matrix* trilogy, for example, our understanding of that universe in the first film was restricted to the virtual world of the Matrix and the protagonist's ship, The Nebuchadnezzar. In the following films, audiences get to see the human base, the robot city, and the inner workings of the Matrix. The stakes are raised for Neo because his new powers make him a greater threat to the system, and Agent Smith's new ability makes him a more formidable opponent. However, although there are new obstacles, there is still the same goal. In *The Matrix*, it was to rescue humanity from the robots. In *Star Wars*, it was to destroy the Empire. Sometimes, part one sets us up with some kind of initial promise that will lead to the ultimate resolution. In *Star Wars*, this was the expectation of Luke becoming a powerful Jedi, which was only partly begun in the first film and not fully realised until *Return of the Jedi*. Part two also typically ends with some kind of cliff-hanger as a delay in fulfilment of the overall goal, such as in *Back to the Future 2* when Doc gets zapped back to 1885 before Marty can get back to the 'recently restored' 1985.

The story of the Exodus in relationship to Genesis is much like these sagas, except that it was not an afterthought, such as with Back to the Future, nor poorly written like the Matrix sequels. Rather, the Mosaic narrative is very much an intentional continuation of the Abrahamic narrative. There was a small victory with Abraham having descendants Isaac and Jacob, owning a part of the land, and his great-grandson Joseph blessing the world with grain from Egypt. However, the overall mission, the redemption of humanity and creation, is still to take place, and we are still yet to see the fulfilled promise of occupation of the land by the descendants of Abraham as a great nation as well. Moreover, as we will see later in this section, the stakes are higher as the goal is greater, and more can go wrong with a nation of people compared to simply dealing with individuals and small families. Thus, in this sense, the Mosaic narrative is not a disconnected, spin-off sequel to the Abrahamic story like *U.S Marshals* is to *The Fugitive.* It is a continuation of the divine protagonist's mission to deliver on his plan to restore creation and fulfil his promises to Abraham, in which the rules, principles, and covenant foundations that govern His actions remain unchanged. The Mosaic Covenant, we will see, is not some disconnected dispensation or new project. It is the intentional theological fulfilment of what God began to do through Abraham to restore fallen creation. We see this in the way God's relationship between the descendants of Abraham, the land they are to inherit, and the outworking of blessing to the nations intertwine and function as a precursor and witness to our creator's restored Kingdom.

Prelude to the Exodus

The book of Exodus begins by passing the covenantal torch onto one who would play a key role in the next significant phase of the fulfilment of the Abrahamic promises. A descendant through the line of Abraham's great-grandson Levi named Moses would become, like Abram, the mediator of a covenant to the offspring of Abraham that furthers the plans and purposes promised in Genesis 12.

But before the reader is introduced to Moses, Exodus begins by describing the fulfilment of the promise of nationhood by explaining how the seventy descendants of Abraham rapidly multiplied and grew to become a large body of people. A new king, who supposedly knew nothing about Joseph and the way he blessed Egypt and the surrounding nations during the great famine, came to power. Responding with fear to their growth, Pharaoh put the Hebrews into slavery to stop them from rising against him and the Egyptians. However, the narrative tells us that "the more they were oppressed, the more they multiplied and the more they spread abroad."[122] As we read on, we find that the people were calling out to God for deliverance. And, as Exodus 2:24 tells us, "God heard their groaning, and God remembered his covenant with Abraham, with Isaac, and with Jacob." This verse describes one of the most foundational motives and driving forces behind the whole Exodus narrative. That the deliverance from slavery and bringing into the Land was an act of faithfulness to Abraham.

When we come across the word 'remembered' in Scripture, we shouldn't read that as God forgetting and ignoring Abraham's descendants until he hears their cries for deliverance at which point he says, 'Oh yeah! Whoops... *Those* guys.' Nor should we read it as some mere mental process, as though He simply thought about the promise He made to Abraham. The idea of God remembering is a much more active process. As an action-oriented language and mindset, to say in Hebrew that God remembered means that he saw and acted. More specifically, it was seeing the situation and acting in faithfulness to a covenant. This is what it means in Genesis 8:1 when 'God remembered Noah' after making a covenant to bring Noah safely through the flood. The principle applies to people as well. When Deuteronomy 8:18-19 says that God's people are to 'remember the Lord', it's not simply

[122] Ex 1:12

an instruction to call to mind that God is there. It is a call to walk in His ways and be faithful to Him in response to the covenant we have with Him.

And so, when God heard the cries of the people and remembered the covenant, Moses the author is telling us that God was about to act and move so as to deliver on his promises to Abraham, Isaac, and Jacob. In Genesis 12, the Lord promised Abram that he would become the father of a great nation. But it's hard for an oppressed people to function as one. Moreover, being away from the Land means that the promise cannot be fulfilled either. As we saw in a previous chapter[123], the Lord told Abram:

> Know for certain that your offspring will be sojourners in a land that is not theirs and will be servants there, and they will be afflicted for four hundred years. But I will bring judgment on the nation that they serve, and afterward they shall come out with great possessions.[124]

Thus, the Exodus was also a promise that formed part of the Abrahamic covenant, since the deliverance of the people from Egypt would be required to fulfil the primary promises. The implication of this is that everything that follows in the Mosaic narrative, and even the history of Israel, can be tied back to these promises made to Abram.

Consequently, the Abrahamic Covenant also serves as the foundational reason for Israel's election. As we saw in *The Promise*, the reason for Abram's election, apart from God simply choosing to, was an absolute mystery as the Bible is completely silent as to why. Israel's gracious election is founded on similar reasons, except we find God through Moses in Deuteronomy making more explicit claims as to why Israel was chosen to be God's people.

123 *Cutting a Covenant*

124 Gen 15:13-14

The reason that is given was because of the Abrahamic promises. This is most clearly communicated in Deuteronomy 4:37, "...he *loved your fathers* and *chose their offspring* after them and brought you out of Egypt with his own presence, by his great power..." Here in this passage, we find that it was because of his love for the patriarchs that God chose their descendants - the people of Israel - to be His chosen people, which he demonstrated with the Exodus. Thus, the promises, love for the patriarchs, the election of Israel, and the exodus are all intertwined. As Peter Enns highlights in his commentary on Exodus, the reality of these repeated references to the covenant with the Patriarchs in the Exodus narrative means that we cannot "properly understand the Exodus if we forget the connection to the patriarchs which is foundational to the book's message. The Exodus is about God's keeping a promise he made to Abraham."[125]

Later in Deuteronomy, Moses elaborates further on this relationship:

> The Lord your God has chosen you to be a people for his treasured possession, out of all the peoples who are on the face of the earth. It was not because you were more in number than any other people that the Lord set his love on you and chose you, for you were the fewest of all peoples, but it is because the Lord loves you and is keeping the oath that he swore to your fathers, that the Lord has brought you out with a mighty hand and redeemed you from the house of slavery, from the hand of Pharaoh king of Egypt.[126]

---

125 Enns, P. *Exodus.* p.387

126 Deut 7:6-8

Here, Moses is explaining to the people that they were chosen to be His treasured possession; not because of anything they had, could, or would do to merit His favour or impress Him, but rather that He chose to love them. We need to understand, as we saw in an earlier chapter, that this election and love are not separate matters. It's not that God elects them, and because they are elected, He consequently loves them. Rather, love and election are almost synonymous. This becomes quite evident when Paul in Romans 9, equates Jacob's election with God's love:

> …in order that God's purpose of *election* might continue, not because of works but because of him who calls - she was told, "The older will serve the younger." As it is written, "Jacob I *loved*, but Esau I hated."[127]

Moses also explains in the above passage from Deuteronomy that just like their election, the Lord doesn't want the people to think that they merited their deliverance. Thus, here we find one of the clearest demonstrations and explanations of grace at the heart of the Mosaic narrative. This grace is further reflected in the way Moses explains to the people that despite their pattern of rebellion, the Lord's ongoing faithfulness to them is likewise based on His commitment to the promises made to the patriarchs:

> Not because of your righteousness or the uprightness of your heart are you going in to possess their land, but because of the wickedness of these nations the Lord your God is driving them out from before you, and that he may confirm the word that the Lord swore to your fathers, to Abraham, to Isaac, and to Jacob.[128]

---

127 Rom 9:11-13

128 Deut 9:5

What this means is that we cannot say that the election of Israel took place at Mount Sinai. It wasn't as though God brought them to the mountain, made a covenant with them, and said, '*Now* you are mine.' Indeed, as Terence Fretheim explains in his commentary, "There is no 'election' of Israel in the book of Exodus; election is assumed."[129] In fact, we find a number of instances throughout the early chapters of Exodus of the Lord already calling the Israelites 'my people' and 'my firstborn.' Such as when Moses was told to tell Pharaoh on behalf of the Lord, "Let *my* people go."[130] And when God was commissioning Moses, He told him to tell Pharaoh: "Israel *is* my firstborn son, and I say to you, 'Let my son go that he may serve me.'"[131] This title of firstborn is very much a part of the language of adoption.[132] There is a popular idea that 'we are all God's children', and in a sense that is true since all people are his creation, but only those who are in a special relationship (covenant), with Him can truly consider themselves His children. And this is effectively what adoption is: conferring upon those that are not children of natural descent, the status of naturally born children.

A liturgical document from the collection of the Dead Sea Scrolls referred to as 'The Words of the Heavenly Lights', reflects this idea of Israel as God's adopted children. In it, the author addresses the Lord with praise, proclaiming "You have adopted us in the sight of all the nations"[133] before quoting Exodus 4:22. What this shows is that the ancient Israelites recognised this declaration in Exodus 4 as a confirmation of their adoption and was for them a point of praise. Therefore, as His firstborn, Israel was to

129 Fretheim, T. *Exodus.* p.208
130 Ex 5:1, 8:1, 10:3-4
131 Ex 4:22-23
132 Cf. Rom 9:4
133 4Q504-6, Col. 3. *The Dead Sea Scrolls.* p.523

enjoy a privileged relationship with their creator, which included the receiving of the inheritance promised in the Abrahamic Covenant. Moreover, as heirs of an inheritance, they were also God's ambassadors in the earth since sons received their inheritance from their father. For in the Ancient world, sons were considered to be representatives of their fathers. Indeed, God was referred to as the Father of Israel a number of times throughout the Tanakh:

> "Children have I reared and brought up, but they have rebelled against me."[134]
>
> "When Israel was a child, I loved him, and out of Egypt I called my son."[135]
>
> "Have you [Israel] not just now called to me, 'My father, you are the friend of my youth…'"[136]

But perhaps, none captures the theme of adoption so descriptively as these words found in Ezekiel 16:

> …on the day you were born your cord was not cut, nor were you washed with water to cleanse you, nor rubbed with salt, nor wrapped in swaddling cloths. No eye pitied you, to do any of these things to you out of compassion for you, but you were cast out on the open field, for you were abhorred, on the day that you were born.
>
> And when I passed by you and saw you wallowing in your blood, I said to you in your blood, 'Live!' I said to you in

134 Isa 1:2
135 Hos 11:1
136 Jer 3:4

> your blood, 'Live!' I made you flourish like a plant of the field. And you grew up and became tall and arrived at full adornment.

If therefore, Israel's election is clearly assumed from the beginning of the Mosaic narrative, then the people belonging to, and being in covenant relationship with God, are not merely a part of the covenant made later in chapter 19. It is in light of this understanding that we begin to feel the real weight and motives of God's resolve to deliver Israel from Egypt. Yes, He wants to be glorified. Yes, He wants to honour his promises to Abraham. But it is not as though He is cold towards Israel. Quite the opposite. As Dumbrell so aptly describes, since God has elected and adopted the descendants of Abraham, He "intervenes as a father to demand the return of his children from a tyrant who has enslaved them."[137] It is against this background that the meaning and structure of the covenant made at Sinai, as we will examine later, finds its richest meaning.

Since Scripture is silent on the when, we could conclude that God had elected and adopted every descendant of Abraham from Isaac onwards, with each individual and generation experiencing the benefits of that adoption differently. Thus, the generation alive at the Exodus were not unique in their adoption, it just so happened that they lived during a unique development of the Abrahamic promises.

Progressive Revelation

Sometimes experiences are opportunities for learning about the character of people. How they respond to difficulties, how they treat people (especially

137 Dumbrell, W. *Covenant and Creation.* p.130

when stressed), what kind of jokes do they make, what they talk about, how they spend their free time. All these things reveal their character.

Whenever I am teaching about characterisation, I get my students to consider three things about a character: their speech, actions, and thoughts. For example, Liesel in *The Book Thief* asks a lot of questions, stares at objects that interest her, and wonders about what things mean. These show her to be a curious person. We see in the story of *Romeo and Juliet* how Romeo so easily and quickly falls in and out of love, marries the girl he met the night before, rashly kills Tibalt, and takes his life when he thinks Juliet is dead. This reveals that he is an impulsive person. For the Israelites in Egypt, the upcoming Exodus and covenant was an opportunity for them to learn something about the character of their God. And this was all centred on the revelation of His Name.

When it comes to 'name' in a biblical sense, we are talking about more than the letters or sounds people make when addressing, getting the attention of, or talking about someone. It is all about character and renown. For example, when talking about the Temple, Solomon said: "Now it was in the heart of David my father to build a house for the name of the Lord, the God of Israel."[138] Here, we find that David wanted God to be honoured and glorified, and so he desired to build a temple to reflect His glory and majesty, albeit imperfectly. Also, in Psalm 8, we see this relationship through the use of parallelism, connecting name with glory: "O Lord, our Lord, how majestic is your *name* in all the earth! You have set your *glory* above the heavens."[139] And through the prophet Isaiah, God laments that "continually all the day my name is despised."[140] Here, the Lord is not upset that people might be making fun of how his name sounds in the way

---

138 1Kg 8:17

139 Ps 8:1

140 Isa 52:5

children are gifted at making anyone's name rhyme with an insult. Rather, because of the oppression and exile under the Assyrians, it appears people were questioning the goodness of God's character. Thus, when we come across references in the Bible to *name*, we need to think beyond the letters and sounds, although they have their relevance, knowing that they point to the glory, renown, and character of God. With this in mind, we now come to another passage that connects the exodus with the Abrahamic covenant.

When Moses and Aaron first confront Pharaoh, it doesn't go very well. He says no, and to demonstrate his indignation at the request, makes them collect their own straw to make bricks. Then to make it worse, the people complain and blame Moses for it. In turn, Moses expresses his frustration to the Lord that not only had He not delivered the people, but He also allowed Pharaoh to oppress the people further. But in response, God reassures Moses of the certainty of their deliverance:

> I am the Lord. I appeared to Abraham, to Isaac, and to Jacob, as God Almighty, but by my name the Lord I did not make myself known to them. I also established my covenant with them to give them the land of Canaan, the land in which they lived as sojourners. Moreover, I have heard the groaning of the people of Israel whom the Egyptians hold as slaves, and I have remembered my covenant. Say therefore to the people of Israel, 'I am the Lord, and I will bring you out from under the burdens of the Egyptians, and I will deliver you from slavery to them, and I will redeem you with an outstretched arm and with great acts of judgment. I will take you to be my people, and I will be your God, and you shall know that I am the Lord your God, who has brought you out from under the

> burdens of the Egyptians. I will bring you into the land that I swore to give to Abraham, to Isaac, and to Jacob. I will give it to you for a possession. I am the Lord.'[141]

Verse three of this passage is interesting, because it says that "by my name the Lord I did not make myself known to them…", yet we find that not only did Abraham (Gen 14:22), Sarai (Gen 16:2), Abraham's servant (Gen 24:12), Isaac (Gen 26:22) and Jacob (Gen 27:20) refer to God as 'Lord', but He, in fact, did declare Himself as Lord to them. For example, in Genesis 15 He said, "I am the LORD who brought you out from Ur of the Chaldeans…" It is important to note that this isn't just a title that is being used, like how a military member refers to an officer as Sir. In that instance, the Hebrew word *Adoni* would be used. However, here in Exodus 6, and the above instances in Genesis, the Hebrew tetragrammaton[142] *YHWH*, often pronounced Yahweh, is being used. Hence, every time we come across the capitalised LORD in our Bibles, behind it is the Hebrew name, Yahweh. That this name is more than a title is seen in the way God referred to it as 'his name' in Exodus 6. It is also used in Moses' initial encounter with God. Earlier in Exodus 3, Moses said:

> If I come to the people of Israel and say to them, 'The God of your fathers has sent me to you,' and they ask me, 'What is his name?' what shall I say to them?

And God answered:

> "I am who I am." And he said, "Say this to the people of Israel: 'I am has sent me to you.'" God also said to Moses,

141 Ex 6:2-8
142 Lit. four letters

> "Say this to the people of Israel: '*The Lord* [YHWH], the God of your fathers, the God of Abraham, the God of Isaac, and the God of Jacob, has sent me to you.' This is *my name* forever, and thus I am to be remembered throughout all generations.[143]

So here, God has declared that Yahweh is His name, or *shem* – the same used to denote proper nouns like Noah, Isaac, and Moses – and that it is His name is forever. As further evidence of the continuity between Abraham and Moses, the Lord has said that He not only their God but also the God of their fathers Abraham, Isaac, and Jacob. He is not some new deity that has come along to claim these people, nor has He moved on from the patriarchs. Rather, by connecting His identity with the patriarchs, He is wanting to reassure the Israelites by connecting them to the promises made to their fathers. In doing so, He is reinforcing the certainty of their deliverance because as Abraham's descendants, they are His special people.

But coming back to the topic of the new revelation of His name, how can it be that the Lord told Moses that He didn't make his name Yahweh known to the Patriarchs when the words of Genesis make it obvious that He had? How are we to make sense of this apparent contradiction? Quite simply, if we understand *name* as *character*, we can see that what God is about to do by redeeming Israel from Egypt in power is a significant aspect of His character He had not previously revealed to the patriarchs. Sure, he told Abram that He would deliver his descendants from captivity in Genesis 15, but the manner in which He would do so was not made known.

For the patriarchs, God was 'God Almighty,' or in Hebrew *El Shaddai*. This revelation of God is more focused on His might and power and sovereignty over creation. *El Shaddai* is the one who brings into existence that

---

[143] Emphasis added

which is not. By His word, all things were created out of nothingness. In his supremacy, He is the one who brought justice with the flood and preserved Noah and His family. For Abraham, *El Shaddai* is the one who protected him throughout His life, the one who is able to fulfil all of His promises, and the one who is able to give a barren couple a child. Interestingly, the first time this title is used is not until Genesis 17 when He commands Abraham to be blameless and changes his name from Abram. What this reveals is that as *El Shaddai*, He has the authority over Abraham to command and instruct Him. Therefore, for Abraham, Isaac, and Jacob, to call on *El Shaddai* is to call on the God of power and majesty. But for Israel from the time of Moses, the Lord was to be primarily a God who redeems. But it is not as though that aspect of God ceased to be revealed or became unimportant, nor does God have a split or shifting personality. On the contrary, when the Lord called Moses, it was to be by a 'mighty hand and outstretched arm' and signs of power that the Lord would deliver Israel from Egypt. Thus, His power was the means by which He would deliver them, and by His power, He would conquer the Promised Land for the people. Additionally, by His might, he would continue to protect them as His people.[144] Moreover, it is not as though the patriarchs did not know Him by His personal and covenantal name Yahweh, and that they did not consider themselves to be His covenant people. Thus, it was not as though God chooses to act as only *El Shaddai* in one instance, and as Yahweh another. The two work together and rely on each other.

What this revelation of His name shows us the reader of Scripture is that we have a God who is mighty and able, as well as personal and relational. Both existed and continue to exist. It is just that as the progressive revelation rolls on through Scripture, the upcoming exodus and covenant

---

144 Ps 91:1 ff.

would place a greater emphasis on the latter. God's people would get an insight into the God who uses His might and power to redeem and rescue His covenant people. Indeed, the Exodus paints a very vivid picture of how the Lord would fulfil the promise made in Genesis 3 to rescue and restore the world from the corruption of the fall. But more importantly, for our purposes in this book, we see that the events of the first Passover, which was the beginning of the Exodus proper, "were integral to God's faithfulness to His covenant with Abraham."[145] For on the one hand, as we saw in the previous section, God told Abram in Genesis 15 that his descendants would go into captivity, but He would rescue them and bring them into the Land. This is because He would have to release Abram's descendants from slavery if they were to become a great nation. It is not as though the Exodus was a whole new project, but rather, another phase in the ongoing fulfilment of the Abrahamic Covenant. And indeed, with great signs, God was able to deliver them from Egypt so that they could begin to experience the fulness of what it means for God to be their God, as was promised to Abraham.[146]

---

145 Jeffery, S. Ovey, M. Sach, A. *Pierced for our Transgressions*. p.41

146 Gen 17:8

WHAT IS THE MOSAIC COVENANT?

The light obtained by setting straw men on fire is not what we mean by illumination.[147]

I find misunderstandings most unfortunate. They create unnecessary conflict, division, and rejection. And when people are trying to resolve that kind of conflict, it's difficult to do. Usually, because both parties are often talking about two different things, or one believes that the other is being dishonest. In an article from Psychology Today, Leon Seltzer outlines nine reasons why people can be misunderstood.[148] Among these reasons include simple factors like the listener's mind wondering, speaking in a way that uses unfamiliar references, or having a different understanding of terms. For example, when

> "complimenting the innocence or spontaneity of someone's behavior, you might employ the word childlike. But

[147] Gopnick, A. "Are Liberals on the Wrong Side of History?" *New Yorker.* 20 Mar 2017.

[148] Seltzer. L "9 Reasons it's so easy to be Misunderstood." *psychologytoday.com*

> someone else may regard this term as synonymous with the much less flattering term childish, and take strong offense."[149]

Or perhaps, because of an accent or inflection, the person's meaning becomes misunderstood. More subconscious reasons for misunderstandings might be because the other person is mad at you, or you have done something that reminds them of a negative experience from their past. These two are related since with the latter, you may have reminded them by no real fault of your own, of another person they are mad at. Or perhaps they are 'negatively sensitised' to you, meaning that no matter what you say it will be taken and interpreted in a negative light. This is typical of deteriorated relationships. Having been on the receiving end of these latter two, the experience feels really unfair. This turns into what is known as negativity bias, and the reason political smear campaigns are so effective. In fact, studies have shown that the human brain "reacts more strongly to stimuli it deems negative."[150] And so, because something someone has said or done has been wrongly interpreted as having a particular meaning or motive, they are deemed to be in the wrong and alienated from people once considered friends. And recovering from this is difficult since not only are they mad at you and will reject any explanation, but also because of the remaining reason given by Seltzer as a cause for misunderstandings. He says that they have

> stringent, intransigent opinions... [unable] to 'take in' any viewpoint other than their own... [and therefore] whatever you might say to someone this uncompromising

---

149 Ibid.

150 Marano, H. "Our Brain's Negative Bias". *Psychologytoday.com*

> will pass through a "filter" protectively held in place and rendering impossible their ability to accurately, objectively, or sympathetically comprehend what you're sharing.[151]

In this case, someone having a deep-seated conviction about a certain issue, matter or event will not logically follow any evidence or arguments to the contrary because they will not really be listening. For example, explaining to the die-hard fan of a losing football team why the referee didn't actually rob them of victory.

Misunderstandings, therefore, have a range of causes. From miscommunication and incomplete information to the more emotionally filtered negativity bias and wilful filtering. It happens in relationships, and it happens in theological discussions too. Sometimes Christians mix up their terms, or use unfamiliar ones, and at times the other person gets distracted and doesn't pick up certain words or tone. Perhaps they use trigger words like *works*, *predestination*, and *prosperity* and the other party immediately assumes they are spouting some kind of heresy. Or perhaps because someone is challenging a strongly held theological conviction, the other person shuts down and tunes out. So, whenever theological conversations take place, it is important to be aware of not only how we are talking, but also to ensure we are tuning in to how the other person is reacting, in order to diagnose where the misunderstanding has taken place.

When it comes to the Mosaic Covenant, I have encountered many negative evaluations and critiques about it from a wide range of a number of Christians. Their negative description usually takes the form of overly conflating it with the Law, hyper-juxtaposing it with the Gospel by saying that it is all about works, that it was a burden to the people, and by saying its principles and foundations are alien to the New Covenant. In doing so,

---

151 Saltzer. *9 Reasons.*

I perceive that they have misunderstood the Mosaic Covenant, typically because they have an overly simplistic about its nature and how it relates to the biblical narrative.

This negative understanding of the Mosaic Covenant is usually the result of two different, albeit related, influences. The first is by reading Pauline polemics against the improper use of the Law with what is known as Covenantal Nomism[152] taught by the Judaisms of the day. The misunderstanding of these passages usually comes about by reading these passages in isolation from what the Tanakh says about the Mosaic Covenant, as well as through the lens of tradition. This tradition has been shaped by an unintended legacy of the Reformation that fought against works-based righteousness in that it created a kind of knee-jerk reaction in some Christians against anything that sounds like 'works' in their misguided attempt to protect the Gospel.

Typically, by approaching the Biblical text through these lenses, they not only cut off this covenant from the rest of Scripture, but also the conclusion is often reached that the Mosaic Covenant was a failed sociological experiment at best, and a costly object lesson at worst. In the first instance, the claim is made that the covenant and Law were there as an offer of reconciliation with God, but *only* ended up showing people they couldn't make themselves righteous. The second, says that it was there *merely* to point people to Christ with no real meaning or purpose for the covenant members. A kind of 1500 years of Daniel San practising 'wax on wax off' under the instruction of Mr. Miyagi, just to teach him how to block. Except in *this* film, Mr. Miyagi, to the shock and horror of Daniel, takes his freshly polished car to the wreckers. In either case, the Mosaic Covenant is seen as some temporary project with limited meaning and significance.

---

152 A term we will define and examine towards the end of Part III

This is why we, if we are to rightly understand this covenant and interpret its relevant passages, need to do two things. The first, as James Dunn encourages us, is to "shift our perspective back from the 16th Century to the first century… to see Paul properly within his own context, to hear Paul in terms of his own time, to let Paul be himself."[153] The other is to look carefully at the Mosaic Covenant in both its historical and literary context and see what it actually says about itself. So, in this chapter, I want us to look broadly and deeply at how the covenant established at Sinai relates to the one made with Abraham. And from this, we can avoid misunderstandings about the Old Covenant, and gain a better understanding of how the different covenants in the Bible relate to one another, as well as grasp the actual essence, purpose, and function of the Mosaic Covenant. Moreover, we will better understand the nature of the Law and its relationship to the covenants and covenant members.

Understanding the Mosaic Covenant

After delivering Abraham's descendants from slavery, as a demonstration of His faithfulness — not only to His promise to Moses earlier in Exodus 3:12, but also His covenant with the patriarch — God brings the people to Mt Sinai three months after they left Egypt. But before delivering on the promise of land, He needs to prepare them for that future by establishing His covenant with them. And as we look at the various elements and details of this covenant, we can see not only a number of parallels between the Abrahamic and Mosaic Covenant. but also that the Mosaic Covenant is very much the result and outworking of the Abrahamic promises.

---

153 Dunn. J. *New Perspective on Paul.* p.103

Until a few years ago, I had never really thought, 'what exactly is the Mosaic Covenant? If a covenant is a relationship based on a promise, what is the promise?' I got the Abrahamic covenant. I got the New Covenant. But not the Mosaic Covenant. For most of my Christian walk, I simply thought that God had established His chosen people Israel, and then gave them rules and commandments to follow. And beyond ensuring that they are holy because God is holy because that's the right thing to do, I never really thought about 'why?' The best I could come up with is, 'make sure you do X Y Z so that you can be blessed, enjoy the land and not die. And while you're waiting for Jesus, here are some sacrifices too.' But it was about ten years ago after reading John Stott's commentary on The Sermon on the Mount that I really began to consider and meaningfully think about the relationship between the 'Old and the New'. I realised that my existing comprehension of the Mosaic Covenant was too simplistic. So, through reading and study, I began to try and understand more. And what I discovered is that the key to the question 'what is the Mosaic Covenant?' is found in Exodus 19, which takes place as the people arrived at the mountain.

Chapter 19 marks the beginning of a new textual phase or section of the book of Exodus. Until this point, indeed even from the beginning of the Bible, we have encountered mostly narrative which focuses on the progression of God fulfilling his promises. The focus now, shifts to covenant establishment, blessings, and obligations. The details of the Mosaic covenant given by God to the people are contained in chapters 19 to 24. Despite belonging to the often considered 'irrelevant old covenant', it is actually a significant section of the text, as seen by the way it is echoed throughout Scripture. Paul House emphasises this in his book on Old Testament Theology:

> There is no way to describe adequately the canonical implications of Exodus 19-24. Everyone from Moses (Deut 5:6-21), to Jeremiah (Jer 7:1-15), to Jesus (Mt 5-7), to Peter (1 Pet 2:9), and every other biblical writer who has anything to say about covenant, morality and relationship to God reflects directly or indirectly on this passage.[154]

Thus, an understanding of this section of Scripture is important to understanding much of the Bible.

In chapter 19, we find that while Israel camped around the mountain, Moses went up to see the Lord. And when he got there, Moses was told the following words which, in essence, summarise the Mosaic Covenant.

> Thus you shall say to the house of Jacob, and tell the people of Israel: 'You yourselves have seen what I did to the Egyptians, and how I bore you on eagles' wings and brought you to myself. Now therefore, if you will indeed obey my voice and keep my covenant, you shall be my treasured possession among all peoples, for all the earth is mine; and you shall be to me a kingdom of priests and a holy nation.'[155]

As discussed in the previous chapter, this covenant was not about making Israel God's people, because they already were. God had elected, adopted, and redeemed them all before reaching this point. Thus, it is important that when we think about the Mosaic Covenant, we do not see it as the old way of getting right with God, or as the way Israel became God's people. The key to understanding the covenant is found in what is best

---

[154] House, P. *Old Testament Theology*. p.117

[155] Ex 19:3-6

described as the covenant prologue. Within the prologue, God invites the people to recall what He had done to the Egyptians in order to bring them to Himself. Note too, that at the beginning of Exodus 19:5, He uses the conjunctive phrase 'Now, therefore…' to link the Exodus to the covenant. This connection is frequently repeated through Scripture when discussing the details of what it means for Israel to be a covenant people. For example:

> I will consecrate the tent of meeting and the altar… I will dwell among the people of Israel and will be their God. And they shall know that I am the Lord their God, who *brought them out of the land of Egypt* that I might dwell among them. I am the Lord their God.[156]
>
> I am the Lord who *brought you up out of the land of Egypt* to be your God. You shall therefore be holy, for I am holy.[157]
>
> You shall stone him to death with stones, because he sought to draw you away from the Lord your God, who *brought you out of the land of Egypt*, out of the house of slavery.[158]

Thus, the Exodus is inseparable from the foundation, obligations, and blessings of the Mosaic Covenant. And since, as we saw earlier in Deuteronomy 7:8, the Exodus was a fulfilment of the promises made to Abraham, it follows that the covenant itself is the result of the fulfilling of the Abrahamic promises. Therefore, what took place in this covenant was not the *creation* of a relationship, but rather a *deepening* of the already existing relationship Israel had with their creator. A relationship that began with the Patriarchs. And, as we will explore later in the chapter,

[156] Ex 29:44-46
[157] Lev 11:45
[158] Deut 13:10

this covenant will outline what it means for the descendants of Abraham to exist as a nation[159] in a covenantal relationship with the Lord as their God.[160] Before going into the specifics of the covenant, I would like to look at its structure and framework in light of this Abrahamic connection, as it helps us to better understand its nature and function.

The Covenant Framework

Influenced by scholarship on the structure of Deuteronomy, the Mosaic Covenant has frequently been considered an adaptation by God of what is known as a Suzerain Vassal Treaty. This type of treaty would be established when a greater King, (Suzerain: overlord) entered into a covenant with a lesser king (Vassal), who was to be subject to the greater King's rule and demonstrate his loyalty by the giving of armies, tribute, and honour. The terms and conditions of their treaty were recorded in a common pattern. It would often begin with the suzerain identifying their name, title, and attributes, which we see at the beginning of the Mosaic Covenant proper: "I am the Lord your God…"[161] Following this came the historical prologue which would outline the basis of their relationship. Often this section would describe the benevolent acts of the suzerain as the foundation of obligation. However, in reality, in extra-biblical treaties these were merely empty words as the real motive for faithfulness is the fear of knowing they would be destroyed. This feature appears in the second half of Exodus 2:20 when God explains that He is the one "who brought you out of the land of Egypt, out of the house of slavery." This section is much more detailed and lengthier in Deuteronomy 1:6-3:29. Next came the stipulations of the

159 Gen 12:2
160 Gen 17:7
161 Ex 20:2

covenant which outlined the vassal's obligations to the King, such as visitation, loyalty, and tax. The *Decalogue* and its subsequent elaborations in Exodus 20:3-23:19 and Deuteronomy 4-26 function as the stipulations of God's covenant nation. In a number of treaties, provision was made for the storage of the treaty document in a temple and the need for regular public reading. Elements of this are found in Deuteronomy 10:2 where Moses is told to put the tablets into the ark.[162] And later in chapter 31, Moses instructs the Levites to keep the law in the ark and have them read it to the people every seven years.[163] After this, deities - and at times deified mountains, rivers or winds, etc… - were invoked as witnesses of the covenant to punish those who did not uphold their obligations. In the Mosaic Covenant, as recorded in Deuteronomy, heaven and earth (another Hittite category of witness) were invoked,[164] which is reminiscent of the covenant ceremony adapted in Genesis 15. In Exodus 24, the twelve pillars erected at the ratification ceremony could also possibly be considered covenant witnesses. And finally, the blessings and curses to be delivered by the gods and other witnesses upon the parties, depending on their faithfulness, were outlined. The blessings for faithfulness in the Mosaic covenant were fruitfulness, protection, provision, and occupation of the land. Unfaithfulness would lead to a lack of provision, conquest, and exile.[165]

However, despite having similar content and structures, the Mosaic Covenant does not strictly follow the pattern of the Suzerain Vassal Treaty, and some of the specifics of the content differ too, which is to be expected when expressed through the lens of a monotheistic worldview. Moreover, there were differences in the foundations, aims, and nature of the two

---

162 Cf. Ex 25:16

163 Deut 31: 9-13, 24-26

164 Deut 30:19; 31:19-22

165 Ex 23:20-33, Deut 28

covenants, in particular the stipulations, as we will consider later in more depth. The general similarities, according to William Dumbrell, seek mainly to highlight the Vassel-type relationship between Israel and their God, rather than to identify the type of covenant.[166]

Although similarities in content and language of the Vassal Treaty are evident within the Mosaic covenant, the familial language of the kinsman-redeemer is much stronger. In numerous places, the Lord is referred to as their redeemer, or in Hebrew: *go'el*,[167] or uses redeemer imagery.[168] The function of the *go'el* was to redeem, or rescue, an enslaved relative, lost property/inheritance, or ensure the continuity of the family line to a relative's childless widow. Essentially, the *go'el* was to preserve the continuity and future of the family. Thus, in redeeming Israel, the Lord, because of His relationship to their ancestor Abraham, has taken on the role as their *go'el*. The Israelites were delivered from slavery to Pharaoh, were to receive the inheritance of the land promised to Abraham (which at that point belonged to the Canaanites), and to be fruitful in childbirth. Recognising the presence of both suzerain and familial language helps to develop a richer picture of Israel's relationship with God. The treaty elements reveal the Kingship and transcendence of God, while the redeemer language shows the personal connection and intimacy with the people. The blending of both seems to indicate to the reader that the two ideas overlap and merge, as the redeemed family member was considered to belong to the *go'el*, which is reflective of the owner and servant language.[169] Thus, while the treaty language and structure are helpful in understanding the Mosaic covenant, the pervasive familial language, especially that of the kinsman-redeemer, means that as

166 Dumbrell. *Covenant and Creation*. p.127

167 E.g. Ex 15:13, Ps 19:14; 78:35, Isa 41 :14

168 E.g. Ex 20:2, Ps 69:18

169 Dumbrell. *Covenant and Creation*. p130-131

King, the Lord is beyond any category of an earthly king. And that the nature of the covenant goes well beyond that of strict legalism and imposition of force. Therefore, as we read the covenant text, it is important to have *both* concepts in mind. As their creator, He has the right to rule. As their redeemer, their relationship is to be one of love, blessing, and gratitude.

The Lord's Covenant

Having examined the structure and nature of the Mosaic Covenant, we can move on to consider what the covenant actually involves, and how it relates to the promises made to Abraham. To answer this, we need to analyse the obligations of the covenant which are summarised in the following passage of Scripture:

> Now therefore, if you will indeed obey my voice and keep my covenant, you shall be my treasured possession among all peoples, for all the earth is mine; and you shall be to me a kingdom of priests and a holy nation.[170]

By having these words follow a summary of the Exodus event, the Lord is saying that as a result of their redemption, the people are to obey His voice and keep His covenant. As discussed in a previous chapter,[171] to *keep* a covenant is to be diligent to fulfil one's required covenantal obligations in order to preserve a positive and good-natured relationship. This wording is reminiscent of the instructions given to Abraham in Genesis 17, who likewise was told to keep the Lord's covenant, not for the purpose of establishing or staying within the relationship, but to maintain a healthy

---

[170] Ex 19:5-6

[171] *Don't Jump Ahead*

relationship. D.A. Carson in his book *The Difficult Doctrine of the Love of God* explains that this maintaining of a positive relationship is described by Jesus[172] and Jude[173] as 'abiding in God's love' by obeying His commands.[174] In light of this conditional statement, Carson clarifies that this "does not have to do with how we become true followers of the living God, but with our relationship with him once we do know him."[175] He goes on to give an example of grounding his children for coming home late and highlights that in comparison to grounding them, taking them out for a meal or fishing "will feel much more like remaining in my love than falling under my wrath." As Scripture explains, "the Lord disciplines the one he loves"[176] and therefore, it is not as though God stopped loving them, it is just that the experience of that relationship is different. This, therefore, is the call of God to His covenant members: keep his covenant and abide in his love.

It might seem like a small thing, but notice that in both Genesis 17 and Exodus 19, the Lord doesn't say '*this* covenant', or '*your* covenant', but rather, '*my* covenant'. The significance of the choice of this possessive pronoun reveals two things to both the covenant members and readers of the covenant text. The first is that it shows that God is sovereign over the covenant and that it was established because of His initiative based on His gracious election and purposes. Moreover, since the conditions, elements, and details of the covenant He dictates are rooted in His eternal nature, they are therefore not some sort of cultural expression.

The second, which is of greater importance for the focus of this book, is that calling it '*my covenant*' shows a continuity in Scripture. It is possible

---

172 John 15:9-10
173 Jd 1:21
174 Carson, D. *Difficult Doctrine of the Love of God.* p.21-22
175 Ibid.
176 Deut 8:5; Prov 3:12; Heb 12:6

that it could be referring to one of many. For example, I could say to a friend of mine that I could drive them somewhere in my car. As a family, we own two cars, and since I consider them both to be technically mine, I could be offering a ride in one of a number of cars. Indeed, Ephesians two refers to the covenants (plural) of promise (singular). However, when we look at the wider narrative of Scripture, we can see one overarching covenant with varying expressions throughout salvation history. This raises the question: how, therefore, are we to understand the exact relationship between what happened at Sinai with Moses and the rest of Israel, and Abraham and his descendants?

One of the clearest teachings on how the covenants relate to one another comes from the book of Galatians:

> ...even with a man-made covenant, no one annuls it or adds to it once it has been ratified. Now the promises were made to Abraham and to his offspring... This is what I mean: the law, which came 430 years afterward, does not annul a covenant previously ratified by God, so as to make the promise void.[177]

Note the explanation at the end: no covenant nullifies or voids the previous one, which means that when a newer covenant is established, the previous remains. In an article on the Mosaic Covenant, Old Testament Professor William Barrick explains that this text from Galatians shows how

> Each covenant advanced the previous without abrogating it. This is part and parcel of the process of progressive revelation. Thus, when the Mosaic Covenant was

177 Gal 3:15-17

> established at Mt. Sinai, it did not nullify the Abrahamic Covenant.[178]

Therefore, we cannot say that at Sinai, the covenant with Abraham was done and dusted and God was now moving onto the next project with Israel. Instead, "the 'covenant' of which the Lord speaks in Exod. 19:5 refers to the covenant previously established by God with Abraham… and not to the institution of an entirely new covenant."[179] Peter Enns elaborates on this as he explains, "what is about to transpire on Mount Sinai is not a new covenant, but the continuation and deepening of an existing covenant, the covenant God made with Israel's ancestors."[180] This continuity can be seen in the repeated references to the Abrahamic promises in passages such as Exodus 32:13 and 33:1. These verses, as Thomas McComiskey points out, show that "the promise to Abraham was regarded as still in effect after the giving of the law; it was not nullified by it."[181] This repetition of the Abrahamic promises in the Mosaic Covenant texts, and the repeated references to 'my covenant' reveals continuity between the two covenants.

However, '*my* covenant' needs to go beyond the Abrahamic covenant since Abraham was not the first one to have been invited into the Lord's covenant. The earliest instance of the phrase is actually found back in Genesis 6:17-18 when the Lord said to Noah:

> I will bring a flood of waters upon the earth to destroy all flesh in which is the breath of life under heaven. Everything that is on the earth shall die. But I will establish *my covenant* with you.

---

178 Barrick, W. The Mosaic Covenant. *TMSJ*. p216

179 Jeffrey, Ovay, Sach. *Pierced for our Transgressions*. p.302 (fn69)

180 Enns, P. *Exodus*. p.388.

181 McComiskey, T. *The Covenants of Promise*. p.67

Again, the Lord did not say establish *a* covenant, but *His* covenant. The question that naturally follows is: is the Lord referring to three different covenants over which He is sovereign, thus making the 'my' merely descriptive, or is this the repetition of one covenant?

The key to resolving this question, I am convinced, lies in the word 'establish'. When God initiates a covenant with people, He uses the language of 'cutting a covenant', or in Hebrew: *karat berit.* This, as we saw earlier, was the language used in Genesis 15:18 when God promised to deliver Abram's descendants from Egypt. It was also used when God made a particular covenant with Israel in Exodus 34:10 when He promised to drive out the occupants of the Promised Land.[182] However, in Genesis 6:18, 'establish a covenant', or *hqum berit,* is used. Whenever *this* phrase is used in Scripture, it always refers to the maintenance or continuation of a covenant; not an inauguration. For instance, the phrase is repeated to Noah after the flood in Genesis 9:9, as a promise to continue His preservation of him and his family as was promised before the flood. The phrase is also used in the context of the Abrahamic covenant in Genesis 17 when the Lord said "I will *establish my covenant* between me and you and your offspring after you throughout their generations for an everlasting covenant..."[183] *Hqum berit* is also repeated in Genesis 17:19 and 21 with regard to promising to pass the covenant promises onto Isaac, and again later in Genesis 26:3 when the Lord fulfils this. This covenant between God and Abraham had been in place for many years, and by chapter 17 was clearly nothing new. Additionally, this phrase is never used in reference to the Abrahamic promises until this point.

The next instance is used in Exodus 6:4-8 when God tells Moses that He was going to fulfil the promises made to Abraham, Isaac, and Jacob

182 "And he said, 'Behold, I am *making a covenant* [*karat berit*]. Before all your people I will do marvels...'"

183 Gen 17:7

by delivering the people from Egypt.[184] Leviticus 26:9 is the next instance where *hqum berit* is used, this time referring to the promise to give peace in the land in response to their obedience, a blessing of the covenant previously expressed in Exodus 19-24.[185] Beyond these instances, the phrase does not occur, demonstrating that it refers to the continuation of prior covenants, and not the establishment of new ones.

This becomes even more evident in the way the word *hqum* is used in relationship to various promises. For example, Saul acknowledges to David that "the kingdom of Israel shall be *established* [*hqum*] in your hand..."[186], a promise God had made to David years earlier. Also, when Moses was talking to the people in Deuteronomy about the people entering the land, he said that the Lord was going to bring them into the land, not because of their own righteousness, but to "confirm [*hqum*] the word that the Lord [previously] swore to [their] fathers, to Abraham, to Isaac, and to Jacob."[187] Therefore, when God establishes His covenant with Noah in Genesis 6, it had to have been a previously established covenant. The closest thing that we can find to a covenant prior to Noah is found in Genesis 1-3.

In the act of creation, it was God's purpose that He rules over creation and His people live and function in accordance with His design and rule. However, the fall in Genesis 3 disrupted this plan, requiring the restoration of creation. This was a process that began when the Lord promised that the seed of the woman would undo what sin had corrupted, and bring about a new creation and perfected humanity. This is what is often known as the Covenant of Redemption, or the Covenant of Grace. This covenant is unique in that it involves a plan made within the Godhead in

---

184 It is also used with regard to this context later in Deuteronomy 8:18

185 Especially Ex 20:12

186 1Sam 24:20

187 Deut 9:5

eternity past.[188] Grudem explains that "this covenant is… different from the covenants between God and man because the parties enter into it as equals… On the other hand, it is like the covenants God makes with man in that it has the elements (specifying the parties, conditions, and promised blessings) that make up a covenant."[189] Indeed, each party had its responsibilities: The Father sent His son to redeem His people[190] and gave Him authority.[191] The Son agreed to come into the world, live in submission to the Father and die on the cross,[192] and gather all the Father had given him before raising them on the Last Day.[193] The Holy Spirit agreed to empower Jesus' earthly ministry and apply the benefits of Jesus' ministry to His followers after the ascension.[194]

Since this is a covenant made within Himself, it is likely that this is what was meant when God talks about 'my covenant.' Therefore, to establish His covenant with Noah prior to the flood was to elect him to be the means of continuity of *this* covenant and its redemptive purposes, after he wipes out the rest of humanity. Dumbrell expands on this by highlighting that when God made his covenant with Noah,

> there had been a flagrant breach resulting in the breakdown within society of a recognized moral order so dire that God, to bring to final fruition his creation intentions, must begin again with selected human representatives.[195]

---

188 Eph 1:4, 1Pet 1:20, Rev 13:8
189 Grudem, W. *Systematic Theology*. p.519
190 Jn 3:16-17, 17:2,6
191 Matt 28:18
192 Phil 2:8
193 Jn 6:38-40
194 Jn 14:16-17, 26; Acts 1:8
195 Dumbrell. *Covenant and Creation*. p.7

Additionally, inviting Abraham and Israel to keep His covenant that He established with them, shows that they too are significant players in God's redemptive plan. Also, that keeping the covenant means living according to the Lord's intentions in creation, as expressed in the obligations of obedience and promises of blessing.[196] So how do things like the Abrahamic and Mosaic Covenants fit into *His* Covenant?

Connecting the Covenants

To understand how the covenants made with Abraham, Moses, and David fit into the larger scope of the biblical narrative, one needs to see them as secondary covenants which serve to advance and propel the Bible's narrative towards the fulfilment of the primary goal of the restoration of creation. If the Covenant of Redemption was the allied invasion of Europe in World War Two, known as D-Day or Operation Overlord, then the subsidiary covenants are Operation Neptune,[197] Operation Astonia,[198] and Operation Cobra.[199] If it were the return of Dorothy to Kansas in *The Wizard of Oz*, they are the journey to the meeting of Scarecrow, Tinman, and Lion, the meeting of The Wizard at the Emerald City, and the defeat of the Wicked Witch of the West. If the Bible were the Marvel Cinematic Universe, the subsidiary covenants are the stand-alone films like *Iron Man*, *Captain America,* and *Guardians of the Galaxy* which lead to their convergence into *Infinity War* and *End Game*. Each subsidiary covenant is both the outworking of God's plan of salvation and the revelation of how that

196 Gen 17:1, Ex 19:5

197 The seaborn invasion of Normandy.

198 Allied attack on the German controlled port of La Havre.

199 US lead offensive for the conquest of the Caen region.

plan was going to be ultimately realised. It is in this role that they provide depth and meaning to that promise.

Unlike the operations of World War Two, or the phases in a film's narrative, a covenant's promises don't stop because the next one has started. They are plans and agreements that work themselves over time towards a goal, and much more than mere historical periods or events. As we saw in Galatians 3:15, no covenant annuls a previous one because they all support the greater objective. God in His sovereign decree decided that the outworking and fulfilment of the Covenant of Redemption was going to happen, not quickly with the birth of Cain or Abel, but rather, set up and played out over many, many generations. As this plan progressed, certain developments of that plan took place which needed further covenants to keep driving them forward in the direction that the Lord wanted. Rather than a quick game of Snap, this plan required the strategic setting up of many moving pieces like chess. The Lord decided to send the promised son through Seth, then Noah, Shem, and eventually Abraham. So, He made a covenant with Abraham that would work towards the ultimate goal of redemption. These promises, as we read in the first chapter, are an outline of the implementation of this plan: the *offspring* of Abram will become a *nation* that will bring *blessing* to all nations. Because those promises were yet to be brought to completion at the time of Moses, that covenant was still in place. One could even conclude that the Mosaic covenant is an evolution of the Abrahamic covenant as it 'defines and amplifies' the Abrahamic promises 'for a new generation.'[200] As McComiskey explains,

> The statement of the promise to Abraham was quite suitable for the nomadic family-clans of the patriarchs, but when Israel became a nation, a new era dawned. Israel was

200 McComiskey, T. *Covenants of Promise*. p.72

> given a covenant that would govern her as a nation for centuries to come.[201]

Thus, as the second phase of that promise to Abram begun at Sinai, at least in an official sense, God made another covenant to not only continue that Abrahamic promise, but to preserve that nation. And in their preservation, drive those covenant people towards the third phase; blessing to all people through the Messiah who would come from that nation.

This progression can be also seen in the fulfilment of another promise that God made to Abraham, namely, that kings would come from his line. We see this beginning with King David who was a part of that covenant nation, to whom was promised a perpetual line that again leads to Christ who as King would bring blessing to all nations by His justice and righteousness.

One way to think about how the covenants relate is to imagine them like transparencies, overlaying one another to create a larger picture of the Covenant of Redemption. These are what Ephesians 2:12 refers to as the Covenants (plural) of the Promise (singular). Although the promise has its ultimate roots in the words spoken to the woman in Genesis 3, Paul is here, more likely because of his audience and context, referring to the promise of blessing that belongs to the Abrahamic Covenant. And within the multiple covenants across Scripture are promises, details, and obligations that find their fullness in the coming and ministry of Jesus who would bring to fulfilment the promise of blessing that also belongs to the Covenant of Redemption. This means that, rather than being disconnected stages of the biblical narrative as though God were saying, 'I've stopped doing that now, I'm moving onto this,' the covenants throughout the Tanakh are all interconnected developments and complexities of the one plan of salvation.

---

[201] Ibid.

So, when we think about the biblical covenants, we should see them as parts of a bigger picture. Fred Klooster explains that just like "the parallel treaties of the ancient Near East, biblical covenants are royal instruments. They are not ends in themselves, but instruments of God's larger kingdom activity."[202]

The dispensational view of Scripture, however, would disagree with such a connection. In his book *Dispensationalism*, Charles Ryrie explains that the progressive revelation in Scripture, which brings to light a new promise or purpose of God, can be divided into specific stages. These stages are typically marked by a change in the nature of God's relationship with humanity. For example, prior to the fall, God had a direct relationship with his image-bearers. Then at Sinai, this relationship became mediated. Ryrie describes these stages as "distinguishable economies or dispensations in... the outworking of God's purpose"[203], which, although sharing some similarities, are quite distinct and separate from others. This model, or hermeneutic, however, was borne not out of any clear teaching in Scripture, but rather out of a desire to completely separate the Law and the Gospel, and as a result, the Jew and the Gentile. In order to achieve this separation, dispensationalists needed to give promises in Scripture strong boundaries and justified this division, at times, with hyper-literalistic interpretations. This division is seen even within the treatment of the Abrahamic covenant. Dispensationalist John Walvoord, in an article on premillennialism and the Abrahamic Covenant, proposes that there is a distinction between the promise to Abraham, his literal seed (Israel), and the 'families of the earth' (the Gentiles):

---

202 Klooster, F. "The Biblical Method of Salvation: A Case for Continuity," *Continuity and Discontinuity*. np

203 Ryrie, C. *Dispensationalism*. p.39

> The promises to Abraham, to Abraham's seed, and to "all families of the earth" are to be distinguished clearly. It breeds utter confusion to ignore these Scriptural divisions and to muddle the whole by reducing it to a general promise… these distinctions [should] be observed…[204]

While the blessing of land does appear to be specific to the literal descendants of Abraham, are we to believe that the blessings promised to and experienced by the 'families of the earth' would not be experienced by Abraham's literal seed? As we will consider in a later chapter, Walvoord's definition and categorisations of seed not only betray his 'literal hermeneutic', they also ignore what the Apostolic Writings have to say about the Gentiles' relationship with Abraham and Israel. As a result of drawing strong boundaries and distinctions, most dispensationalists, "draw the strongest possible contrast between the Abrahamic and Mosaic eras. Sometimes they have perceived the difference to be so great that they have charged Israel with making a grave blunder by promising God, through Moses, that...'all that the Lord has spoken (in giving the law) we will do' (Exod. 19:8)."[205] We find this practice of strong division reflected in the writings of dispensationalist Lewis Chafer who, in his book on systematic theology, went so far as to insist that,

> [Israel's] choice [of accepting the law] was in no way required by God… Israel deliberately forsook their position under grace, which had been their relationship to God until that day, and placed themselves under law.[206]

---

204 Walvoord, J. "The Abrahamic Covenant and Premillennialism."

205 Fuller, D. *Gospel and Law – Contrast or Continuum.* p.125

206 Chafer, L. *Systematic Theology IV.* p.162

This negative view of the Law comes not from the teachings of Scripture, but rather a commitment to a theological model and tradition. One only needs to consider the words of Genesis 18:18-19 in which God explains that obedience to His law is required to enjoy the blessings of the Abrahamic covenant. As David Fuller explains,

> "...not only was the enjoyment of the blessings of the Abrahamic Covenant made certain by God's electing work, but also the obedience needed by its beneficiaries in order to enjoy the blessings."[207]

Thus, Israel's agreement with the covenant terms was very much an important part of the fulfilment of the Abrahamic promises for Israel. Moreover, it did not change the nature of God's relationship with Abraham's descendants since this principle was always there. Especially in the way a genuine relationship with the Lord that allows them to experience His blessings has always been demonstrated through obedience. Also, consider too how Paul said quite explicitly in Galatians 3 that the Law was not contrary to the promises made with Abraham. Thus, to declare the law anathema to the promises betrays the teachings of Scripture.

If the strong dispensational view is correct, then the developments in the story of Israel, for example, could not be the fulfilments of God's promises he made with Abraham. We would also have to assume that at the time of Moses, God had completed his promises to Abraham, his seed, and the families of the earth. But the record of Scripture, as we have seen, shows that this is clearly not so. Therefore, rather than seeing the Mosaic Covenant be completely distinct, it is more accurate to see it as a natural progression and development of the Abrahamic Covenant. Indeed, as God

[207] Fuller, D. *Gospel and Law.* p.142

fulfilled his promises to Abram, we can see a kind of development and evolution. When God gave Abraham a child, he became a family. When that family grew and grew, it became a nation. When Yahweh became God to that nation, they became a *qehal*.[208] And the Mosaic Covenant explained how that *qehal* was to function.

The Covenant Specifics

So far, we have looked at the structure of the Mosaic Covenant as a kind of hybrid between a Suzerain Vassal Treaty and the agreement between a kinsman-redeemer and their relative. We have also considered its relationship with the wider context of Scripture, namely, as a subsidiary covenant of God's plan of salvation and as a consequence of the fulfilment of the promise to turn Abram into a great nation. It is in light of these details that we can begin to understand the purpose of the Mosaic covenant and appreciate what it was trying to achieve.

The common belief is that the covenant's *sole* purpose was to point to the person and work of Jesus. And although that is a significant function, we still need to consider what it meant for those who were standing at the base of the mountain, and their descendants, in a meaningful and practical way. If this covenant was nothing more than some kind of dress rehearsal for the Messiah, then the curses and punishments given for their disobedience were unnecessarily excessive and redundant. But more than any kind of appeal to logic or emotion, the text itself shows that the covenant had a real and concrete purpose. For the people of Israel, it provided an outline of what it means for the descendants of Abraham to function as a nation in a covenantal relationship with the Lord as their God.

---

[208] Hebrew word often translated assembly, or congregation.

In verses five to six of Exodus 19, the Lord declares three interrelated promises (like He did with Abram), that form the relational foundation of the Mosaic Covenant. God said that if they obey Him, they would be a treasured possession, a kingdom of priests, and a holy nation. These three functions, or roles, of covenant members, describe the responsibilities that require a whole of life commitment and define their relationship with their neighbours and God, as well as the quality of their life. And what one finds is that the people are to be not merely set apart from the nations, but also dedicated as priests for the Lord's service to them.

The first role, a treasured possession, shows that they belong to God as His 'royal property'. Peter Enns explains that "they are God's purely by virtue of his own will and desire, as emphasised by the phrase, 'the whole earth is mine (Ex. 19:5); the Lord can do as he pleases…"[209] But it also shows the intimacy and closeness of that relationship and the affection the Lord has for His people. In his commentary on Exodus, Victor Hamilton explains that in an ancient Ugaritic letter, a Hittite King uses the same wording to the King who preceded him, Hammurapi. He wrote: "You belong to the Sun [king], your master; you are his servant and his friend/personal property/treasure."[210] Two things from this letter are worth highlighting. The first is that the term servant is used here not so much as a demonstration of inferiority, but more as a term of endearment. The Lord uses this term of Israel, for example, when addressing them through Isaiah saying "you, Israel, my servant, Jacob, whom I have chosen, the offspring of Abraham, my friend",[211] when he talks about protecting them. He also uses it of Moses when defending his role of prophet against Miriam and

209 Enns. *Exodus*. p.388

210 Hamilton, V. *Exodus: An Exegetical Commentary*. p.303

211 Isa 41:8

Aaron,[212] and of David when He tells Samuel to speak to him about the temple and Davidic covenant.[213] The second is that the term treasure in the letter, *sglthat*, is very similar to the Hebrew *segula*, which again is more about describing the affection the King has towards his predecessor than about hierarchy and ownership. Therefore, as God's treasured possession, Israel enjoys a special relationship with Him, and the nature of that relationship is developed in the two remaining roles.

As the second role, a Kingdom of Priests, Israel was to function as the mediator of God's revelation to other peoples. The role of a priest was a representative one in two directions. One was to represent the people before God through the practices of the various sacrifices and intercessions, the other was to represent God to the people. Priests were set apart from the remainder of the people with higher standards of holiness placed upon them, and various grounds for restriction from priestly service were given in the Law based essentially on the importance of reflecting God's holiness and perfection. Priests were also responsible for teaching and interpreting the law. As Malachi 2:7 explains, "For the lips of a priest should guard knowledge, and people should seek instruction from his mouth, for he is the messenger of the LORD of hosts." Since the people were never instructed to intercede or sacrifice for the nations, it is the second representative/revelational role that is in view. In fact, this is at the very heart of the calling to be a light to the nations. And this was not a task just for the priestly clans of the Levites but was the calling of all the people. We find the following description in Psalm 114:1-2 "When Israel went out from Egypt, the house of Jacob from a people of strange language, Judah became his sanctuary, Israel his dominion." Calling Israel 'the Lord's sanctuary' was the

---

212 Num 12:6-9

213 2Sam 7:4-16

ancient world's equivalent of saying they are His embassy on Earth where He would be represented to the nations. And the people were to fulfil this role as a kingdom of priests by living as a holy nation.

By living holy lives, the people would be reflecting the holiness of God to the nations. Interestingly, in calling the people a holy nation, the Hebrew uses the word *goy*, which as we saw in an earlier chapter, is often used for nations other than Israel. God had also done this when He promised in Genesis 12 that Abram would become a great nation. By using this irregular term, we find the author identifying that this covenant is a further fulfilment of the Abrahamic promises, revealing that his descendants were to be a Holy Nation who were to be ambassadors of God's blessing to the other nations. Moreover, the declaration of "For all the earth is mine" within these covenant promises is a further demonstration of the connection with the global purposes of the Abrahamic covenant.

In light of these covenant promises, which are essentially functions and roles, it becomes quite clear that the Mosaic Covenant was a vocational covenant. A kind of job description of how Israel was to operate as God's vice-regents and image-bearers who were His representatives on the Earth. This calling is nothing short of a picture of the restoration of creation, whereas in the beginning humanity was made in God's image to be His representatives in the earth before our first parents turned their back on that vocation. N.T Wright in his book, *The Day the Revolution Began*, describes this connection:

> ...creation itself is understood as a kind of Temple... where humans function as the 'image-bearers' in the cosmic Temple... This is how creation was designed to function and flourish... Humans are called not just to keep certain moral standards in the present and enjoy God's presence

> here and hereafter, but to celebrate, worship, procreate and take responsibility within the rich, vivid developing life of creation. According to Genesis, that is what humans were made for… The priestly vocation [reaffirmed with Israel in Exodus] consists of summing up the praises of creation before the Creator; the royal vocation, in turn, means reflecting God's wisdom and justice into the world. This is a direct outworking of Genesis 1:26-28, where humans are created in the divine image.[214]

The essence of the covenant relationship and the obligations of Israel can be best understood by looking at what is known as the *Shema*: "Hear, O Israel: The Lord our God, the Lord is one. You shall love the Lord your God with all your heart and with all your soul and with all your might."[215] In what is considered the central creedal statement of the Tanakh is a description of the God they are in covenant with, and their obligations to Him as covenant members. It begins by declaring the name of God, Yahweh, and declaring that He is their God; a fulfilment of the promise made to Abraham in Genesis 17:7-8. As Moses explained at the end of Deuteronomy as part of the covenant renewal at Moab:

> You are standing today, all of you, before *the Lord your God*… so that you may enter into the sworn covenant of *the Lord your God*, which t*he Lord your God* is making with you today, that he may establish you today as his people, and that he may be *your God*, as he promised you, and

214 Wright, N.T. *The Day the Revolution Began*. p.76-77,78-79

215 Deut 6:4-5

> as he swore to your fathers, to Abraham, to Isaac, and to Jacob.[216]

This theme of the Lord as Israel's covenant God who dwells among them is the climax and goal of the Exodus narrative, and a major purpose to which the Mosaic Covenant points. We can see this in how the book of Exodus concludes with the dramatic event of the Lord's glory filling the Tabernacle.[217]

The *Shema* also declares that He is 'one', and in so doing emphasises the unique nature of their God as the one true God. Here, Israel is being called to accept and believe His uniqueness. They are to acknowledge his sovereignty "as the One Who redeemed her from Egypt and made her His own…", that He is the one true God in a pagan world of false gods, and that He is "the eternal God Who exists without reference to time" [218] as revealed in the use of the tetragrammaton: YHVH. As Yahweh, this name is significant as its meaning declares that:

> …the One Who always has been, Who is, and Who always will be, the Unchangeable One, is Israel's God. This relationship (emphasized by the possessive "our"), is one which was initiated by God, is maintained by God, and will inevitably bring glory to God. He is able to keep His eternal, covenant promises primarily because of Who He is—the unchangeable One. Nothing affects change in Him—He is the unmoved Sovereign of the universe.[219]

216 Deut 29:10-13
217 Ex 40:34-38
218 Hegg, T. *Deuteronomy*. p.56
219 Ibid.

The title *Shema* is the Hebrew for the first word in the declaration: hear. But since Hebrew is an action-oriented language, the word means to hear *and* obey, which is reminiscent of James' teaching in his letter, "...be doers of the word, and not hearers only..."[220] In accepting the self-revelation of God as 'one', they are to respond by loving "the Lord their God with all their heart and with all their soul and with all their might." Here, the Israelites are called to use their heart (the centre of their intellect and will), soul (the collective individuality), and might (ability to affect others) — a summation of their entire being — for the purposes of glorifying God and therefore fulfil their created purpose. What we find in the *Shema* is that their relationship with and loyalty to God, are to be demonstrated by their obedience. In fact, Jesus quotes this second part of the Shema when asked what the most important commandment is. He concludes that loving God is one of the two 'hooks' upon which the entire law hangs.[221] John likewise explains that obedience to God is a demonstration of our love for Him.[222] And the obedience to which they were called, as a response to God's unique nature, and demonstration of their covenant relationship with Him, is expressed in the Law, or *Torah*.

The Law was initially given in Exodus 20:1-17, in what is often called the Ten Commandments, or the *Decalogue.* The latter term seems to be more scriptural as the commandments are referred to in the Bible as the 'Ten Words.' In Exodus 34:28, and Deuteronomy 4:13, most English Bibles translate the phrase *aseret hadevarim* as Ten Commandments. However, the root of *hadevarim* (*dabar*) means words or speech. While commandments are technically the words of God, the *Decalogue* is more than a list of commandments. The first 'word' is the prologue, declaring that the Lord is

---

220 Js 1:22

221 Matt 22:36-40

222 1Jn 5:3

their God who brought them out of Egypt, and the remaining nine are commandments that are based on the prologue. For example, the second 'word', which is the prohibition against other gods and idols, is an expression of the fidelity that the people were to show to God both as an expression of gratitude for redeeming them, and the fact that they now belong to Him. In short, the *Decalogue* was God's way of saying, 'because I am your God who delivered you, this is how you are to live.' Thus, in this covenant, the people were called not into a new relationship or revelation, but rather to acknowledge what they already knew, and to worship Him as God and saviour with their praise and obedience from grateful, loving hearts. What this means is that this covenantal aspect of the *Decalogue* emphasises that the primacy of one's purpose is found in being in a relationship with the Lord, rather than simply being created by Him. The physical creation is merely a facilitation of location for that friendship to take place, as seen in the way the creation of humanity as image-bearers of God is the pinnacle act of creation. Thus, creation was not the ultimate goal of God, but rather the material universe is there to facilitate a relationship between a creator and His creation.

The Ten Words of Exodus 20 are a summary of the Torah. And, as one reads through the remainder of the Law, the commandments given are elaborations of these initial ten words, in what we today might refer to as 'case laws'. For example, "If ever you take your neighbor's cloak in pledge, you shall return it to him before the sun goes down"[223] is an application of 'do not steal' and 'do not take the name of the Lord your God in vain', which is a commandment about swearing falsely. And the instructions on provisions for the poor are a response to the nature of God revealed in the first word, as are the instructions on sacrifices. We, therefore, have

---

223 Ex 22:26

three levels of elaboration in the law. At the root level is a call to love God and love neighbour. Next are the demonstrations of this call that are summarised in the *Decalogue*, and then further elaborated on in the remaining commandments. As we read a couple of verses further into the *Shema* in Deuteronomy 6, we find Moses telling the people that the commandments were a *sign* of the covenant: "You shall bind them as a sign on your hand, and they shall be as frontlets between your eyes."[224]

As I have written elsewhere,[225] this explanation of the covenant obligations help makes better sense of the actual nature and purpose of the Law. As alluded to at the beginning of the chapter, the negative descriptions that I hear from some Christians about the Law seem to be based on misunderstandings of what the Law is. But this discussion should help make it evident that the Law was given by God not merely to show sin, nor was it to simply reveal their need for a saviour. Instead, the Law was given as a part of the Mosaic Covenant to reveal to His covenant people what it looks like to function as a covenant member. It is also important to understand that these Laws were not some arbitrary commands that seemed to be good for that time. They existed as a revelation of God's moral character and Holiness. Therefore, by keeping the Torah, the covenant people of God were not only responding appropriately to their redeemer and creator but fulfilling their call to reveal His character to the surrounding nations.

And this is how we are to understand the conditional statement in the Covenantal conditions: "if you will indeed obey my voice and keep my covenant, you shall be my treasured possession…" This is not: 'if you obey you will be accepted.' Rather, 'if you obey, you will be functioning as, and demonstrating to the world that you are my Holy People.' And the reward

224 Deut 6:8

225 *Why then the Law.* 2020

for obedience is that they get to experience the blessing of Land as promised to Abraham. For he too was required to obey the Lord to demonstrate his faith which allowed Him to enjoy the blessings of the divine promises.

What is fascinating is that we see the continuity between Abraham and Moses when God commends Abraham to Jacob, saying he "obeyed My voice and kept My charge (*mismarti*), My commandments (*miswotay*), My statutes (*huqqotay*), and My laws (*terotay*)." In Deuteronomy 11:1, with one exception, these same words are used to describe faithfulness to the Mosaic Covenant: "You shall therefore love the Lord your God and keep his charge (*mismarti*), his statutes (*huqqotay*), his rules (*mispataw*), and his commandments (*miswotay*)."

Given the existence of the Torah before Sinai, such as the way Cain is condemned for murdering his brother, the Law of God is the standard of blamelessness to which Abraham was charged to keep in Genesis 17. And therefore, what we find in Exodus 19:5 with the imperative to obey God and those commandments outlined from Exodus 20 onwards was the official and formal incorporation of the pre-existing law into the pre-existing covenant with Abraham as a kind of job description for his descendants of how to function as God's Holy Nation; the nation promised to Abraham.

COMPARING THE COVENANTS

I don't reconcile friends.[226]

In the two previous chapters, I have attempted to highlight the strong connection and continuity between the Abrahamic and Mosaic Covenants. With the latter being the product and outflow of the first, despite being different kinds of covenants, there are several parallels between them. In this chapter, I hope to demonstrate that in the giving of the Law and the covenant ratification process at Sinai, there are several elements that are reminiscent of God's encounters with Abraham in Genesis.

A connection is found not simply by the introduction of obligations to the relationship,[227] but also in the description and imagery of the events of Exodus 19 and 20. For instance, as the reader encounters the smoking mountain and its terrifying appearance at Sinai, they should be reminded of the smoking pot and the dark atmosphere of Abram's covenantal ceremony in Genesis 15.

---

226 C.H. Spurgeon

227 See *Don't Jump Ahead*

The relationship between Abraham and Israel is made more apparent in the words of Moses in response to the people being terrified by the appearance and voice of God.[228] To try and comfort the people, Moses explained that the Lord's terrifying appearance was a test to see if the people 'feared God'. What makes this significant is that, as Hamilton explains, this combination of *test* and *fear* appears only twice in the Bible: here, and in Genesis 22:12 when the Lord tested Abraham to see if he 'feared God' with the sacrifice of Isaac.[229] What this similarity reveals is that a 'fear of the Lord' was an expectation by God in both covenants.

There is also a very significant connection between Abraham and Israel seen in the ratification of the covenant in Exodus 24.

Covenant Ratification

After the people refused to listen to the voice of the Lord because they were afraid, Moses went up on the mountain where God gave him the covenant obligations in the Law. After descending, Moses recounted 'the words and ordinances' - the Ten Words and their elaborations, as recorded in the preceding three chapters, to the people. The narrative tells us that "all the people answered with one voice and said, 'All the words that the Lord has spoken we will do.'"[230] What is interesting is that previously in Exodus 19:8, the people had already said this, even before the Law was revealed to them. As we saw in the previous chapter of this book, some describe this as a brash and thoughtless commitment to a covenant that would only bring about their demise. This understanding, however, ignores the narrative's wider context. Fretheim explains that the pledge in 19:8 and 24:3-7 is "a

228 Ex 20:18-20

229 Hamilton, V. *Exodus.* p.356

230 Ex 24:3

pledge to the God with whom they are *already* closely related."[231] Thus, it is more about a declaration of commitment to their already existing relationship, more than any given commandment, especially in the way that the pledge in chapter 19 lacked any specificity.[232] It was as though God was saying to the people: 'I have some things that I expect of you as my covenant people.' And they responded with: 'Yes. We trust you, we love you, and we're grateful for our deliverance; we'll do what you ask.' Then after they were given the specifics, they reaffirmed their commitment by saying, 'Sure. We'll do those things.'

After this, Moses wrote down the words the Lord had given him, which became known as the Book of the Covenant. The next day, Moses prepared for the ratification ceremony, and again, we find a similar exchange. "Then [Moses] took the Book of the Covenant and read it in the hearing of the people. And they said, 'All that the Lord has spoken we will do, and we will be obedient.'"[233] Note how this time, we have the added words of 'we will be obedient.' This phrase in the Hebrew literally translates to 'we will hear', using the word *shema.* Hence, they were speaking in the same spirit they had earlier in Exodus 19, as explained by Fretheim, in that they had promised to wait for God's commandments, were willing to obey the revelation thus far, and anything that may come later. This is a demonstration not only of an 'Abrahamic faith' that is willing to obey their redeemer and creator, but also reinforces that obedience and the Law are not the foundation or prerequisite of the Israelite's relationship with Him. Rather, it is the fruit and outflowing of that relationship.

The reason that this exchange was repeated is somewhat of a formality as it needed to be included in the ratification ceremony because of its rela-

231 Fretheim. *Exodus*. p.210. Emphasis added.
232 Fretheim. Exodus. p.211
233 Ex 24:7

tionship to the covenant. The ceremony at Sinai, much like that of Genesis 15, is also a bizarre and odd ritual for modern readers. Firstly, we see in verse four that Moses constructed an altar and erected twelve stone pillars, each one representing each of the twelve tribes, quite possibly with the purpose of being witnesses to the covenant. This practice is seen, for instance, at the end of the book of Joshua, after the partial conquest of Canaan. There, Joshua sets up a stone having established a covenant with the people that they would not worship foreign gods, but rather be devoted to the Lord alone. Joshua explained that "this stone shall be a *witness* against us, for it has heard all the words of the Lord that he spoke to us. Therefore it shall be a witness against you, lest you deal falsely with your God."[234] Thus, it is quite likely that these pillars fulfil a similar function.

After these pillars were erected, sacrifices were made to God on the altar. What needs to be highlighted here is that they were burnt and peace offerings; not sin offerings. This ceremony has nothing to do with forgiveness or atonement. As I said in the previous chapter, this covenant is not a salvific covenant; it is a vocational one. The burnt offerings were representative of Israel's whole-hearted devotion to God, and the peace offerings were a recognition and celebration of Israel's communion with their redeemer. Thus, the sacrificial elements of the ceremony were nothing short of grateful worship. The sacrifice of the animals is also reminiscent of the ceremony of Genesis 15; however, their purpose is clearly different.

From the sacrifice of these animals, blood was collected and sprinkled on the altar and pillars. The word sprinkle is somewhat misleading, giving the idea of a quick little splash. However, the Hebrew for sprinkled, *zaraq*, is best understood in this context as meaning to 'throw profusely.' The same word is used in Exodus 9 when Moses threw the soot in the air, carrying the

---

[234] Josh 24:27

idea of throwing handfuls as opposed to sprinkling with a finger. It might seem irrelevant and unnecessary to know how much blood was used, but it seems that the volume is reflective of the significance of the event. That a lot of blood was used and not some tiny flick and sprinkle means that this was a meaningful event. And once the people agreed to the covenant obligations, Moses covered them with blood and declared, "Behold the blood of the covenant that the Lord has made with you in accordance with all these words."[235]

There is some speculation as to what these ritual actions and the significance of the use of blood might mean. There are those who would claim that the blood represents purification from sin. Indeed, just as the people were sprinkled with blood, as Hebrews 9 explains, Moses also "sprinkled with the blood both the tent and all the vessels used in worship. Indeed, under the law almost everything is purified with blood."[236] Considering, however, that this covenant was vocational rather than salvific, the purification in mind here in Exodus 24 was most likely more about sanctifying and setting apart the people for His purposes, rather than actual forgiveness of sins. Others would suggest that the blood was a symbol of the imparting of life. Some might even say that the sprinkling of the people binds them to a blood oath. Victor Hamilton explains that the "dashing of the blood first on the altar (v. 6) and then on the people, or their representatives (v. 8), is a symbolic act, binding both parties of this covenant to each other, Yahweh to Israel…"[237] While all are reasonable theories, the fact of the matter is that, as Childs points out, the meaning of the ceremony is not explained. And unlike the incident in Genesis 15, there are no historical parallels to compare it with. Nonetheless, the ritual's "effect in sealing the covenant

---

235 Ex 24:8

236 Heb 9:18-22

237 Hamilton. *Exodus*. p.441

is fully obvious." Thus, it is the effect and not process or function that is the focus of the author.[238] The best we can conclude with certainty is that blood is a significant element in sealing covenants and was used by God in the Mosaic Covenant to set His people apart for His vocational purposes.

Moreover, the symbology of the ceremony most likely contains a combination of meanings. As Peter Enns suggests:

> The nature of these two offerings [burnt and fellowship] parallels how the blood of the sacrifices was used. One half was sprinkled on the altar, while the other half was put in bowls (v. 6) and was sprinkled on the people (v. 8). The former represents sin atonement, the latter fellowship... This blood that was sprinkled... indicates that fellowship between them and God has been confirmed. That is why it is called the 'blood of the covenant.'[239]

The significance of this ratification, as it was with the Abrahamic covenant, was not that it created the relationship between the descendants of Abraham and the Lord, or that it was here that God bound Himself to Israel. But rather, it was putting the vocational covenant into effect. Nahum Sarna in his commentary on Exodus elaborates on this, saying that the blood ceremony brought the people to "a higher level of intimate relationship with the Deity."[240] A similar act is described when God in Genesis 17:2 said that he was 'making His covenant' with Abraham. As we saw in an earlier chapter, this phrase means that 'He is about to set into motion the covenant made in Genesis 15:8.' In the same sense, this ratification ceremony meant that God was now beginning to set into motion

238 Childs. *Exodus*. p.505

239 Enns. *Exodus*. p.152

240 Sarna, N. *The JPS Commentary: Exodus*. p.152

His purposes for His Holy Nation and their role in blessing people from all nations. A promise and purpose not only established with Israel in Exodus 19 but also with Abraham in Genesis 12.

Circumcision

Just as the Abrahamic Covenant had the sign of circumcision to demonstrate covenant membership and loyalty by symbolically reflecting the essence of the covenant, the Mosaic Covenant also contains signs that demonstrate that Yahweh is their creator, redeemer, and sanctifier.

What is interesting is that within the Mosaic Covenant texts (Exodus to Deuteronomy), circumcision is hardly mentioned at all. When it is mentioned, it comes across more as a side note, rather than the direct, explicit instruction as it was given to Abraham. Its earliest mention is when Moses was circumcised by Zipporah, sometime after their departure from Midian.[241] The next is in Exodus 12 as a prerequisite to keep the Passover,[242] either for the descendant of Abraham, or the stranger living among them. The next is in Leviticus 12 in the context of purification after birth saying that the male child is to be circumcised on the eighth day, which is a repetition of the commandment given originally in Genesis 17:12. In this context, it is merely given as a time marker in connection to the duration of the mother's unclean status, and not a new commandment.[243] And that's it. This minimal discussion, especially its absence from Exodus 19-24 shows that circumcision does not stand as an obligation to, nor a sign of, the Mosaic Covenant. The covenant text's handling of the practice, especially

241 Ex 4:25

242 In this context (verses 43-46), the keeping refers to the eating of the sacrificed lamb itself, not the memorial meal as a whole.

243 Gen 21:4

its lack of explicit, direct instruction, strongly suggests that for Moses and the Israelites, the act of circumcision was simply a given. This is because the people recognised that their identity was connected to being descendants of Abraham, and their existence as a nation belonging to God is a fulfilment of the promises made to the patriarch, which are embodied in the practice of circumcision.

The continuity of not just the practice but also the symbolism, further shows the continuity of the Abrahamic covenant into the Mosaic, especially in its requirement for Passover which was also a fulfilment of the Abrahamic promises.[244] But what is new here in the relationship between Passover and circumcision is not so much a redefinition, but an expansion of meaning. I think of it as being like Remembrance, or Veterans Day (depending on where you live). The original purpose was the acknowledgement of the end of World War 1 on November 11, but as other wars come and go – World War 2, Vietnam, Afghanistan, etc… - they become a part of the day's reflection too. It's not that the latter superseded the first, but the elements of what's involved expanded.

Circumcision at the time of Abraham, as we saw, pointed to the gracious fulfilment of the promise of a descendant, ultimately leading to the promised Messiah – a hope and expectation that obviously carried over into the Mosaic era and beyond. But it has now expanded to include the fulfilment of the promise of land and blessing, which required their gracious deliverance from Egypt, which is why circumcision - proof of covenant membership - was required to celebrate Passover. Therefore, circumcision was not a sign of the Mosaic Covenant, but rather the Abrahamic Covenant, which carried over into the Mosaic era and beyond. And the only reason Israelites

[244] Gen 15:13-16, 18-21

were expected to be circumcised was that they were still members and beneficiaries of the Abrahamic Covenant.

The other expansion of the meaning of circumcision is not so much in its symbology, or practice, but rather in its location. In the book of Deuteronomy, we find the following instruction: "Circumcise therefore the foreskin of your heart, and be no longer stubborn."[245] This is a commandment that pertains to obedience. Just a few verses prior to this, Moses told the people:

> Israel, what does the Lord your God require of you, but to fear the Lord your God, to walk in all his ways, to love him, to serve the Lord your God with all your heart and with all your soul, and to keep the commandments and statutes of the Lord, which I am commanding you today for your good…[246]

This instruction is rooted in the fact that Yahweh is Lord of heaven and earth, and He has chosen Israel as His special people. In short, they were told: 'demonstrate your love for the Lord and obey him and love your neighbour[247] because He loves you' — a reiteration of the great commandment.[248] This is the wherefore of the commandment to circumcise one's heart. Thus, this is a metaphorical circumcision, and an instruction to change one's inclination towards God and neighbour by removing those thoughts, beliefs, and attitudes that make one resistant, or 'stubborn' to loving God, leading to a love for His instructions and ways. As Duane Christensen explains in his commentary,

---

[245] Deut 10:16

[246] Deut 10:12-13

[247] Deut 10:18-19

[248] Deut 6:5 cf. Matt 22:37-38

> What Moses legislated for the people of Israel is not legalism, or ritual, or the external minutiae of religious observance, or even a creed. What Moses emphasized was simply a vital relationship with God that is worked out in terms of specific responsibilities toward our neighbors.[249]

This understanding of the Mosaic Covenant is quite contradictory to popular descriptions that paint it merely as the observance of 'external matter' to satisfy God in order to get blessings.[250] This is because such a misrepresentation of the covenant is the consequence of the hermeneutics required to defend hyper-dispensationalism. Even at this point in the Bible's narrative, obedience that is expected and satisfactory for a covenant member is obedience that comes from the heart and is motivated by love. As we read further in Deuteronomy, we find that this act of circumcision of the heart is not something that was to be done by the Israelite's efforts, but rather a promise of something God would do. As Moses told the people, "the Lord your God will circumcise your heart and the heart of your offspring, so that you will love the Lord your God with all your heart and with all your soul."[251] Again, contrary to the stereotype that God expected the Israelites to strive after obedience under their own strength and efforts, God promised to empower them supernaturally to fulfil their vocational covenant. Although it was never described or defined explicitly as a sign of the Mosaic Covenant, one could consider a circumcised heart as a sign of a genuine relationship with the Lord that could belong to those living under that covenant.

---

249 Christensen, D. *Deuteronomy* 1-21:9. p 469

250 E.g. Stanley, A. *Irresistible*. p.235

251 Deut 30:6

Signs of the Mosaic Covenant

There are two significant practices, or rituals, that were to be considered signs of the covenant. One is the celebration of the Passover and the subsequent week of unleavened bread. After explaining how they are to be observed, Moses says:

> And it shall be to you as a sign on your hand and as a memorial between your eyes, that the law of the Lord may be in your mouth. For with a strong hand the Lord has brought you out of Egypt. You shall therefore keep this statute at its appointed time from year to year.[252]

Here, the celebration of Passover as a memorial of when God fulfilled His promise to Abraham to deliver the people from Egypt and bring them into the land given to him and his descendants, is to function not merely as a reminder of the covenant relationship they have with Yahweh, but also to point to the reality that the Lord is their redeemer. We see the memorial function in the language choices of this passage. Douglas Stuart in his commentary explains that the phrase 'on your lips' describes something well known and thought about, and being on the hand and forehead was a metaphorical reminder of what the Lord had done,[253] which was the foundation of their relationship. This language is also used in the *Shema* and in Deuteronomy 11:18 where the people are told to remember the commandments and promises of God. Thus, the celebration of the feast was a sign not simply of who they are, but *whose* they are, since "Israel's identity is a function of what God has done for them."[254] It is quite likely, therefore,

252 Ex 13:9-10

253 Stuart, D. *The New American Commentary: Exodus.* p.315

254 Enns. *Exodus.* p.252

that the keeping of the feast was to also be a reminder to 'keep the covenant' since according to Exodus 20 their deliverance was the foundation of their obligation to obey God.

The other sign of God's covenant with Israel is the Sabbath. In Exodus 31, the Lord declared:

> Above all you shall keep my Sabbaths, for this is a sign between me and you throughout your generations, that you may know that I, the Lord, sanctify you. You shall keep the Sabbath, because it is holy for you. Everyone who profanes it shall be put to death. Whoever does any work on it, that soul shall be cut off from among his people. Six days shall work be done, but the seventh day is a Sabbath of solemn rest, holy to the Lord. Whoever does any work on the Sabbath day shall be put to death. Therefore, the people of Israel shall keep the Sabbath, observing the Sabbath throughout their generations, as a covenant forever. It is a sign forever between me and the people of Israel that in six days the Lord made heaven and earth, and on the seventh day he rested and was refreshed.[255]

The Sabbath is a day packed with many theological concepts, principles, and meanings. Much like the other signs, the Sabbath reminds the people of who God is, and the nature of their relationship with Him. The first is that as a day that is holy and set apart,[256] the people are reminded not only of the holiness of God, but more specifically that this Holy One

---

255 Ex 31:13-17

256 Gen 2:3

sanctifies his people: 'be holy as I am holy.' Thus, to profane the Sabbath, was to deny a significant aspect of the nature of God – holiness.

Another is that it is a reminder that God is the creator of the heavens and the earth, which is also expressed as the foundation of the Sabbath in the Ten Words given in Exodus 20. Not only is this role of creator the basis of the authority from which God gives instructions to His people and evidence of His holiness, but also the pattern of creation was to be reflected by His image bearers who had been restored to their vocational purpose. This is why the seventh day was the Sabbath; because that was the day on which God rested. And by resting on the Sabbath, the people were not only reminding themselves but communicating to the world, that the Lord is the one true creator of all things.

The third layer of symbolism in the Sabbath is a reminder of the act of redemption. In Deuteronomy, when Moses repeats the Ten Words, the justification for the Sabbath there is the redemption of the people from Egypt. They were once slaves, but now they can have a day of rest to honour their redeemer. This is related to the act of sanctification in that by rescuing Israel, He set them apart, which was a significant element of the Mosaic Covenant; to be a holy nation. They had been redeemed from their harsh taskmasters, and restored into their role as servants of Yahweh. Peter Enns highlights the purposes of giving the detailed instructions for the Sabbath right after the construction of the Tabernacle, which serves to emphasise the relational basis of the Sabbath. Moreover, it also serves to connect the holy space with holy time, as a reminder that the entire lives of the Israelites are to be holy as God is holy. He explains:

> It is most fitting that the Sabbath be a sign of this covenant. Israel... is a new creation. This is a new people of God, whom he intends to use to undo the work of the first man.

> Also, the tabernacle is a microcosm of the created order, a parcel of Edenic splendour established amid the chaos of the world. The Sabbath is not just a reminder of the original creation in Genesis 1 and 2, but a reminder of God's re-creation of the cosmos in the tabernacle.[257]

Therefore, the Sabbath not only has the people looking back and remembering, but also looking forward and hoping, reminding His people of their purpose in the biblical narrative. The Sabbath, as described by the author of Hebrews, was a sign of the ultimate rest humanity has from God's redemption and being in covenant with Him. A covenant that brings refreshment and peace. A sign of rest from working for salvation, and rest and peace from guilt and condemnation. Moreover, it points to the eternal sabbath.[258] In light of these details, it is no wonder that the sabbath was to be 'a sign forever.'

If we were to summarise the purpose of the signs of the Passover and Sabbath, it would be that they are signs that the people are indeed God's people and that He is their creator, redeemer, and sanctifier.

Over the last few chapters in Part II, my goal has been to demonstrate that rather than being a new project or idea, the Mosaic covenant, as well as the Exodus, was a part of the fulfilment of the promises made to Abram that he would become the father of a great nation and that the Lord would be God to those people. In the following chapter, we will continue to look at the ongoing fulfilment of the Abrahamic promises for the Israelites, in particular the promises of land and blessing to all nations.

---

257 Enns. *Exodus*. p.544-5

258 Heb 4:9-10

ENJOYING THE LAND

Entering a world of trials.

Narrative structures are a fantastic tool when it comes to understanding a story. Being able to map out the development of the plot and characters certainly helps to make sense of what is happening, why it is happening, and what to expect. A narrative structure that I have been studying lately is Joseph Campbell's The Hero's Journey, or, as it is sometimes referred to, the Monomyth. This narrative structure was originally a seventeen-stage outline (others have since created simpler versions), that follows a hero's adventure into a different 'world', where they experience trials, some kind of victory, and transformed through the process. Although much of Campbell's explanation of this theory draws from and delves into Jungian and Freudian psychology and comparative religious studies, it is a model that is quite representative of so many stories. Whether consciously or unconsciously, the monomyth can be seen in so many stories and films. In fact, while I was studying it and then watching movies, I couldn't help but recognise it. One significant stage of this plotline for the protagonist is the crossing of the threshold, as they enter into their new situation. This is Neo's awakening in the real world, Jake Sully's first time in his avatar body, Luke Skywalker's escape from Tatooine, and

Frodo and Sam leaving the Shire. Campbell in his book *The Hero with a Thousand Faces* describes it like this: "With the personifications of his destiny to guide and aid him, the hero goes forward in his adventure until he comes to the 'threshold guardian' at the zone of magnified power."[259] And this is very much the experience of Israel as they entered the land promised to Abraham about five hundred years earlier.

Having gone through the 'refusal of the call'[260] with the bad report of the spies, the nation born from the seed of Abram was now ready to leave their old experience of being landless nomads without an inheritance. They were ready to enter the Land and conquer the 'threshold guardians' (the Canaanites) to enjoy the treasure of the land and dwell with their covenant God. Now, I should be clear here. My point is not that the Bible was written according to a mythological, Freudian formula — far from it! My purpose in making this comparison is to emphasise how the occupation of the land, rather than being some new project, was still very much a continuation of a yet to be completed story that begun in Genesis.

Conquest of the Land

As we saw in an earlier chapter, the promise and instruction to occupy the land were frequently anchored back, not to Moses, but Abraham. When the Israelites were moved on from Sinai where the Mosaic Covenant was established, "The Lord said to Moses,

> Depart; go up from here, you and the people whom you have brought up out of the land of Egypt, to the land of

[259] Campbell, J. *The Hero with a Thousand Faces*. p. 64.
[260] Ibid p.49

> which I swore to Abraham, Isaac, and Jacob, saying, 'To your offspring I will give it.'[261]

This highlights that although faithfulness to the Lord through the Mosaic Covenant was one of the prerequisites of entering the Land, the promise and giving of Land is actually rooted in Abraham. Thus, as we see the Israelites crossing the Jordan and defeating the Canaanites, Hittites etc…, we see not so much the success of the Exodus — although that is definitely in view — but more significantly, God's faithfulness to the oath He swore to Abram centuries earlier. In fact, it was Moses' appeal to the patriarchal promises that spared Israel from destruction after the Golden Calf incident,[262] allowing them to enter the land in the first place.

The next generation, as they were east of the Jordan River, received a similar message as they anticipated their entrance into the promised land:

> See, I have set the land before you. Go in and take possession of the land that the Lord swore to your fathers, to Abraham, to Isaac, and to Jacob, to give to them and to their offspring after them.[263]

The instruction here, in the Hebrew, to go and possess the land has the sense of 'possess by dispossessing.'[264] This was a somewhat implicit part of the promise made to Abram in Genesis 15:16; 'they shall come back here in the fourth generation, for the iniquity of the Amorites is not yet complete.' Here, the idea is that Israel's occupation of the land was to also serve as an instrument of God's justice against the wickedness of the land's inhabitants.

---

261 Ex 33:1

262 Ex 32:13-14

263 Deut 1:8

264 Christensen, D. *Deuteronomy*. p.16

Just prior to this verse in Genesis 15, was a description of the boundaries of the Promised Land that "reflects the patriarchal covenant to Abraham, in which God promised to give his descendants the land from 'the river of Egypt to the great river Euphrates' (Gen 15:18)."[265] It would be a great error to disconnect the Patriarchs from the monumental event of crossing the Jordan and taking the land.

The author of the book of Joshua wants to be sure that the reader is quite aware of this. At the end of Joshua's campaign, once the land was divided among the tribes, the author reiterates that the many victories and occupation of the land (albeit incomplete) is a fulfilment of the Abrahamic promises:

> Thus the Lord gave to Israel all the land that he swore to give to their fathers. And they took possession of it, and they settled there. And the Lord gave them rest on every side just as he had sworn to their fathers. Not one of all their enemies had withstood them, for the Lord had given all their enemies into their hands. Not one word of all the good promises that the Lord had made to the house of Israel had failed; all came to pass.[266]

Marten Woudstra in his commentary on Joshua explains that this passage demonstrates how the "conquest and settlement in the land which God had given must also be seen against the background of the patriarchal stories which first mention the oath made to the forefathers."[267] Moreover, he also explains that the victory over Israel's enemies is a fulfilment of the promise made back in Genesis 12:3, namely, that God would curse those

---

265 Ibid. p.17

266 Josh 21:43-45

267 Woudstra, M. *Joshua.* p.314

who curse Abram. This formula was later applied to the people of Israel in Exodus 23:22: "I will be an enemy to your enemies and will oppose those who oppose you."

Joshua was also careful to ensure that the generation that conquered the land were aware that their situation and victory is the culmination of the Abrahamic promises. At the ceremony when Israel renewed their covenant with God at Shechem, Joshua, in a typical fashion, gave the historical background to that covenant. However, instead of beginning with Moses, he began much earlier:

> 'Long ago, your fathers lived beyond the Euphrates, Terah, the father of Abraham and of Nahor; and they served other gods. Then I took your father Abraham from beyond the River and led him through all the land of Canaan, and made his offspring many. I gave him Isaac. And to Isaac I gave Jacob and Esau. And I gave Esau the hill country of Seir to possess, but Jacob and his children went down to Egypt. And I sent Moses and Aaron, and I plagued Egypt with what I did in the midst of it, and afterward I brought you out.[268]

That the Lord, through Joshua, wanted to ensure the people understood and knew that their inheritance of the Promised Land was founded not in their military skills, obedience, faithfulness and efforts, or even Joshua's leadership could not be clearer. He wanted the people to know that their inheritance was based on His faithfulness to the patriarchs and the patriarchal promises.

[268] Josh 24:2-5

Remembering the Covenant

In His wisdom, God gave the people a liturgy and ritual to make sure they do not forget this truth. In Deuteronomy, Moses passed the following instruction onto the people:

> When you come into the land that the Lord your God is giving you for an inheritance and have taken possession of it and live in it, you shall take some of the first of all the fruit of the ground, which you harvest from your land that the Lord your God is giving you, and you shall put it in a basket, and you shall go to the place that the Lord your God will choose, to make his name to dwell there… And you shall make response before the Lord your God, 'A wandering Aramean was my father. And he went down into Egypt and sojourned there, few in number, and there he became a nation, great, mighty, and populous. And the Egyptians treated us harshly and humiliated us and laid on us hard labor. Then we cried to the Lord, the God of our fathers, and the Lord heard our voice and saw our affliction, our toil, and our oppression. And the Lord brought us out of Egypt with a mighty hand and an outstretched arm, with great deeds of terror, with signs and wonders. And he brought us into this place and gave us this land, a land flowing with milk and honey. And behold, now I bring the first of the fruit of the ground, which you, O Lord, have given me.' And you shall set it down before the Lord your God and worship before the Lord your God.[269]

---

[269] Deut 26:1-2, 5-10

The significance of this ritual and declaration that the people — whether native-born Israelite, Levite, or the foreigner who lives among them[270] — were to make at the presentation of the first fruits of the harvest during the Feast of Weeks and the Feast of Booths is seen in the way that "[t]he declarations here and in vv 13b– 15 are the only addresses to God with prescribed wording, which ordinary folk are to recite in a formal liturgical setting, to be found within the Torah."[271] In this prescribed liturgy is the confession that "the land [is] a gift from God in fulfillment of his promises to the fathers, a land described as 'flowing with milk and honey.'"[272] This imagery of 'milk and honey', is more than merely a description of high quality and enjoyable products. Earlier in Deuteronomy 8:8, Moses describes the land as having 'wheat and barley, of vines and fig trees and pomegranates.' These products of the land are the result of the efforts, wisdom and work of the farmer. Milk and honey, on the other hand, are products that require no effort on the part of the inhabitants as cows and bees produce these for them. At the heart of this declaration, therefore, is a recognition of God's sovereignty and ownership of the land, and the gracious nature of the inheritance for the descendants of Abraham. The land belongs to the Lord, it is His to give, and as the passage states explicitly. And in this ritual, the people were acknowledging He is giving it to them.

The prescribed liturgy, like that of Joshua's recital of God's mighty works, begins with the declaration 'A wondering Aramean was my father.' The description given here matches the depiction of their ancestor Jacob who went to Egypt during the time of Joseph and sojourned there until 'he became a nation, great, mighty, and populous.' There is also most likely an allusion to the journey of Abram into Egypt as well. When Abraham sent

---

270 Deut 26:11

271 Christensen, D. *Deuteronomy* 21:10-34:12. p.632

272 Ibid.

his servant to find a wife for Isaac, he was emphatic that the servant was to go only to 'his country.' Later on, we read that he 'went to Mesopotamia to the city of Nahor'[273], which is most likely the city of Abram's birth, named most likely after one of his fathers.[274] Where the English translators have used 'Mesopotamia', which means 'between the rivers', is actually the translation of the Hebrew *Aram naharayim,* meaning 'Aram of the two rivers.' Thus, as an Aramean, Abraham was definitely in mind in this figure. So how are we to make sense of this? Quite simply, the figure functions almost like a pun, where both patriarchs are conflated into the one, especially since the people trace their heritage to Abraham, while also calling Isaac and Jacob their father too. Thus, the wandering Aramean is a symbol of the patriarchs who were yet to inherit the land promised to their descendants.

This designator of Aramean appears to be quite significant in meaning as well. It is most likely that when formulating this liturgy, God intended to do more than merely identify Abram's origins; He wanted to explain its significance and meaning. As I mentioned earlier, this liturgy was given to all who live in the land, the Levites, the native-born and the sojourner, or *ger.* And this is just one of many passages where an instruction was given to both the native-born who had blood lineage back to the patriarchs *and* the foreigner who lived among them (something that is often looked over). The stranger from among the nations was to likewise acknowledge God's provision to them as a fulfilment to the promises made to Abraham. In his commentary on Deuteronomy, Tim Hegg explains that in this liturgy:

> the native born as well as the ger confesses both that Abraham, Isaac, and Jacob are his forefathers, and that the covenant promises made to them have passed to him

---

273 Gen 24:10

274 Gen 11:22-25

> through God's faithfulness… In fact, all who came into the Land, regardless of their physical lineage, were to rehearse the gracious and sovereign acts of God in leading Israel out of Egypt, through the wilderness, and into the Promised Land. All are viewed as one people, with One God, and with one purpose—to worship Him in all of life. This, in fact, is the primary purpose of creation.[275]

This is why the liturgy does not say, 'my Father was a wandering Jew.' Abraham was a Gentile, a *ger*, and the people were reminded of this every time they recited it. Although the Abrahamic promises would result in the birth of a nation that descended from Abram, the benefits of those promises were not limited to 'the Jews' but the whole world. This is why the foreigner was invited to participate in Israel's worship as an equal member.

On the one hand, the land of Canaan was to be the place where the Israelites dwelt as a place to call their own, as well as provide them with food, a sense of belonging, and protection from the nations. However, as we read through the laws and commandments in the Torah, including this thanksgiving ritual, there is a repeated connection with the land. For example:

> "But you shall keep my statutes and my rules and do none of these abominations, either the native or the stranger who sojourns among you (for the people of the land, who were before you, did all of these abominations, so that the land became unclean), *lest the land vomit you out* when you make it unclean, as it vomited out the nation that was before you."[276]

---

275 Hegg, T. *Deuteronomy*. p.177-178.
276 Lev 18:26-28

> "Therefore you shall do my statutes and keep my rules and perform them, and then *you will dwell in the land* securely."[277]

> "I will tell you the whole commandment and the statutes and the rules that you shall teach them, that they may *do them in the land* that I am giving them to possess."[278]

> "But when you go over the Jordan and *live in the land* that the Lord your God is giving you to inherit, and when he gives you rest from all your enemies around, so that you live in safety, then to the place that the Lord your God will choose, to make his name dwell there, there you shall bring all that I command you: your burnt offerings and your sacrifices, your tithes and the contribution that you present, and all your finest vow offerings that you vow to the Lord."[279]

As we read these conditional statements regarding obedience and staying in the land, the ultimate purpose for the land is revealed: God's restored sanctuary where His Holy people will serve and worship Him. This becomes particularly evident in the way the final quote above from Deuteronomy 12 shows how in this new experience, the sacrifices that were made without geographical restriction, would now be centred on one location. This was to be in contrast with the idolatrous worship practices of those who were previously living in the land. The land existed primarily for the glorification of God as He restored His created order. And because

277 Lev 25:18
278 Deut 5:31
279 Deut 12:10-11

foreigners were living in that land, they too were called to worship the one who ruled over it.

Another example of Israel's worship acknowledging the patriarchal origins of their inheritance is found in Psalm 105:

> Seek the Lord and his strength;
> seek his presence continually!
> Remember the wondrous works that he has done,
> his miracles, and the judgments he uttered,
> O offspring of Abraham, his servant,
> children of Jacob, his chosen ones!
>
> He is the Lord our God;
> his judgments are in all the earth.
> He remembers his covenant forever,
> the word that he commanded, for a thousand generations,
> the covenant that he made with Abraham,
> his sworn promise to Isaac,
> which he confirmed to Jacob as a statute,
> to Israel as an everlasting covenant,
> saying, "To you I will give the land of Canaan
> as your portion for an inheritance."...
>
> He opened the rock, and water gushed out;
> it flowed through the desert like a river.
> For he remembered his holy promise,
> and Abraham, his servant.

So he brought his people out with joy,
his chosen ones with singing.
And he gave them the lands of the nations,
and they took possession of the fruit of the peoples' toil,
that they might keep his statutes
and observe his laws.
Praise the Lord![280]

This Psalm is what is known as a historical psalm, which has the worshippers proclaim and reflect on significant historical events, in particular, the mighty works of the Lord. In this Psalm, the covenantal promises made with the patriarchs are given as the foundational motivation for God's actions in the past, and therefore the lens through which they are to be understood. In fact, we could consider this to be actually a song of praise about God's faithfulness to the Abrahamic covenant. As Artur Weiser explains in his commentary on the Psalms,

> The theme of the hymn… is the fulfilment of the promises made to the forefathers, to which the account given in vv. 12-41 is devoted… In these statements God is almost always the subject of the action…; the story serves to prove his 'faithfulness and grace.'[281]

The Psalm makes the worship personal by connecting the worshippers to the covenant. It addresses them as the 'offspring of Abraham' and 'children of Jacob,'[282] and has them recount the promise made with the

280 Ps 105:4-11, 41-45
281 Weiser, A. *The Psalms: A Commentary*. p.674-675
282 Ps 105:6

patriarchs that the Lord would give Abraham and his descendants the land of Canaan as an inheritance. Here, the Psalm describes this promise as everlasting and declares that the Lord 'remembers His covenant forever.' Additionally, the Psalm demonstrates the covenantal reciprocal pattern of remembering in the way that the "promised remembrance of the Lord follows immediately after the call for the people to remember, in turn, the covenant that the Lord has wrought on their behalf."[283]

The psalm then recounts God's protection of the patriarchs in the land and Egypt, before describing the plagues and subsequent exodus. Then in the last historical section of the Psalm, the worshiper reflects on God's provision for Israel in the wilderness of protection, food and water. The psalmist reiterates the promise made in verse 8 as the reason for this provision: 'For he remembered his holy promise, and Abraham, his servant.' This, together with the introduction makes the underlying message of this psalm clear: the "Lord remembers, and so too must we."[284] In reciting this psalm as a congregation, the people were not only praising God for His faithfulness to the patriarchs in fulfilling His promises, they were also reminding themselves of this great reality: that the land they were standing on, the food they were eating, and that they even exist as a people who call Yahweh their God, is evidence of God's faithfulness to the Abrahamic promises. And these two liturgies were given to not only allow the people to articulate a thankful recognition that they are the beneficiaries of the Abrahamic promises, but to help remind themselves of this as well.

---

283 Van Harn, R; Strawn, B. *Psalms for Preaching and Worship: A Lectionary Commentary*. p. 276. Kindle Edition.

284 Ibid. p.277

Exile and Restoration

But their enjoyment of the land was not without some form of obligation. One of the conditions of dwelling in the land, as discussed in a previous chapter, was their obedience and faithfulness to the covenant established at Sinai. Should they rebel against their God, they would experience exile from the land. This is because of the connection between a lack of faith, and rebellion. In Numbers 14, after the spies who were sent into the land came back with a pessimistic report, the people complained and wanted to go back to Egypt. This lack of faith was described by Joshua as rebellion.[285] Likewise, the author of Hebrews connects obedience and faith with regards to occupation of the land when they wrote:

> For good news came to us just as to them, but the message they heard did not benefit them, because they were not united by faith with those who listened... Let us therefore strive to enter that rest, so that no one may fall by the same sort of disobedience.[286]

What this means is that when the people turned to false gods, they did so because they did not have the faith that the Lord would preserve them in the Land, which was a demonstration of faithfulness to the Abrahamic covenant. And as history and the ongoing narrative of the Tanakh demonstrates, this was indeed the outcome of the people of Israel as they fell into unrepentant idolatry. Having abandoned the God who brought them out of Egypt and gave them conquest over the land, the Lord sent many prophets warning them to repent until 722BC when Assyria took the Northern

---

285 Num 14:9

286 Heb 4:2,11

Kingdom into captivity, and 586BC when the Babylonians destroyed Jerusalem.

Often when God warned about exile, it was balanced with an explanation that it would not be permanent. In Leviticus 26, after warning the people of the threat of exile for disobedience, the Lord explained:

> But if they confess their iniquity and the iniquity of their fathers in their treachery that they committed against me, and also in walking contrary to me, so that I walked contrary to them and brought them into the land of their enemies—if then their uncircumcised heart is humbled and they make amends for their iniquity, then I will remember my covenant with Jacob, *and I will remember my covenant with Isaac and my covenant with Abraham, and I will remember the land…* when they are in the land of their enemies, I will not spurn them, neither will I abhor them so as to destroy them utterly and break my covenant with them, for I am the Lord their God. But I will for their sake remember the covenant with their forefathers, whom I brought out of the land of Egypt in the sight of the nations, that I might be their God: I am the Lord.[287]

Here, we find that God promises to restore the repentant nation, not simply because they said sorry, but as a demonstration of his faithfulness to the eternal promise He made to the patriarchs. This message is also found in the words of the prophet Micah. After promising judgement against Israel because of their oppressive, corrupt rulers, and false prophets, the

287 Lev 26:40-42, 44-45

Lord promises to restore a remnant and the nation. In the final verses of the prophetic book, we find this declaration:

> Who is a God like you, pardoning iniquity and passing over transgression for the remnant of his inheritance? He does not retain his anger forever, because he delights in steadfast love. He will again have compassion on us; he will tread our iniquities underfoot. You will cast all our sins into the depths of the sea. You will show faithfulness to Jacob and steadfast love to Abraham, as you have sworn to our fathers from the days of old.[288]

Here the unfaithful Israelites are given a reminder of the enduring faithfulness of their God. But more significantly, the remnant is given a foundation and anchor for the hope they have for their promised restoration; His faithfulness to the Abrahamic promise. For the sake of His glory, the Lord intended to prove Himself faithful to His promise to give Abraham and his descendants the land to dwell in, in perpetuity.

This has implications for us as readers of the biblical narrative as we go through the exilic and post-exilic narratives. What we are intended to recognise is that the Israelites' preservation and restoration are about God remaining true to His goals and purposes of restoring the world. A mission He wants to accomplish via the people of Israel, which He declared many centuries earlier that He would do through the Abrahamic promises. When we see the Lord blessing Daniel in Nebuchadnezzar's palace, or delivering the Jews through the influence of Esther, we are meant to recognise God's preservation of the remnant because of His oath to Abraham. And when we see Him restoring the people through the covenant renewal and returning

---

[288] Mic 7:18-20

them to the land where they can begin to rebuild under the leadership and direction of Nehemiah and Ezra, we need to recognise that this is about more than just forgiveness. It is because of the faithfulness of the Lord to Abram, overflowing to his descendants, that the people were brought back to the land. Quite clearly, the Abrahamic covenant can be seen to unite the entire narrative of the Tanakh.

BLESSINGS AND CURSES

I will bless those who bless you, and him who dishonors you I will curse, and in you all the families of the earth shall be blessed."[289]

The fulfilment of narrative promises often takes time to play out and become realised by the hero and other characters. In the Matrix trilogy, humanity's deliverance by Neo does not happen until the end of the third film. Frodo's destruction of the ring of power is also a long journey from the saga's opening pages. And Luke Skywalker's mastery of the force takes at least a trilogy to achieve. But along the way, we see small glimpses of the promise being played out: Neo's discovery of his powers, Frodo's protection by the fellowship, and Indie finding the clues required to discover the lost ark. But that is not to say that the final goal is completely foreign to the narrative that leads to the plot's resolution. Neo is able to defeat agents and save individuals from death, Frodo constantly keeps the ring safe from evil, and Luke can use the force in small doses to give him advantages over his enemies. This is similar to what theologians describe as the 'now but not yet' reality of the promises of the Gospel. This

---

[289] Gen 12:3

is not limited to the expectation of Christ's return and the establishment of His kingdom; it is true of the Abrahamic narrative too.

Thus far, we have seen the way the Lord has fulfilled His first two promises of descendants and land through the Tanakh. In particular, the way the Lord blessed the Patriarchs and the Israelites materially through the provision of food and wealth, and protection from enemies and armies. However, is this the best the covenant members in the Tanakh can expect? If you were to ask the hyper-dispensationalist, they would most likely tell you that any spiritual blessing hinted at in the Abrahamic covenant would not be unlocked until Christ, especially the blessing for all nations. They claim that 'the Old Testament beneficiaries of the Abrahamic covenant are for the Jews, and any inclusion of the Gentiles or spiritual blessings would have to wait until the arrival of Christ.' The narrative of the Tanakh, however, demonstrates that this is not the case. As we will find, many of the people of Israel experienced God's supernatural blessing, and that more than those who were descended from Abram shared in this gift.

Supernatural Protection

Blessing, as we defined earlier in chapter one, is God making possible the achievement of His purposes in people's life. He blessed Adam and Eve by empowering their call to be fruitful and subdue the Earth and provided wealth and protection for Abram and the Israelites that they might become a great nation. Yet, there is more than merely a material, or physical, narrative being played out in the Tanakh. God's restoration of creation is more than a fresh paint job and new carpet. It requires healing at a spiritual level, and spiritual forces were working in opposition to God's purposes. This brings us to the story of Balaam.

Towards the end of the forty years of wondering the desert, Israel camps in the plains of Moab, and the Moabites freak out both because they "saw all that the Israelites had done to the Amorites" and in response to their vast number.[290] And so, Balak, the King of Moab, sent for a prophet called Balaam to curse the Israelites because he was convinced that this was the only way to defeat them. Not a lot is known about Balaam. From the limited descriptions provided, the best we can surmise is that he is an Ammonite of great importance and renown and is known for having power in his words. Dennis Olen offers this creative depiction: "…a professional seer or prophet who travels about and curses military enemies for money. He is a kind of unattached hired gun, a mercenary, but his only weapons are words that have the power to curse or bless."[291]

The narrative makes it clear that he does know Yahweh and acknowledges Him as sovereign. As he explained to Balak:

> Did I not tell your messengers whom you sent to me, 'If Balak should give me his house full of silver and gold, I would not be able to go beyond the word of the Lord, to do either good or bad of my own will. What the Lord speaks, that will I speak'?[292]

It is quite significant that we have here in the Torah, a foreigner who "acknowledges Yahweh as his divine lord whose will he must follow in all that he says and does."[293] But is he a worshipper of God like Melchizedek? History and clues in the biblical account would suggest not. The discovery

---

290 Num 22:1-3
291 Olson, D. *Numbers*. p.140.
292 Num 24:12-13. Cf. Num 22:18,38; 23:12
293 Noth, M. *Numbers: A Commentary*. p.174

of inscriptions at Deir Alla, which is in the Jordan Valley, gives us an insight into his practices:

> Balaam, son of Beor, is visited at night by gods, who communicate to him an ominous message. Balaam gathers his comrades and informs them as follows: certain gods convened a council, and commanded a goddess... to cover the heavens with sense cloud... Balaam proceeds to interpret this omen by depicting the disaster which it predicts.[294]

Apart from being dated to the eighth-century BC, not much is known about the origins of this story. Nonetheless, it does support the understanding that Balaam was someone merely aware of Yahweh's identity and nature, and not a devoted covenant member. Rather, he was deeply involved in pagan cultic practices. Consider too how Scripture describes Balaam. In Joshua, Balaam is referred to as 'the diviner'[295] which is from the Hebrew word *qasam*; a term related to the mystical arts and necromancy[296] and is denounced alongside witchcraft in Deuteronomy 18. Additionally, while condemning false prophets, Peter compares these teachers with Balaam saying, "They have followed the way of Balaam, the son of Beor, who loved gain from wrongdoing."[297] Clearly, Scripture does not see Balaam as a regular prophet of God.

The benefit for us is that through the oracles of Balaam, we are provided with insight into the realities of spiritual warfare. Tim Hegg, in his com-

---

294 Levine, B. T*he Deir Alla Plaster Inscriptions.* p.195-196

295 Josh 13:22

296 1Sam 28:8

297 2Pet 2:15

mentary on the event, suggests that Balaam is in fact a messenger of Satan[298] by offering the following evidence. The first is when Balak says to Balaam in Numbers 22:6 "I know that he whom you bless is blessed, and he whom you curse is cursed." This ability that Balaam was obviously well known for, that could very well have been on his business card, is an obvious reference to the Lord's words to Abram in Genesis 12:3; that He would 'bless those who bless him and curse those who curse him.' In this quote from Genesis, it is clear that the act of blessing and cursing is a deed and function reserved for God. However, like Satan, Balaam is attributing "to himself what could only be the work of the Almighty."[299] The other evidence is found when the Lord said to Balaam, "You shall not go with them. You shall not curse the people, for they are blessed."[300] Because of God's divine purposes and will, as expressed in the Abrahamic promises, the descendants of Abraham are already blessed, meaning that Balak's request was to go against the work of the Lord, which likewise, is the mission and purpose of Satan. It appears that Balaam would have willingly gone and fulfilled Balak's request for a good pay cheque, but is restrained by God's decree.

The Lord's rebuke against Balaam on his way to Balak is an incident that has often puzzled me. For a long time, I had wondered 'why was God mad at Balaam for going when He had just told him to go?' A possible explanation for this, and it seems quite reasonable, is related to the intentions and inclinations of Balaam's heart. Before leaving, the Lord said, "If the men have come to call you, rise, go with them; but only do what I tell you."[301] However, it is quite likely that with a desire to obtain riches and notoriety with Balak, Balaam had it in his heart to actually curse Israel,

---

298 Hegg. *Balaam – Prophet or Sorcerer?* p. 2

299 Ibid.

300 Num 22:12

301 Num 22:20

and it is for this reason the Lord was angry with him. As the Angel of the Lord said to Balaam, "I have come out to oppose you because your way is perverse before me."[302] Thus, as Tim Hegg explains, "permission to allow Balaam to accompany the messengers of Balak was given in order to disclose his true intentions."[303] The terrifying encounter with the angel - a motif not unfamiliar in Scripture – would have definitely revealed the folly of this attempted deceit against God, and instilling him with the fear of the Lord ensured he spoke only according to what the Lord told him.

It seems odd that a sorcerer would be concerned with the Lord's instructions. But as one who is involved in divination, Balaam would have had reverence for the gods, and recognised their authority. And this is no different to Satan, as we see in the book of Job when he asks God for permission to test Job and does so within His prescribed parameters. Hegg explains that

> ...there have always been those who appear to have a connection with God, and who even appear to obey Him, who in fact, are enemies of God and His people. Balaam understood that God existed, and that His will was sovereign. James tells us that the demons also 'believe in God and tremble' (James 2:19). But Balaam has no regard for God's ways – he despises God's covenant, because he disregards God's covenant people.[304]

Thus, although Balaam appears to believe in God, his belief is clearly one of ascent to knowledge and superstitious reverence rather than genuine faith. Nonetheless, the Lord uses Balaam to bless His people and demon-

---

302 Num 20:32

303 Hegg. Balaam. p.4-5

304 Hegg. *Balaam –Prophet or Sorcerer*. p.3

strate His sovereignty to him, King Balak, and the nations. This lesson was foreshadowed to the reader with the incident involving the talking donkey. By having the animal see the Angel of the Lord standing in the road, but Balaam remaining oblivious, his 'spiritual vision' as a diviner is being mocked. This encounter shows how even the forces of evil are unable to thwart the Lord's commitment to fulfil His promises to bless the descendants of Abraham. This truth is further emphasised in the oracles given by God through the sorcerer Balaam.

Looking at the general themes and message of each oracle, we can see that each of the blessings uttered by Balaam flow together to culminate in the ultimate fulfilment of God's covenant promises. The first oracle declared that Israel was set apart for God and that their election is the reason for their blessing. The second is about the faithfulness of God to his covenant promises, which is the foundation for their victory over their enemies. The third alludes to the Abrahamic promise, emphasising the covenant promise of blessing and the danger of cursing God's covenant people. The fourth and final oracle is about the coming Messiah who is described as a conquering King who will come from Israel:

> I see him, but not now; I behold him, but not near: a star shall come out of Jacob, and a scepter shall rise out of Israel; it shall crush the forehead of Moab and break down all the sons of Sheth.[305]

Following this, Balaam went on and declared that no nation will defeat Israel. This final oracle has great significance because it describes the

[305] Num 24:17

Messiah as "the pinnacle of [Israel's] blessings - indeed, the very source of all [Israel's] blessings",[306] which is the goal of the Abrahamic promises.

By having someone like Balaam proclaim these blessings, the Lord was demonstrating that the enemy will never stop God from fulfilling His purposes for His people and the world. For through Balak and Balaam, Satan tried to stop the fulfilment of the Abrahamic covenant, reflecting what Paul wrote to the Ephesians:

> we do not wrestle against flesh and blood, but against the rulers, against the authorities, against the cosmic powers over this present darkness, against the spiritual forces of evil in the heavenly places.

Nonetheless, the Lord was able to use the enemy's attack and turn it to His purposes. Not only were Balaam's oracles words of blessing, but also by protecting the descendants of Abraham from spiritual attack, the Lord was blessing them also. Hidden here is a foreshadowing of how the enemy, when they think they are cursing God's anointed on the Earth, blinded like Balaam to God's workings and greater purposes, are in fact working towards the blessing of God's people. The enemy, Satan, worked to attack the Messiah by having Him killed, thinking He could thwart His mission, only to discover that this act is what brought God's greatest blessings and purposes to fruition. Such is the sovereignty of Yahweh.

All Nations will be Blessed

Whenever people talk about the old covenant people of God, a number will often describe them as 'the Jews', made up of the descendants of Abraham,

---

306 Hegg. *The Balaam Oracles: 'I will bless you…'* p. 2

Isaac and Jacob. This view results in the belief that anything spoken by God to the people in the Tanakh is only for the native-born, blood descendant Jews, and not the Gentiles. In his book *Dispensationalism*, Ryrie claims that both Jews and Gentiles as fellow heirs on equal footing was "not known or experienced by God's people in Old Testament times or even during the earthly lifetime of our Lord."[307] Rather, this was only something that began at Pentecost. But does this correspond with the biblical record? The short answer is no. Granted, a clear majority of the people of Israel were physical descendants of the patriarchs, but the narrative of the Tanakh reveals that they were not exclusively so.

This becomes clear when we recognise that from the Exodus onwards, we begin to find Gentiles being included into that body of people as a partial fulfilment of the promise made to Abram that 'in him, all the families of the earth shall be blessed.' As these Gentiles joined the people of Israel, they experienced and shared in their covenant blessings. Moreover, not only were the same rights afforded to them; the same obedience and faithfulness was expected of them.

> There shall be one law for the native and for the stranger who sojourns among you.[308]

> You shall treat the stranger who sojourns with you as the native among you, and you shall love him as yourself, for you were strangers in the land of Egypt: I am the Lord your God.[309]

---

307 Ryrie, C. *Dispensationalism*. np.

308 Ex 12:49

309 Lev 19:34

> And if a stranger is sojourning with you, or anyone is living permanently among you, and he wishes to offer a food offering, with a pleasing aroma to the Lord, he shall do as you do.[310]

> For the assembly, there shall be one statute for you and for the stranger who sojourns with you, a statute forever throughout your generations. You and the sojourner shall be alike before the Lord.[311]

There are three significant moments where one finds the inclusion of Gentiles amongst the Israelites; the Exodus, the destruction of Jericho, and the marriage of Ruth.

A Mixed Multitude

The first is at the moment of the Exodus. It is a little-known passage, that many quickly read over, but it has significant implications. In Exodus 12 we find, "And the people of Israel journeyed from Rameses to Succoth, about six hundred thousand men on foot, besides women and children. *A mixed multitude* also went up with them…"[312] What this means is that the descendants of Abraham, Isaac and Jacob left Egypt along with 'a huge ethnically diverse group'[313] for Mt Sinai. That they are not natural descendants is seen in the way the Hebrew grammar clearly sets the mixed multitude apart from the sons of Israel. According to Philo, they were comprised of people who had also been slaves in Egypt, the product of intermar-

310 Num 15:14
311 Num 15:15
312 Ex 12:37-38
313 Stuart. *Exodus.* p. 303, cf. Enns. *Exodus.* p.251

riage between the Egyptians and Hebrews, and those who had abandoned the worship of the Egyptian gods after the plagues and began to worship Yahweh.[314] All of which are reasonable candidates for the identity of this group, however, no one can say for certain. In his commentary, Douglas Stewart favours the latter group, explaining that they "had observed the miraculous work of Yahweh... and had become convinced that conversion to him and like among his people would represent their best hope for the future."[315] Regardless of their specific identity, the inclusion of the mixed multitude has a number of theological implications.

In his article on this group, Aaron Sherwood suggests that because of its proximity to the plunder narrative, the crowd who were brought out along with the Hebrews can be considered God's spoils from Egypt as His victory over Pharaoh. As he explains,

> The mixed multitude of 12:38 thus marks an implicit instance of the nations being unified with Israel to be God's people... The narrator simply supplies as a given that God's prize of Israel was made up of both Israelites and non-Israelites who were united in and as worship of him.[316]

Thus, their inclusion with those redeemed from Egypt demonstrates that the bringing in of the nations into Israel is an intrinsic quality of those who belong to the restored people of God. The inclusion of the Gentiles here is a demonstration that even as far back as Exodus, a "lack of proper

---

314 Philo. *Moses.* 1.27

315 Stuart. Exodus. p. 303

316 Sherwood, A. "The Mixed Multitude in Exodus 12:38: Glorification, Creation, and Yhwh's Plunder of Israel and the Nations." p.153

bloodlines and heritage does not bar one from God's kingdom…"[317] This concept is reflected most clearly in the Lord's extension of hospitality and mercy to foreigners who 'bind themselves to the Lord' in Isaiah 56. The implications of this are that when the people stood at Mt Sinai and entered into covenant with the Lord, it was not just 'the Jews', but the mixed multitude as well. It is not as though the mass of people were considered to be divided into different groups either. As the narrative continues, the term is never used again, and they are only ever called 'Israel'. When God speaks to Moses from the mountain, He did not see Hebrews over here and Gentiles over there, He saw Israel.

One significant figure who is an example of this is Caleb. The book of Numbers explains that this faithful spy was the son of a man called Jephunneh, who was a Kenizzite.[318] Yet, when the representatives of each tribe are being selected to go into the land to spy it out, Caleb was not regarded as a representative of the Gentiles or the Kenizzites, but rather, he was a representative of the tribe of Judah. What is interesting, and you can make of this what you will, but the two spies who demonstrated faith in the Lord's ability to deliver the people into the land were comprised of Joshua, a descendant of Ephraim, and Caleb, the integrated Gentile. And in these two we have an image of the true Israel; the native-born and the stranger united in faith.

It is most likely that this integration of the mixed multitude is partly why the Law contains so many instances where the same standard is applied to the native-born and the stranger, especially when it comes to instructions of worship. In particular, just a few verses after the mention of the mixed multitude, it was commanded by God that when it comes to

---

317 Hamilton. *Exodus*. p.195

318 Num 32:12

the celebration of the Passover, "There shall be one law for the native and for the stranger who sojourns among you."[319] The foreigner who becomes a part of Israel participates, not by a change in their ethnicity, but rather by becoming united in their faith in the God of Israel and His promises, as demonstrated by their having received circumcision.[320] Therefore, as well as explicitly fulfilling His promise to give Abram land and a nation, by including the mixed multitude in the Exodus, God was implicitly fulfilling the first fruits of His promise that in Abraham would the families of the earth be blessed.

Rahab

The next character of note is Rahab. We are introduced to her in the book of Joshua as Israel is preparing to conquer Jericho. Joshua had sent out two spies, and they had ended up at Rahab the prostitute's house in Jericho. Word had gotten out to the king that they were in the city, so he sent his guards to find them, but Rahab kept the spies hidden from them and lied about them leaving the city. Was this just good hospitality? Did Rahab hate the leaders of the city and therefore welcomed the invaders in? Why did she help out the enemy of her people? The following words of Rahab to the spies helps us to understand why she invited them in:

> I know that the Lord has given you the land, and that the fear of you has fallen upon us, and that all the inhabitants of the land melt away before you. For we have heard how the Lord dried up the water of the Red Sea before you when you came out of Egypt, and what you did to the two kings

319 Ex 12:49
320 See *Don't Jump Ahead*

> of the Amorites who were beyond the Jordan, to Sihon and Og, whom you devoted to destruction. And as soon as we heard it, our hearts melted, and there was no spirit left in any man because of you, for the Lord your God, he is God in the heavens above and on the earth beneath.[321]

This recount of the Exodus shows how far and wide the miraculous events had spread through the Ancient Near East, and how after forty years, people were still talking about it. But what is fascinating is that this account from Rahab is very similar to the words of Moses in Deuteronomy 4. As he was encouraging the people to obey the Lord by reminding them of God's amazing fulfilment of the Abrahamic promises, he said:

> …has any god ever attempted to go and take a nation for himself from the midst of another nation, by trials, by signs, by wonders, and by war, by a mighty hand and an outstretched arm, and by great deeds of terror, all of which the Lord your God did for you in Egypt before your eyes?… because he loved your fathers and chose their offspring after them and brought you out of Egypt with his own presence, by his great power, *driving out before you nations greater and mightier than you*, to bring you in, *to give you their land* for an inheritance, as it is this day, know therefore today, and lay it to your heart, that *the Lord is God in heaven above and on the earth beneath*; there is no other.

---

[321] Josh 2:9-11

Rahab recognised by the miraculous signs and wonders the Lord had done in bringing the people out of Egypt, that the Lord is Lord of all. This is nothing less than a declaration of faith. James Boice in his commentary on Joshua explains that Rahab no doubt knew very little of Israel's history with God beyond the Hebrews' deliverance from Egypt, 'but that was enough!'[322] This depth of faith was sufficient for her to hide the spies, for which Hebrews and James commend her.[323] However, this faith was incomplete and is evident in her confession. Notice how at the end of Deuteronomy, Moses had made the declaration 'there is no other.' Despite recognising the Lord's supremacy, this significant aspect of understanding God was missing from Rahab's words. As Robert Hubbard explains, the silence in Rahab's confession of Yahweh as the sole deity, and the reference to Him as 'your God' means 'Yahweh is not yet her God.' At this point, Yahweh is merely added to the Canaanite pantheon, making her theology henotheistic[324] rather than monotheistic.[325] Nonetheless, although she was not yet an Israelite theologically, she was on her way there. John Calvin likewise recognised the beginning of Rahab's 'conversion' if you will, through her confession:

> For it is perfectly clear that when heaven and earth are declared subject to the God of Israel, there is a repudiation of all the pagan fictions by which the majesty, and power, and glory of God are portioned out among different deities... I deny not that her faith was fully developed, nay... that it was only a germ of piety which, as yet, would have been

[322] Boice, J. *Joshua*. p.31

[323] Heb 11:31, Js 2:25

[324] Henotheism is the worship of a single, supreme god while not denying the existence or possible existence of other lesser deities.

[325] Hubbard, R. *Joshua*. p.121

> insufficient for her eternal salvation… [N]evertheless… however feeble and slender the knowledge of God which the woman possessed may have been, still in surrendering herself to his power, she gives proof of her election, and that from that seed a faith was germinating which afterwards attained its full growth.[326]

Could it be possible that Rahab's faith was sufficient to be counted righteous, just as Abram was? It is difficult to say with certainty as we do not know the full extent of that faith, or what exactly that faith entailed. All we know is that she recognised the sovereign supremacy of Yahweh and submitted to Him, as demonstrated in her protection of the spies. As highlighted above, the author of the Book of Hebrews, as well as James, applauded her faith at that point, which makes it quite possible. What is clear is that after the attack and destruction of Jericho, once Rahab and her family had been spared as promised by the spies, we find that she had become part of the covenant people of Israel.

> …the young men who had been spies went in and brought out Rahab and her father and mother and brothers and all who belonged to her. And they brought all her relatives and put them outside the camp of Israel. And they burned the city with fire, and everything in it… But Rahab the prostitute and her father's household and all who belonged to her, Joshua saved alive. And she has lived in Israel to this day, because she hid the messengers whom Joshua sent to spy out Jericho.[327]

---

326 Calvin, J. *Commentaries on The Book of Joshua.* p. 32-33

327 Joshua 6:23-25

What this shows is that Rahab's assimilation into the community was a process. At first, she and her family were placed outside the camp. This is based on God's instructions in Numbers 2 about the arrangement and layout of the camp. It was arranged with the Holiest at the centre; the Ark within the Tabernacle, then the Levites, then the remaining tribes arranged to the north, south, east and west on the outer circle, making one's place in the camp about their degree of holiness. Thus, while at first, it looks like Rahab and her family were not fully welcome, there was, however, a practical reason. In several places in the Torah, 'outside the camp' was prescribed as the place of spiritual quarantine. For example, Numbers 5:2-3, explains:

> Command the people of Israel that they put out of the camp everyone who is leprous or has a discharge and everyone who is unclean through contact with the dead. You shall put out both male and female, putting them outside the camp, that they may not defile their camp, in the midst of which I dwell.

Outside the camp was also the location for the slaughter and burning of certain sacrifices like the red heifer, the ashes of which were used in purification rituals. This preparation of the red heifer left the one burning it unclean until evening, requiring them to wash before returning to the camp. Thus, Rahab and her family needed to go through a time of purification. Perhaps it was because of their contact with the dead, or proximity to and even participation in idolatry. We find a more detailed instruction in Numbers 31 when, after defeating the Midianites, Moses instructed the soldiers: "Encamp outside the camp seven days. Whoever of you has killed any person and whoever has touched any slain, purify yourselves *and your captives* on the third day and on the seventh day."[328] This is most likely the process Rahab and her family went through.

Then after seven days, "…having been purged from their defilement's, they began to be regarded in the very same light as if they had originally belonged to the race of Abraham."[329] This inclusion becomes evident from the language choice made in our passage in Joshua 6. The phrase, 'And she has *lived in* Israel to this day' uses the Hebrew words *yashab* and *qereb*. *Yashab* means to permanently dwell and settle, and was also used in Genesis 13:7 to describe the Canaanites *dwelling* in the land, which doesn't just mean amongst but as a part of. And *qereb* means to be a part of something. As a bit of a visual metaphor, *qereb* is also the word that is translated as entrails, and the abstract inward place of a person, such as the place in which David asks for a steadfast spirit in Psalm 51. This word is used in Exodus 31:14 to describe how someone will be cut off and no longer *among* their people, and in Deuteronomy 17:20 to describe the King's children living *in the midst of* Israel. Thus, Rahab did not simply dwell among the people in the land, she lived with the same status as a native-born Israelite. One only needs to look at the Gospel accounts to confirm Rahab's covenant status. What could be more affirming of Rahab's full covenant membership than her inclusion in the genealogical line of the Messiah?[330]

With regards to her covenant status, Boice insightfully comments:

> [Rahab] was not a Jew. But since she believed in the Jewish God, she now instinctively understood that her place was with this new people rather than her own… In fact, since not even all Jews believed as genuinely as she did, she

[328] Num 31:19
[329] Calvin. *Joshua*. p.79
[330] Matt 1:5-6

> actually became more Jewish, spiritually speaking, than many of her new fellow citizens.[331]

Her identity and status as an Israelite and full covenant member was established, not by bloodlines, nor some kind of ritual or observance of cultural practices, but by her faith. Even at the time of the Mosaic Covenant, the experience of Rahab shows that covenant membership was still by faith, even for the Gentiles. Woudstra in his commentary emphasises this lesson:

> The purpose of [verse 25] is to celebrate the goodness of God exhibited in Rahab's rescue. Perhaps the writer also means to remind later readers that at some significant points in Israel's history, other non-Israelite stock was added to the nation's life. Purely racial components have never defined the people of God under the 'old dispensation.'[332]

Thus, Rahab's rescue and assimilation into the people of Israel is not only a fulfilment of the third covenant promise made to Abram, but also a key marker in the biblical theme of Gentiles worshipping the Lord.

Ruth

The third event is the migration of Ruth the Moabite with her Jewish mother in law, Naomi, to Israel. During the time of the Judges, Naomi and her husband Elimelech left Bethlehem in the midst of a famine and went to Moab. While they were there, Elimelech died and her sons married two Moabite women, Orpah and Ruth. But eventually, Naomi's sons died as well, leaving her with her daughters-in-law. It was at this point that Naomi

---

331 Boice. *Joshua*. p.32-33

332 Woudstra. *Joshua*. p. 115-116

decided to return to Judah. Orpah and Ruth wanted to come with her, but Naomi insisted that they return to their homes because she believed that with her, they would have no future. Orpah did end up leaving Naomi, but, as the text reads, 'Ruth clung to her.'[333] Naomi said to her, "See, your sister-in-law has gone back to her people and to her gods; return after your sister-in-law." However, Ruth would not have it. She replied saying that she wanted to stay with Naomi. She wasn't interested in returning. She didn't want to be a part of those people or worship those gods. She goes on to make a significant confessional statement: "your people shall be my people and your God my God."[334] This wasn't some empty promise, sentiment, or wishful declaration. By referring to 'Naomi's God' as Yahweh, and making an oath in His name in the following verse shows that she knows about the Lord and who He is. By joining that family, she had joined the covenant community and didn't want to leave. This commitment is made evident by the oath she swore in verse seventeen: "Where you die I will die, and there will I be buried. May the Lord do so to me and more also if anything but death parts me from you." This is a foretaste of what would be later taught in the book of Jeremiah. After condemning the Israelite's neighbours for seizing the people's inheritance the Lord says: "And if they learn well the ways of my people and swear by my name, saying, 'As surely as the Lord lives'—even as they once taught my people to swear by Baal—then they will be established among my people."[335] This welcomed inclusion of the Gentiles who would renounce their old gods and call upon the name of Yahweh among the covenant people of God seems to be a principle that predates Jeremiah. Ruth was not only aware of its reality, it was something

---

333 Ruth 1:14

334 Ruth 1:16

335 Jer 12:16

she experienced. Clearly, this is a Moabite who genuinely belonged to the people of Yahweh.

The formal inclusion of Ruth into the nation of Israel happens a little later. After catching the attention of Boaz, a wealthy relative of Naomi, while gleaning his field, she appeals to him as a kinsman-redeemer by requesting marriage. This petition happens through the strangely foreign ritual of 'uncovering Boaz's feet' at the threshing floor in the middle of the night.[336] After confirming that the unnamed, more eligible redeemer did not want to take up the role, Boaz agreed to both take Ruth as his wife in a levirate marriage as well as acquire the land belonging to Naomi. This as a package deal is not required by the Law, although, as John MacArthur suggests, "maybe the redemption of land and marriage had been combined by local tradition."[337] Or perhaps Boaz is fulfilling his obligations as a redeemer to both his relative Mahlon, Ruth's former husband, as well as Naomi. It appears that because of their poverty, Naomi needed to sell her land. And as her Kinsman Redeemer, Boaz buys it. This practice is the fulfilment of the redeemer law set out in Leviticus 25:25, "If one of your fellow Israelites becomes poor and sells some of their property, their nearest relative is to come and redeem what they have sold."

The principle behind both the levirate marriage and redeeming the land is the perpetuation of family lineage and preservation of their inheritance; intrinsic elements of the Abrahamic covenant. We see this motive in the words of Boaz when he proclaimed:

> You are witnesses this day that I have bought from the hand of Naomi all that belonged to Elimelech and all that belonged to Chilion and to Mahlon. Also Ruth the

336 Ruth 3:7-9

337 MacArthur, J. *The MacArthur Bible Commentary*. p.295

> Moabite, the widow of Mahlon, I have bought to be my wife, to perpetuate the name of the dead in his inheritance, that the name of the dead may not be cut off from among his brothers and from the gate of his native place.[338]

In response, the elders and witnesses at the gate recognised the transaction by giving the following blessing:

> May the Lord make the woman, who is coming into your house, like Rachel and Leah, who together built up the house of Israel. May you act worthily in Ephrathah and be renowned in Bethlehem, and may your house be like the house of Perez, whom Tamar bore to Judah, because of the offspring that the Lord will give you by this young woman.[339]

The significance of this blessing is that there is both an explicit and implicit recognition of Ruth's inclusion among the people of Israel. The explicit is seen in the explanation that Ruth is entering into Boaz's house. The word used for 'your house', *beteka*, can refer to a literal structure, but it is also used for a household. This usage is found, for example, in Genesis to denote Noah's household on the ark[340] and the people who belonged to Abraham who were to be circumcised.[341] Considering the occasion, the more symbolic meaning appears to be primarily in mind, especially since only a few words later the elders refer to 'the house (*bet*) of Israel.'

---

338 Ruth 4:9-10

339 Ruth 4:11-12

340 Gen 7:1

341 Gen 17:13

The implicit recognition is found in the blessings the elders bestowed on her. Their desire is that like Racheal and Leah (Israelites), Ruth would add to the building up of the nation of Israel through bountiful childbirth. Similarly, the people make mention of the house of Perez, wishing that Boaz's house would grow like Perez's. There seems to be a dual purpose for mentioning him. The first is that Perez was an ancestor of Boaz, thus making the blessing personal. The second is that Perez was the offspring of Judah to Tamar. Although of unspecified origin, it appears that based on the limited description in Genesis 38, she was a Canaanite, which makes her an outsider like Ruth. And like Ruth, was also the beneficiary of a levirate marriage. Therefore, Ruth's inclusion among the people of Israel began with faith in and knowledge of Yahweh but was later formalised in her marriage to Boaz. Indeed, Yahweh truly was her God, and the people of Israel were truly her people. Moreover, her story shows a true fulfilment of the Lord's promise to Abram that "I will bless those who bless you, and him who dishonors you I will curse, and in you all the families of the earth shall be blessed." Ruth was blessed because, as we read repeatedly through the narrative, she was a blessing to Naomi by leaving her home, (as did Abram), and caring for her. As a descendant of Abram, blessing Naomi was like blessing her ancestor. When Boaz learned of this, he protected and provided for her, even though – as Ruth recognised – she was not one of his servants.[342] Yet Boaz explained to Ruth:

> All that you have done for your mother-in-law since the death of your husband has been fully told to me, and how you left your father and mother and your native land and came to a people that you did not know before. The Lord repay you for what you have done, and a full reward be

---

342 Ruth 2:13

> given you by the Lord, the God of Israel, under whose wings you have come to take refuge![343]

What is interesting in the case of Boaz is that his father, Salmon, was the husband of Rahab. Perhaps, having a mother who was a stranger brought into the covenant people of God, made him sympathetic to Ruth's situation and could appreciate what she had given up. And indeed, the Lord did bless Ruth in his sovereign provision through Boaz and bringing them together in marriage. By blessing a descendant of Abram, the Lord fulfilled his promise and blessed her.

Moreover, she was also blessed through her offspring. At the conclusion of the book of Ruth, we are told that their child, Obed, became the father of Jesse, who was the father of David. And from David came a great line of Kings, leading ultimately to the Messiah. This is another fulfilment of God's promises to Abraham. As discussed in an earlier chapter, the Lord promised that he and Sarah would become the parents of kings.[344] How fascinating that the fulfilment of this would occur through two Gentile women who were brought into the nation of Israel. A far cry from the dispensational view that natural Israel and the Gentile believers are two distinct groups throughout history. Moreover, it is a contradiction of Ryrie's claim that a Gentile's equality with the 'Jews', "was something unknown in the Old Testament times; it is a distinct entity in the present age."[345] In fact, he goes so far as to say that a singular body "composed of Jews and Gentiles was [not] in existence in Old Testament times."[346] Yet, the inclusion of the

---

343 Ruth 2:11-12

344 Gen 17:6, 16

345 Ryrie. *Dispensationalism Today*. p135

346 Ryrie. *Dispensationalism*. np.

mixed multitude, Rahab and Ruth show this to be false. Rather, the inclusion of Gentiles was a welcomed reality from the beginning.

Granted, we are unaware of the scale of how many Gentiles were considered a part of the covenant community. However, the presence of characters through Israel's history like Uriah the Hittite, Obed-Edom,[347] and the non-Israelite judge Shamgar,[348] suggests there were more than just the occasional handful. And the Lord did not consider them as 'second class citizens', or under a different covenant and promises than the native-born. As he expresses through the prophet Isaiah:

> Let not the foreigner who has joined himself to the Lord say,
> 'The Lord will surely separate me from his people'…
> And the foreigners who join themselves to the Lord,
> to minister to him, to love the name of the Lord,
> and to be his servants,
> everyone who keeps the Sabbath and does not profane it,
> and holds fast my covenant—
> these I will bring to my holy mountain,
> and make them joyful in my house of prayer;
> their burnt offerings and their sacrifices
> will be accepted on my altar;
> for my house shall be called a house of prayer
> for all peoples.[349]

347 A Philistine who housed the Ark (2Sam 6)

348 Jud 3:31. Being the son of Anath (named after a Canaanite goddess) suggests Canaanite ethic origins.

349 Isa 56:3-7

Passages like this suggest that there was some uncertainty about the place of Gentiles among the covenant community. Whether this was imposed from the native-born, or personal doubt from the foreigner, is unclear. What is clear is that the Gentile who follows Yahweh is not separated or distinct from the native-born, and free to participate in the sacrifices, worship at the Temple, and sabbaths.

Moreover, that there was also those outside of Israel who worshipped Yahweh, such as Naaman the Aramean,[350] the Widow of Zarapeth,[351] and the sailors who threw Jonah into the sea,[352] shows that before Christ, this was not something restricted to the Israelites. Nonetheless, although their percentage was undoubtedly small, the prophets predicted a time when this number would grow significantly. In fact, following the above quote from Isaiah 56, the prophet writes: "The Lord God, who gathers the outcasts of Israel, declares, 'I will gather yet others to him besides those already gathered.'"[353]

There are many other prophecies through the Tanakh that show the extended inclusion of the Gentiles. Here is just a sample:

> 'It is too light a thing that you should be my servant
>   to raise up the tribes of Jacob
>   and to bring back the preserved of Israel;
> I will make you as a light for the nations,
>   that my salvation may reach to the end of the earth.'
> Thus says the Lord,
>   the Redeemer of Israel and his Holy One,

---

350 2Kg 5:1-14
351 1Kg 17:8-24
352 Jonah 1:15-16
353 Isa 56:8

to one deeply despised, abhorred by the nation,
    the servant of rulers:
"Kings shall see and arise;
    princes, and they shall prostrate themselves;
because of the Lord, who is faithful,
    the Holy One of Israel, who has chosen you."[354]

In that day I will raise up
    the booth of David that is fallen
and repair its breaches,
    and raise up its ruins
    and rebuild it as in the days of old,
that they may possess the remnant of Edom
    and all the nations who are called by my name,"
    declares the Lord who does this[355]

O Lord, my strength and my stronghold,
    my refuge in the day of trouble,
to you shall the nations come
    from the ends of the earth and say:
"Our fathers have inherited nothing but lies,
    worthless things in which there is no profit.
Can man make for himself gods?
    Such are not gods!"[356]

---

354 Isa 49:6-7 cf. Acts 13:47
355 Amos 9:11-12 cf. Acts 15:16-17
356 Jer 16:19-20

> It shall come to pass in the latter days
> that the mountain of the house of the Lord
> shall be established as the highest of the mountains,
> and it shall be lifted up above the hills;
> and peoples shall flow to it,
> and many nations shall come, and say:
> "Come, let us go up to the mountain of the Lord,
> to the house of the God of Jacob,
> that he may teach us his ways
> and that we may walk in his paths."
> For out of Zion shall go forth the law,
> and the word of the Lord from Jerusalem.[357]

> And in the place where it was said to them, "You are not my people," it shall be said to them, "Children of the living God."[358]

As highlighted in the footnotes, a number of these prophecies were recognised by the Apostles as the scriptural foundation for what they were observing in the early church: the mass conversion of Gentiles to worshippers of Yahweh through their faith in Jesus. As Mark Seifrid comments on Paul's use of Hosea 1 in Romans 9:

> Through Jesus Christ, the Son of God..., both Jews and Gentiles... have become 'sons of the living God.' As he did with Israel in the past, so now God calls those who were not his people, his people, both Jews and Gentiles.[359]

---

357 Micah 4:1-2

358 Hos 1:10 Cf. Rom 9:25-26

359 Seifrid, M. "Romans". *CNTUOT*. p.648

This is the promise envisioned from Genesis 12, experienced in part through the Tanakh, and fully realised in the person and work of Christ. The question of how the promise of blessing for all nations would be realised, and how the Gentiles can become the sons of Abraham through faith in Jesus will be the focus of Part 3: The Messiah.

Part III
THE MESSIAH

ABRAHAM AND CHRIST

Now the promises were made to Abraham and to his offspring. It does not say, "And to offsprings," referring to many, but referring to one, "And to your offspring," who is Christ.[360]

Foreshadowing is a fascinating device in literature and many other types of texts as the writer gives an advance hint of what is to come later in the story. Foreshadowing often appears at the beginning of a story, or a chapter, and helps the reader develop expectations about the coming events in a story.[361] It is a great way of writing because not only does it help create tension, it offers a kind of reward for those who have been engaged with the story.

A classic example of foreshadowing is found in Shakespeare's Romeo and Juliet, when, in the prologue, we are told, "From forth the fatal loins of these two foes / A pair of star-crossed lovers take their life..." Here, the audience is given the narrative promise that the story will involve two people

360 Gal 3:16

361 https://literarydevices.net/foreshadowing/

from opposing families, falling in love and ending their lives in suicide. But we don't know who, why, or how until we get into the play. Greater clarity comes later in the story when, before attending the Capulet's party, Romeo says to Mercutio that he fears this party will somehow result in his own untimely death. Yet, although we have a greater understanding of how it may unfold, there are still many questions about how and why. The next day, when Romeo visits Friar Lawrence, we are given a more hidden foreshadowing of the means of their death when, after Romeo enters, Lawrence explains that within the flower he is holding contains a powerful poison. The significance of this soliloquy is not realised until later in Act 4 when Friar Laurence proposes Juliet use a sleeping potion to make her look dead, and in Act 5 when Romeo commits suicide by drinking poison upon hearing about Juliet's supposed death. The unpacking and discovery of the full scope and purpose of the poison that was hidden in the play by Shakespeare, required the development and outworking of the narrative to give us progressively more information about its role in the story.

We can see how each mention and development of the theme of death functions as a signpost that points us to the conclusion of the story. Therefore, when the narrative promise 'this story will end in death' is realised and fulfilled, the progressive revelation of how this will happen makes the narrative's climax more meaningful. On the one hand, Shakespeare has appealed to his audience by not bombarding them with too much information at once, which in turn makes the story more enjoyable by creating tension and rewarding those who discover these signposts along the way. More importantly, he is showing his control over the story and its outcome. How much more significant therefore is the foreshadowing God provided in the millennia before the coming of Christ as a way to demonstrate His sovereignty over history in the real world.

As we enter Part Three of this book and come to the Apostolic Scriptures to consider the relationship between its content, and the Abrahamic promises, we are able to examine the climax and fulfilment of the promises of God given in the Tanakh. As I explained in much more detail in the chapter *Don't Jump Ahead*, some of these promises are explicit. Others are more implicit as patterns of people, events and institutions function as a kind of typological foreshadowing of the means and method of God's dealing with sin and the resolution of God's narrative. The implication of this is that when we, for example, read Genesis 25 and 26, what we encounter

> ...is not so much about [Jacob] and [Esau], or [Isaac] and [Rebecca]. It is about the covenant. The Promise of the Coming One (Gen 3:15) is being worked out event by event, unfolded to us in the pages of Moshe's writings, filling in the picture by each stroke of the divine brush.[362]

What this means is that, contrary to the dispensational position, what unfolds from Matthew 1:1 is not some plan C or brand-new project. Instead, as we saw in the chapter '*What is the Mosaic Covenant?*', just as the Mosaic covenant was the fulfilment and deepening of the ongoing relationship between God and the descendants of Abraham, rather than being anything new, the same can be said about the New Covenant. What I hope to achieve in this final section of this book is to examine and explain what the Apostolic Scriptures have to say about the connection between the Abrahamic promises and Christ, the Gospel and the church.

---

362 Hegg, T. "Parashah 27." Commentary on Genesis. p.1

Fulfilment of the Promise

When we look at the person and ministry of Jesus, and His relationship to the Tanakh, we are to see in Him the fulfilment of all of God's promises, which especially includes the covenantal promises. Jesus Himself said that He came to fulfil the 'Law and the Prophets',[363] which is a short-hand way to describe the Tanakh. Likewise, as Paul writes to the church in Corinth: "For all the promises of God find their Yes in him."[364] But what does it mean to be the 'fulfilment of a covenant'? Quite simply, it means to be the one in whom all the depths and realities and fullness of the promises can be understood and experienced. This is definitely the case when it comes to the Abrahamic Covenant, as we find Abraham being used as the foundation of the identity and ministry of Christ in several places in the Apostolic Scriptures.

That Jesus is the anticipated fulfilment of the Abrahamic promises is communicated, I believe, most explicitly in Paul's letter to Galatia:

> Now the promises were made to Abraham and to his offspring. It does not say, "And to offsprings," referring to many, but referring to one, "And to your offspring," who is Christ.[365]

This verse sits in the middle of the Book of Galatians' discussion of 'justification by faith alone' and how the covenants build upon each other as opposed to replacing the one before,[366] culminating in the person of Christ. Here in verse 16, we are given an explanation as to how one can

---

363 Matt 5:17
364 2Cor 1:20
365 Gal 3:16
366 Gal 3:15

participate in the promises of blessing made to Abraham. I will focus on details of this participation in a later chapter, but for now, we shall focus on how here, Paul is making the point that the promises were with Abraham and his singular seed, Christ.

Douglas Moo in his commentary on Galatians explains that "Paul's Christological interpretation of the 'seed'… is a very significant claim for his overall argument about the way the promise to Abraham becomes applicable to Gentile believers."[367] Those familiar with the Abrahamic promise passages being alluded to by Paul will, at a glance, scratch their heads and wonder 'did Paul actually read the original?' To make sense of Paul's interpretation, we need to answer a few questions. The first is: *to which specific source text is Paul referring?* After all, the Abrahamic promises were spoken, elaborated on and reiterated a number of times. Perhaps there's a singular usage there? Douglass Moo suggests that the original promise is most likely Genesis 15:18 or 17:8 since they are the places where 'seed' and 'covenant' occur together. But, since Genesis 17 is more focused on Abraham's lineage, this is most likely the one in Paul's mind.[368] According to Paul here in Galatians 3, the promised beneficiary of the Abrahamic promises was to be a singular 'seed', or offspring. The problem is that the singular noun 'seed' is also a collective noun, in the same way fish and sheep are used as both singular and plural in English. And in both of these passages suggested by Moo and many others, the collective is the one in view, such as when the Lord says to Abram that his 'descendants will be as numerous as the stars.'[369] So how are we to make sense of this? Is this just sloppy hermeneutics on Paul's behalf?

---

[367] Moo, D. *Galatians. Baker Exegetical Commentary on the New Testament.* np.

[368] Ibid.

[369] Gen 15:5; 22:17

This brings us to our second question: *how can Paul say the promise was made to a singular seed even though the source text says differently?* There are two related aspects to this answer. The first is that the best way to understand this verse is to understand that although the Abrahamic texts make much use of the plural sense of offspring, it does make use of the singular too. This is also a valid interpretation of seed, in particular when referring to Isaac, albeit not explicitly. When God explained to Abraham that Ishmael would become a great nation, He said that this blessing was given because he is Abraham's 'seed.' It stands to reason, therefore, that we could make the same application to Isaac. The second aspect of the answer is to understand that Paul is making a typological interpretation, meaning that in this passage, Paul has the ultimate, eschatological expectation of the promise mind. In this context of explaining that the inheritance of the covenantal promises depend on faith, Paul is denying any claim to them via bloodlines alone by saying that it is in Christ that one experiences them. This is because, as John Davis in his article on the Abrahamic Covenant explains, Jesus, as "the quintessential seed of Abraham, ...inherited all the promises given to Israel."[370] Thus, it is in Christ that we find the ultimate fulfilment of the promises made to Abraham, which especially in the context of Galatians 3, is the promise of blessing.

So, whether we apply the plural or singular to Christ depends on what aspect of His foreshadowing one focuses on. The plural shows us that Abraham's line, the collective descendants, were types and foreshadows of the ultimate descendant who would bring to fruition all the Abrahamic covenant was intended to achieve: the blessing of redemption for all the families of the earth by the forgiveness of sins, imparting of life, and reconciliation with our creator. And in the singular, which is the focus of

[370] Davis, J. "Who are the Heirs of the Abrahamic Covenant." *ERT*. p.149

Galatians 3:16, we can understand Isaac to be a 'type' of Christ, thus making Jesus the true[371] and ultimate son of Abraham. Isaac by no means experienced anything close to the fulness of the Abrahamic promises. He may have enjoyed some blessings, but the fact he never saw his descendants become a great nation and conquer the land, nor was he able to bring blessing to all the families of the earth. When we consider the failures of Esau and Jacob, we see Isaac struggled to even do this for his household. So, Isaac was not the ultimate beneficiary of the promises. The narrative points us forward telling us in the words of Yoda, 'No, there is another.' Jesus, as Paul tells us, is that seed. And the Gospel accounts make that clear.

The Son of Abraham

The book of Matthew, the Gospel account that seeks to demonstrate how Jesus was the anticipated Messiah from the Tanakh, begins with a genealogy:

> The book of the genealogy of Jesus Christ, the son of David, the son of Abraham.
>
> Abraham was the father of Isaac, and Isaac the father of Jacob, and Jacob the father of Judah and his brothers, and Judah the father of Perez and Zerah by Tamar, and Perez the father of Hezron, and Hezron the father of Ram, and Ram the father of Amminadab, and Amminadab the father of Nahshon, and Nahshon the father of Salmon, and Salmon the father of Boaz by Rahab, and Boaz the father of

371 By using the term true, I'm not implying that Isaac is somehow invalid or irrelevant. Rather, Christ and his ministry embodies everything that Isaac was pointing towards.

> Obed by Ruth, and Obed the father of Jesse, and Jesse the father of David the king.
>
> And David was the father of Solomon by the wife of Uriah, and Solomon the father of Rehoboam, and Rehoboam the father of Abijah, and Abijah the father of Asaph, and Asaph the father of Jehoshaphat, and Jehoshaphat the father of Joram, and Joram the father of Uzziah, and Uzziah the father of Jotham, and Jotham the father of Ahaz, and Ahaz the father of Hezekiah, and Hezekiah the father of Manasseh, and Manasseh the father of Amos, and Amos the father of Josiah, and Josiah the father of Jechoniah and his brothers, at the time of the deportation to Babylon.
>
> And after the deportation to Babylon: Jechoniah was the father of Shealtiel, and Shealtiel the father of Zerubbabel, and Zerubbabel the father of Abiud, and Abiud the father of Eliakim, and Eliakim the father of Azor, and Azor the father of Zadok, and Zadok the father of Achim, and Achim the father of Eliud, and Eliud the father of Eleazar, and Eleazar the father of Matthan, and Matthan the father of Jacob, and Jacob the father of Joseph the husband of Mary, of whom Jesus was born, who is called Christ.
>
> So all the generations from Abraham to David were fourteen generations, and from David to the deportation to Babylon fourteen generations, and from the deportation to Babylon to the Christ fourteen generations.

When we as modern Western readers come across genealogies in the Bible, we tend to switch off and wonder about their relevance. I'm sure many of us acknowledge that they do have a purpose and that they're not irrelevant; we just get a little stumped on how they are relevant to us, or what their exact purpose is. The significant purpose of genealogies for the original audience of the Tanakh was to "authenticate hereditary succession and inheritance rights, biological descent, and geographical or ethnological relationships."[372] In short, they were tied to their identity and defined their relationship to God, one another, and the nations. For example, it showed who was entitled to live in particular plots of land and who was eligible for the office of priest or King. But for modern readers, they not only reveal how the biblical narrative is tied and founded in historical reality, but also confirm the fulfilment of prophecy. Since God promised that Abraham would become a great nation, the census information at the beginning of the books of Numbers or in Chronicles shows the growth of a large nation. It also reveals God's concern for individuals, and it is this second purpose that will be our focus here.

Matthew could have, like Luke, begun with Adam and showed how the whole Tanakh narrative was lining up and preparing for Jesus, which indeed it was. However, Matthew was focusing on something more specific than that. Craig Keener in his commentary on Matthew explains that many ancient biographers began with ancestry and prophecy to paint their subject in a glorious light by stirring up in their reader what they knew about the person's predecessors and origins. Matthew "does this by listing Jesus' ancestors who evoke Israel's rich Old Testament heritage…"[373] In particular, he focuses on two key figures by introducing his reader to Jesus as the son of Abraham and the son of David. However, this is about more

[372] Harrison, R. "Genealogy." *ISB Encyclopedia Vol 2.* p.424

[373] Keener. C. *The Gospel of Matthew - A Socio-Rhetorical Commentary.* p.73

than lineage, it's about prophecy and identifying Jesus as the culmination of the messianic promises.

Being a 'Son of David' is a reference to the promise made by God in 2 Samuel:

> When your days are fulfilled and you lie down with your fathers, I will raise up your offspring after you, who shall come from your body, and I will establish his kingdom… I will establish the throne of his kingdom forever. I will be to him a father, and he shall be to me a son… And your house and your kingdom shall be made sure forever before me. Your throne shall be established forever.[374]

This is what is known as the Davidic Covenant, which was the promise that one of David's sons would rule over Israel as King forever. Thus, as a Son of David, Jesus is being identified as the rightful heir to the throne. Moreover, "'Son of David' was a standard messianic title for the rabbis… [which] developed, no doubt, from the messianic expectations such as 'sprout of Jesse' (Is 11:10)…"[375] Much more could be said about Jesus as the fulfilment of the Davidic covenant, however that is beyond our purposes. I want us to focus more on the other title, Son of Abraham.

This title carries with it a combination of meanings. One has to do with Abraham being the father of Israel. Repeatedly in the Gospels, appeals are made by the Jews that being Abraham's offspring gives them a position of pride and privilege. This presumptive attitude, however, was challenged by God's mouthpieces. For example, John the Baptist rebukes those who hope in their bloodline as a guarantee of God's forgiveness and salvation:

---

374 2Sam 7:12-16

375 Hegg, T. *Matthew.* p.18

> ...do not presume to say to yourselves, 'We have Abraham as our father,' for I tell you, God is able from these stones to raise up children for Abraham.[376]

Also, when Jesus was talking to the Jews about setting them free by the truth, they responded with, "We are offspring of Abraham and have never been enslaved to anyone..."[377] This high-status attitude is also reflected in the apocryphal texts, such as in 4 Maccabees:

> Let not us who are children of Abraham be so evil advised as by giving way to make use of an unbecoming pretense; for it were irrational, if having lived up to old age in all truth, and having scrupulously guarded our character for it, we should now turn back, and ourselves should become a pattern of impiety to the young, as being an example of pollution eating. It would be disgraceful if we should live on some short time, and that scorned by all men for cowardice, and be condemned by the tyrant for unmanliness, by not contending to the death for our divine law. Therefore do you, O children of Abraham, die nobly for your religion...?

Although not a part of Scripture, this first-century Jewish text describes the attitudes of the people Jesus ministered to, and not all are bad. This portion shows the belief that it would be unfitting and improper for a 'son of Abraham' to succumb to Antiochus' threats of arrest, torture and death to sin by eating food sacrificed to idols. In short, a Son of Abraham is a

[376] Matt 3:9

[377] Jn 8:33

descriptor of the 'ideal Jew',[378] and this is how Matthew wanted his audience to understand Christ's identity.

The other aspect of this identity is covenantal. As already discussed, the promises of blessing were made to Abraham and his seed, and therefore, to be called a 'son of Abraham' is to be considered a chosen member of the Abrahamic Covenant. However, more than a mere covenant member, as the culmination of the Abrahamic promises, "Jesus is thus the heir of Abraham par excellence, who can communicate Abraham's promised blessings to his people."[379]

This leads to our third purpose. When God made his promise to Abraham, it was not only for those who were descended from him but for all the families of the earth. This means that Matthew was indicating that Jesus was the one by whom salvation would be made possible for the Gentiles. This is amplified when we consider that the genealogy includes four mothers (not including Mary), all of which are either Gentiles (Tamar, Rahab and Ruth) or gentile by association and marriage (Bathsheba). This, according to Richard France, demonstrates the universal relevance of Jesus' incarnation and ministry.[380]

The opening verse, identifying Jesus as the son of both Abraham and David strongly suggests that Matthew also wanted us to see the connection between the Abrahamic and Davidic covenant in Jesus' identity. Much has been made by various commentators suggesting that the repetition of fourteen in the genealogy is drawn from the use of the *gematria*[381] of David's name. In Hebrew, David is spelt DWD which is 4+6+4=14, suggesting Matthew's focus is on the Davidic promises. Sounds interesting and 'it'll

[378] Keener. C. *Matthew*. p.73

[379] Ibid. p.73

[380] France, R. *The Gospel According to Matthew*. p.74

[381] The numerical value of a word based on the values of letters within a word.

preach', but there's not much to suggest that this is the case since the time *gematria* is used is with the number of the beast in Revelation, and there it is explicitly introduced as being so. Another reason to reject this interpretation is that the counting of fourteen generations is based on the pre-existing genealogical lists in 1 Chronicles 1-3. If we are to find any symbolic meaning from the use of fourteen, the most reasonable interpretation would be fourteen as two times seven; the number of completion.[382]

Nonetheless, it is safer to base our exegesis on what is explicit, rather than any implicit symbology. By choosing to structure the genealogy the way he has, Matthew is drawing a line between the Abrahamic promises, the Davidic covenant, the failure of the Davidic line and exile, and Jesus as the answer to both.

The relationship between the Abrahamic and Davidic covenants are seen in the words of Zechariah, the father of John the Baptist. After the birth of John, "his father Zechariah was filled with the Holy Spirit and prophesied, saying,

> "Blessed be the Lord God of Israel,
>   for he has visited and redeemed his people
> and has raised up a horn of salvation for us
>   in the house of his servant *David*,
> as he spoke by the mouth of his holy prophets from of old,
> that we should be saved from our enemies
>   and from the hand of all who hate us;
> to show the mercy promised to our fathers
>   and to remember his holy covenant,

382 Seven days of creation, days of Levitical Priesthood ordination (Lev 8:33), days circling Jericho, number of washings for the purification of Naaman (2Kgs 5:10), and the seven spirits of God (Rev 1:4).

the oath that he swore to our father *Abraham*, to grant us
    that we, being delivered from the hand of our enemies,
might serve him without fear,
    in holiness and righteousness before him all our days.
And you, child, will be called the prophet of the Most High;
    for you will go before the Lord to prepare his ways,
to give knowledge of salvation to his people
    in the forgiveness of their sins,
because of the tender mercy of our God,
    whereby the sunrise shall visit us from on high
to give light to those who sit in darkness and in the shadow of death,
    to guide our feet into the way of peace."[383]

We see here again in this Benedictus the themes of the Davidic and Abrahamic covenant being merged. Commenting on this passage, David Pao and Eckhard Schnabel explain how:

> 'He has shown the mercy… promised to our ancestors,' echoes Mic. 7:20… [which] provides the conceptual framework for the various elements in the immediate context of 1:72. These include the preceding note on the victory over God's enemies (1:71; Mic. 7:8-10) and the explicit mentioning of Abraham that follows.[384]

[383] Lk 1:67-79

[384] Pao, D and Schnabel, E. "Luke." *CNTUOT.* p.264

Thus, as discussed and demonstrated above, the expectation of a Davidic heir[385] with the power of salvation who would bring about the Abrahamic promises of deliverance and forgiveness to his descendants has its origins, not in some new program, but in the Tanakh itself. And Zechariah prophesied that this was to be fulfilled in his nephew, Jesus. It is worth highlighting that the reference to the Abrahamic covenant in this Benedictus is primarily focused on the aspect of the provision of land and the flourishing of the nation, which goes hand-in-hand with the protection of Abraham's descendants and the freedom to worship God.

The relationship between the two covenants also merges in their global scope. With Abraham, it was promised that he would be the father of many nations, and the Scriptures point to a Davidic King who would reign over the earth, especially within the psalms. For example, in Psalm 2 we read:

> The Lord said to me, "You are my Son;
>   today I have begotten you.
> Ask of me, and I will make the nations your heritage,
>   and the ends of the earth your possession.
> You shall break them with a rod of iron
>   and dash them in pieces like a potter's vessel.[386]

This royal liturgy explains how "God's response to the rebellion of the nations is to act in and through the Davidic king."[387] And the king is able to do so because of his conquest and global reign. On the other side of this reality, those who are under His reign will experience the blessing of justice,

---

[385] Ps 132:17-18, "There I will make a horn to sprout for David; I have prepared a lamp for my anointed. His enemies I will clothe with shame, but on him his crown will shine."

[386] Ps 2:7-9

[387] Van Harn, R. and Strawn, B. *Psalms for Preaching*. p.56

protection and provision. As stated, for example, in Psalm 72, where God is petitioned to exercise justice and righteousness through the king, it is also said: "May his name endure forever; may it continue as long as the sun. Then all nations will be blessed through him, and they will call him blessed."[388] This language of global blessing is reminiscent of the language used in Genesis 12:3, and intentionally so. Thus, when the Lord established his covenant with David, it can be understood that the true and ultimate Davidic King was the one through whom the global realities and blessings of the Abrahamic covenant would be realised. Indeed, the opening of the Gospel of Matthew makes this clear, as does its conclusion.

The final words of Jesus in this book, known most commonly as the Great Commission, demonstrate Christ's success in realising his role as the Son of Abraham and the Son of David:

> All authority in heaven and on earth has been given to me. Go therefore and make disciples of all nations, baptizing them in the name of the Father and of the Son and of the Holy Spirit…[389]

As a result of His death, burial and resurrection, Christ was given victory over the forces of evil,[390] given dominion and authority over all things in heaven and on earth, and declared the head of the church.[391] By using the word 'therefore', Jesus connects his authority and rule with the 'go' of the Great Commission. Not only is His rule the basis from which He can command His people to proclaim the Gospel, but His universal authority over all creation means that universal mission is now possible.

---

388 Ps 72:17

389 Matt 28:18-19

390 Eph 4:8, Col 2:15

391 Phil 2:9-11, Eph 1:20-23

In fact, the etymological origin of evangelism, *euaggelion* (good message), was the message of a king's victory over his enemies.[392] Moreover, the Great Commission goes on to explain that His ambassadors are to teach his disciples 'to observe all that [He had] commanded [them],' thus indicating that part of the Great Commission means bringing people under Christ's rule and authority too. Thus, as the anticipated Davidic-Messianic King over all creation, the Abrahamic blessings of forgiveness, redemption, and reconciliation with Yahweh, is now possible for 'all the families of the earth' through the true and ultimate son of Abraham.

Isaac and Jesus

As well as Matthew's bookending of the Abrahamic expectation and fulfilment, Luke's Gospel also makes a typological connection between Christ's identity and Abraham. Or to be more specific, his son Isaac. In Luke chapter 1, we learn from the angel Gabriel's conversation with Mary about the supernatural origins of Jesus' conception. While the conception of Isaac in Sarah was miraculous in that God supernaturally empowered it through the natural means, just as it was with Mary's cousin Elizabeth, the conception of Christ was to be at the next level. Since she was unmarried and a virgin, Jesus' conception was completely of the Holy Spirit, making His earthly origins not merely similar to Isaac's, but greater. This is not the only similarity between the Abrahamic narrative and this conversation.

The first is in the question, "How will this be, since I am a virgin?" Here Mary is questioning the mechanics of this promise, just as Abraham did in Genesis 15. As we saw in the chapter '*Cutting a Covenant*', this was a question about filling in the gap between knowledge and faith. Abraham knew

392 E.g. Appian. *Civil Wars.* 4.4.20

God would achieve everything He promised; he just couldn't understand how. In a similar way, Mary was no doubt confused by this proclamation. Being familiar with the narratives of the Tanakh, her knowledge of such a promise was based on the miraculous, but natural, conceptions like that of Isaac and Samuel, hence her question.

As evidence that her question came from a good place, Gabriel gives Mary a rather comprehensive answer to the question, 'how?' If for example, someone asked: 'How does that Olympian lift such heavy weights?', there's two ways to answer. One is the 'practical', or the Captain Obvious, how of: 'with his arms.' The other answer is the more causational kind of how. 'They can lift because they are so strong from exercising and training regularly, and being genetically predisposed to good muscle mass, and from a proper diet etc…' Gabriel's answer encompassed both senses of the word 'how.' He started by explaining how God would do it by the Holy Spirit, and how even Elizabeth had conceived in her barrenness. He then concluded with a causational statement that Jesus' conception is possible 'For nothing will be impossible for God.'[393] This, David Pao and Eckhard Schnabel point out,[394] is reminiscent of Genesis 18 when the three strangers come to visit Abraham and Sarah's tent. There, the Lord said to Abraham, "I will surely return to you about this time next year, and Sarah your wife shall have a son."[395] And in response to this promise, she laughed to herself. Now this was not humorous laughter, it was a sceptical reaction to what was "from her viewpoint the audacity of the man's claims…"[396] The text explains that she had laughed because "The way of women had ceased to be with Sarah" (a euphemism for menopause). In response, the Lord challenged this

---

393 Lk 1:37

394 Pao, D and Schnabel, E. "Luke." *CNTUOT*. p.260

395 Gen 18:10

396 Mathews, K. *Genesis 11:27-50:26*. p.218

laughter and asked rhetorically, "Is anything too hard for the Lord?" rendering her scepticism unfounded. It is important to note, as John Walton explains, that the Greek word for 'hard' "is not a quality that can be connected to human endeavours. Even applied as a description of the temple (2 Chron 2:9), it refers to that which goes beyond what human workmanship can attain… beyond 'wonderful or 'astonishing' to something more like 'mystical' or 'supernatural.'"[397] In other words, is there anything that is too mind-blowing and amazing that the Lord can't do it? This theme of the power of God is repeated in Luke by having Gabriel use similar wording that the Lord used in Abraham's tent. The use of this reference, most likely, was intended to help both Mary and Luke's audience to not only see the correlation between Jesus and Isaac's origins, but also to remind us of all that the Lord accomplished through Abraham and His demonstration of power in fulfilling His promises. Having been reminded of the omnipotence of God, Mary trustingly accepted the message of Gabriel.

The typological parallels between Jesus and Isaac do not end with Christ's miraculous conception and birth, but also in His death. We find this similarity in the narrative event recorded in Genesis 22 and referred to by Jews as the *Akedah,* or in English, 'the Binding of Isaac'. It is a well-known story and the foundation of many sermons encouraging Christians to be willing to trust God by putting Him first and make the necessary sacrifices needed to do so. And of course, these are great lessons and valid reminders, but I believe there is a deeper point and purpose to this narrative.

The story goes that one day God spoke to Abraham and told him: "Take your son, your only son Isaac, whom you love, and go to the land of Moriah, and offer him there as a burnt offering on one of the moun-

[397] Walton. *Genesis.* p.454

tains of which I shall tell you."[398] Now this, the reader is told, is a test of Abraham's faithfulness and trust in God and His covenant promises. The deeply connected relationship of this event to the covenant is seen firstly in the Hebrew of verse one. John Walton points out that this verse could be translated as: 'After these things, *that* God tested Abraham…' He continues by explaining how 'that God' is a reference back to 21:33 where the Lord is called the Everlasting God. Thus, verse one can be paraphrased as, 'After these things, *the Everlasting God* tested Abraham…'[399] That this is intended to remind the reader of God's covenant with Abraham becomes clear when we look back at Genesis 17:18. There, Yahweh told Abraham that He would establish his covenant with Isaac, the son in Genesis 22, as an *everlasting* covenant. And to maintain an everlasting covenant requires an everlasting God. With the reality of God's faithfulness to the covenant in mind, perhaps the right question one should ask as they encounter this story for the first time is not, 'why on Earth would God ask Abraham to offer up the long-awaited fruit of the covenant promises?', but rather, 'in offering Isaac, what is God's faithfulness going to look like?' Just like Mary's questioning and Abraham's curiosity, we too can ask: 'I know that the Lord will come good on His promises. But in this circumstance, I don't know how?' This is the test of Abraham. And we can see in the following two declarations and responses by Abraham that he was passing.

The first, after the Lord called his name, is his response of 'Here I am'. This phrase is an example of a Hebrew idiom meaning 'I am ready to listen and obey', and is used in Scripture by people who were about to receive instruction. Samuel, for example, said it multiple times to Eli, believing it was he and not the Lord calling his name in the tent.[400] That this phrase

398 Gen 22:2

399 Walton. *Genesis*. p.509

400 1Sam 3:3-18

could be a demonstration of a willingness to listen and obey comes from Eli's instruction once they worked out that God was calling Samuel. He told Samuel to say: 'Speak, Lord, for your servant hears.' And so Samuel did, and the Lord told him to prophecy against Eli and his household, which he was faithful to do. Jacob also said it just before the angel of the Lord told him to return to his family, as did Ananias before he was sent to preach the Gospel to Saul. In every situation, even before they know what was coming, they were effectively saying, 'yes, Lord.' This was the intention behind Abraham's response since after receiving the instructions from the Lord, Abraham rose early to fulfil what he was told to do. This walking out in obedience is our second example.

When the group was near the mountain God told them to travel to, Abraham and Isaac left the servants with the donkey. Abraham told them, "Stay here with the donkey; I and the boy will go over there and worship and come again to you."[401] Note how Abraham was confident they would *both* be coming back. We don't see anything here in this narrative to explain why, but Hebrews provides us with an explanation:

> By faith Abraham, when he was tested, offered up Isaac, and he who had received the promises was in the act of offering up his only son, of whom it was said, 'Through Isaac shall your offspring be named.' He considered that God was able even to raise him from the dead…[402]

Here, the author of Hebrews explains that although Abraham probably didn't understand how, he was confident that even in this test, God's faithfulness to His covenant promises would still come true. He figured that

---

401 Gen 22:5

402 Heb 11:17-19

since the Lord was able to bring life to Sara's dead womb, there's no reason why He couldn't raise the fruit of that womb from the dead too. This is a significant reason why Abraham was willing to obey. The Lord had been faithful to His promises; therefore, Abraham would remain faithful too.

After intervening and acknowledging that Abraham does fear Him, we are given another confirmation that this test was about the covenant promises. In response to Abraham's faithfulness, the Lord reaffirmed his covenant promises with Abraham to bless him, vastly multiply his offspring, and that his offspring would occupy the land promised him and be the source of blessing for all nations. It is important to reiterate that, as was the case for the previous occurrences of God affirming His covenant, Abraham's obedience was not the prerequisite for God's fulfilment of His promises as though they were a reward. Rather, as explained in a previous chapter, Abraham's obedience acted out in faith was a demonstration of the genuine relationship Abraham had with the Lord where such blessings take place.

The declaration of "…and in your offspring shall all the nations of the earth be blessed"[403] in this narrative, which is based on the promise of blessing in Genesis 12:3, brings us back to our discussion earlier in this chapter about Galatians 3:16. In this context, we are pointed forward to the descendant of Abraham whose sacrifice would bring about the blessings of forgiveness and reconciliation with Yahweh for all the nations of the earth. By borrowing the wording of Genesis 22:16 in his letter to the Romans, Paul appears to be making a connection to the *Akeda*: "He who *did not spare his own Son* but gave him up for us all, how will he not also with him graciously give us all things?"[404] Just as it was on the mountain in Genesis 22, on the cross we see a greater connection between sacrifice and blessing

403 Gen 22:18
404 Rom 8:32

to the nations. At the crucifixion, God the Father exchanged roles with Abraham when He took His son, His only son, whom He loves and offered him as a sacrifice.[405] However, instead of sparing the Son, He was delivered over. There was no voice from Heaven yelling 'stop!' This time, the knife of God's wrath and justice came down, and Jesus was slain on the cross. By this shedding of blood, as John records from the lips of the saints singing before the throne, He "ransomed people for God from every tribe and language and people and nation."[406] The difference between the *Akeda* and Calvary is, as Mark Seifrid aptly points out, "…the surrender of the 'beloved son'… is occasioned not by divine testing of faith, but by the unbelief, deceit, and violence of fallen humanity (see Rom. 3:10-18)."[407] Isaac was not fit for this role. He was not 'worthy to open the scroll'. Instead, Isaac was a type and shadow, pointing to Christ, the true son of Abraham who would be the perfect sacrifice. And this connection is more than a coincidence of patterns; the prophetic words within the narrative themselves help to make that link.

The well-known response of Abraham to his son's question 'where is the lamb for a burnt offering?' hints at something more: "God will provide for himself the lamb for a burnt offering, my son."[408] The word for provide, *ra'ah*, is an interesting one. Essentially at its root level, it means 'to see.' Walton suggests that this means that God will 'see to' the situation, meaning that "Abraham is convinced that the Lord will work out the

[405] Cf. Gen 22:2

[406] Rev 5:9

[407] Seifrid, M. "Romans." *CNTUOT.* p.634

[408] Gen 22:8

details."[409][410] And indeed, we do find that the Lord saw to intervening and stopping Abraham and providing this substitute of a ram as a sacrifice.

This ram is also a type of Christ for two key reasons. One is that like the ram caught in the thicket, Christ is the substitute not only for Isaac, but all humanity since none of us are worthy to atone for our own sins, let alone the sins of people from all nations. The other is seen in the symbolism of the sacrifice. According to Leviticus, rams are the chief[411] requirement for guilt offerings,[412] the burnt offering required for the ordination of the High Priest[413], and general burnt offerings. Since no reasons or causes for burnt offerings are given[414] they are considered to be 'free will offerings' that are simply given as an elaborate act of worship, and a declaration of obedience. All these images relate to the sacrifice of Christ: His quality as a sacrifice was greater than the lamb anticipated by Isaac and Abraham,[415] as well as the multitude of sacrifices to follow through the generations; Christ's role in the atonement is described in the book of Hebrews to be a High Priestly one, making him the perpetual High Priest; and Jesus offered Himself freely in obedience to the Father. By God's sovereignty, He took care of the details in the provision of the blessing for all the families of the earth with an ultimate sacrifice for sins.

Tim Hegg takes a different, albeit complimentary, angle to the word 'see.' The word can also mean to choose, or select, or find something or

---

409 Walton. *Genesis*. p.511

410 *Ra'ah* is used in this sense when David asks the Lord to 'see to' his deliverance from Saul's hand (1Sam 24:15)

411 Allowances were made for the offering of other animals 'from the flock' for those who may not be able to afford it, but a ram is the highest standard.

412 Lev 5:18, 6:6

413 Lev 8:22-29

414 Lev 1

415 Gen 22:7-8

someone. It is used when the Lord explains to Samuel: "I have *provided* for myself a king among [Jesse's] sons…"[416] as well as when Saul's servants suggest they "*seek out* a man who is skilful in playing the lyre…"[417] In the first instance, we know by the end of that narrative that God's selection of David is based on the quality of his heart[418], and in the second, they were looking for a person with a certain skill. Thus, this understanding of *provide* means the provision of something that meets a certain quality or standard. This is partly what Abraham was hinting at in his answer to Isaac. As Moses' commentary after Abraham offered up the ram explains: "it is said to this day, 'On the mount of the Lord it shall be provided.'",[419] revealing that there was an expectation and anticipation of a future sacrifice that would be suitable for what God requires. One can say that this was on the one hand partly fulfilled by the future sacrifices at the temple, but it was definitely the case for the provision of Christ as the ultimate and perfect atoning sacrifice. Tim Hegg explains this typological trajectory by suggesting that when Abraham said 'God will provide the lamb', what he was saying is:

> God will provide for Himself a Lamb, a Lamb that meets His criteria, and a Lamb that will in every way suffice to bring about a full and perfect redemption. Every lamb offered up in sacrifice, from Passover lambs of the exodus, to the daily sacrifices in the Tabernacle and Temple, foreshadowed the Lamb that God Himself would provide as the final and perfect payment for sin. Yes, surely God

416 1Sam 16:1
417 1Sam 16:16
418 1Sam 16:7
419 Gen 22:14

> will provide for Himself a Lamb, One chosen, One known from all eternity, His own beloved Son.[420]

But as we know, unlike the ram, Christ did not stay dead. Instead, God rose Him from the dead, as vindication that He was indeed the provision for our sins, and that those who put their faith in Him may share in His victory over death. And we see in this story of the *Akeda* a foreshadowing of this resurrection. At its conclusion, we find an interesting omission of Isaac's return. In verse 19, it only mentions Abraham returning to the servants, even though Isaac never died. Since we know that Isaac never died, especially since we have Isaac living with Abraham after Sarah's death and his father finding him a wife in chapter 24, it seems almost like a contradiction in the text. However, perhaps we can consider this to be a foreshadowing of the pattern of the crucifixion and resurrection: the father takes His Son to the sacrifice, however, only the father walks away, only to have the son reappear later. This idea of resurrection can also be seen when we consider the passage from Hebrews 11 that we looked at earlier. The full verse says Abraham "considered that God was able even to raise him from the dead, from which, figuratively speaking, he did receive him back."[421] Because Abraham had resolved to fully obey God, it was perhaps in his mind that Isaac was going to die, but because it was only a test since God finds human sacrifice abhorrent, it was like he had figuratively returned from the dead.

As the one appointed to bring about and make possible the promise made to Abraham of blessing to the nations, whose birth, death and resurrection reflect those of Isaac, it is very difficult to separate Jesus' life and

---

420 Hegg. *Genesis.* p.158

421 Heb 11:19

ministry from the Abrahamic covenant. In the chapters to follow, we will look at the relationship between Abraham and the New Covenant inaugurated by Christ, and the connection between Abraham and the church.

ABRAHAM AND THE GOSPEL

And the Scripture, foreseeing that God would justify the Gentiles by faith, preached the gospel beforehand to Abraham, saying, "In you shall all the nations be blessed."[422]

One of the most interesting elements of history that I love is the idea of continuity and change over time. I am fascinated by looking at old photos of cities and familiar places to see how things have transformed while realising that it is still the same place. I remember some time ago seeing 'before and after' images on the Facebook page of the Historical Society for my home town. For instance, there would be a current photo of a particular street and an old building from years ago superimposed into the photo. They were very interesting to look through.

But it's not just house colours, buildings and landscapes that change. Societies, politics, and technology all change in an interconnected way as well as in response to external events and developments. The wealth, peace

[422] Gal 3:8

and prosperity under Queen Elizabeth I, for instance, allowed for significant development in the arts by people like William Shakespeare. It also led to the age of discovery and opened up access to new materials. The expanding necessity of access to goods made from these materials from the expanding European imperialism of the time spawned the Industrial Revolution, resulting in numerous social changes and technological developments of which we are beneficiaries today. The invention of the malaria vaccine, for example, was a product of necessity during the construction of the Panama Canal. It is interesting to think about what life was like without many of the advancements we enjoy today, or freedom from the complexities some of them bring us, to imagine life before electricity, cars, and portable music. On the same taken, it is difficult to imagine what life will be like after them too. Will people one day wonder how we survived the primitive ways of the 21st century?

This way of thinking about history is on the one hand helpful if we want to understand the how and why of the way things are in society. But it can be confusing when we want to use it to understand salvation history. I remember in the early days of my faith asking a question I've been asked a number of times myself: What about people who lived before Jesus? How were they saved? And this is a valid question. If faith in the death and resurrection of Jesus is the only way to salvation and forgiveness of sins, then how could those who came before Him be saved? How could the promises of the New Covenant be realised for the 'Saints of the Tanakh' like Moses, Elijah, and Abraham, if at all?

It has been pointed out repeatedly in this book that the promise of blessing in the Abrahamic Covenant finds its fulfilment of the New Covenant established by Christ, but how exactly are we to understand the chronological relationship between the two? By looking at what exactly the

New Covenant is, we can then understand its relationship to Abraham and answer the question of how those before Jesus could be saved.

The New Covenant

The New Covenant is the promise that those who put their faith in Jesus as the divine and obedient mediator whose atoning sacrifice dealt with sin can be forgiven, reconciled as sons and daughters to God, and given the Holy Spirit as a seal of the eternal life they now have as citizens of God's Kingdom. And that this is all of grace through faith, and not of works. Moreover, this is not limited to any one people group, or nation or culture, but instead "now [God] commands all people everywhere to repent."[423] But there is even more to it than that. Paul explains that "if anyone is in Christ, he is a new creation. The old has passed away; behold, the new has come."[424] Being a new creation means there is a change in desires. As Paul in Romans 6 explains, before we are united to Christ by faith, we are slaves to sin and its desires. By nature, we are children of wrath[425] from birth because our sinful nature wants to disobey the Lord for it finds rebellion appealing. As James explains in his letter: "each person is tempted when he is lured and enticed *by his own desire*. Then desire when it has conceived gives birth to sin, and sin when it is fully grown brings forth death."[426] There is something in us that wants to dethrone God and make ourselves the 'captain of our own destiny', the one who defines what is right and wrong. This is what happened in the fall; sin entered the world and now our hearts are corrupt. But what Paul goes on to explain in Romans is that

423 Acts 17:30
424 2Cor 5:17
425 Eph 2:3
426 Js 1:14-15

we have been set free from sin. It no longer has any control over those in Christ because we have now become slaves to righteousness. The new heart and desires that we are given in our regeneration, having been born again, mean that we 'hunger and thirst for righteousness' and we delight in the things of God. This is a fulfilment of what was promised through the prophets.

Jeremiah 31 is the first place we encounter the phrase 'new covenant' and is one of the few places that explicitly explains and outlines its obligations and promises. Yes, we have the Apostolic Scriptures where people like Paul unpack the new covenant blessings in great detail, but as a foundational equivalent like Genesis 12 and Exodus 19, Jeremiah 31 is our best text. In fact, the phrase 'new covenant' only appears eight times in the totality of Scripture. Two are in Hebrews discussing Jeremiah 31, and the one in 1 Corinthians is a quotation of Luke 22:20. So, what is the 'new' in the new covenant? What does Scripture say about the difference between the 'old' and the 'new' covenants?

I believe that by looking primarily at Jeremiah 31 and 2 Corinthians 3, which contain the most extensive explanations, we can begin to build a much richer understanding of what the New Covenant is actually about.

In Jeremiah, the Lord says through the prophet:

> Behold, the days are coming, declares the Lord, when I will make a new covenant with the house of Israel and the house of Judah, not like the covenant that I made with their fathers on the day when I took them by the hand to bring them out of the land of Egypt, my covenant that they broke, though I was their husband, declares the Lord. For this is the covenant that I will make with the house of Israel after those days, declares the Lord: I will put my law within

> them, and I will write it on their hearts. And I will be their God, and they shall be my people. And no longer shall each one teach his neighbor and each his brother, saying, 'Know the Lord,' for they shall all know me, from the least of them to the greatest, declares the Lord. For I will forgive their iniquity, and I will remember their sin no more.[427]

Here in this passage, we see a demonstration of both discontinuity and continuity. This passage concludes with what is commonly known about and associated with the New Covenant, namely, the forgiveness of sins which makes a personal and covenantal relationship with the Lord possible. The declaration 'I will be their God, and they shall be my people' in verse 33 is not merely an echo, but a reiteration of what was promised to Abraham regarding his descendants back in Genesis 17:7-8, and to Moses regarding Israel, the descendants of Abraham, in Exodus 29:45. This reveals the continuity of God's ongoing plan and intention to restore fallen humanity to Himself through His singular promise expressed and worked out through His subsidiary covenants.

What is interesting is that this offer of forgiveness and restoration of relationship is also an echo of a promise from Leviticus 26:40-45 to restore Israel after exile for their disobedience on the basis of the Abrahamic Covenant.[428] That this New Covenant promise of restoration in Jeremiah 31 is actually a fulfilment of a promise made centuries earlier through Moses is evident in the fact that Jeremiah is prophesying to the generation that would see the fulfilment of the consequences for disobedience that Leviticus 26 was warning against. Similarly, through the prophet Hosea, the Lord promised: "I will say to Not My People, 'You are my people';

---

[427] Jer 31:31-34

[428] See '*What is the Mosaic Covenant?*'

and he shall say, 'You are my God.'"[429] Thus, this line of continuity from Abraham to Moses, to Jeremiah of a relationship between Creator and covenant people reveals that this offer in the New Covenant is nothing short of the fulfilment of what was originally promised to Abraham.

Jeremiah 31, however, indicates discontinuity as well. Verse 32 points out that the New Covenant will not be like the covenant that God made with those He brought out of Egypt, i.e. the Mosaic Covenant. And it is at this point that those who want to separate Jesus from Moses will say, 'See. They're different. They have *nothing* to do with each other.' But note that what Jeremiah actually says disagrees with this conclusion: "I will put my law within them, and I will write it on their hearts."[430] In the New Covenant, the laws that were written on stone will instead be written on the hearts of those who are members of the covenant. This is similar to what was spoken through Ezekiel:

> I will give you a new heart, and a new spirit I will put within you. And I will remove the heart of stone from your flesh and give you a heart of flesh. And I will put my Spirit within you, and *cause you to walk in my statutes* and be careful to *obey my rules*.[431]

In both passages, we see the promise that in the New Covenant, the Law, the Torah, that was once external will become internal. And by writing it upon a new, malleable heart that is shaped by the Spirit, the nature of the covenant member is transformed from one that is predisposed to disobedience into one of obedience. This solution addresses the problem introduced by Jeremiah in verse 32: those under the Mosaic covenant kept

---

429 Hos 2:23
430 Jer 31:33
431 Ez 36:26-27

breaking the Law and consequently breaking their covenant. God's solution, therefore, was not to change the Law to make it easier, nor to abandon it. The problem isn't with the Law. As Paul himself says, "the law is holy, and the commandment is holy and righteous and good."[432] The problem is the people. This has been the problem from the beginning. Since sin entered the world, humanity has been by nature rebellious creatures. It isn't enough to simply forgive. For God to restore what was lost in Genesis 3 and gain even more glory and praise, His image-bearers need to be transformed at the heart level. This is, essentially, the promise of the sanctification of believers as they become transformed into the image of Christ.

We find this element of the New Covenant fleshed out in the book of Romans. After declaring our freedom from condemnation for sin because of what Christ did in his crucifixion and resurrection, Paul explains that,

> God has done what the law, *weakened by the flesh*, could not do. By sending his own Son in the likeness of sinful flesh and for sin, he condemned sin in the flesh, in order that *the righteous requirement of the law might be fulfilled in us, who walk not according to the flesh but according to the Spirit.*[433]

An external law has no power to transform people. Because of 'the flesh' (a short-hand term used by Paul to describe our sinful, unredeemed, depraved state), we are unable to obey and live righteously. However, by Jesus receiving God's judgment against sin on our behalf, we can be declared righteous. But more than that, this passage also declares that those who belong to Christ will walk 'according to the Spirit.' A few verses later,

---

432 Rom 7:12

433 Rom 8:3-4

Paul elaborates by saying: "For the mind that is set on the flesh is hostile to God, *for it does not submit to God's law*; indeed, *it cannot*." Thus, walking according to the Spirit is to live in obedience to the Law written on our hearts, as prophesied by Jeremiah. And this is possible because God, in Christ, 'condemned sin in the flesh.' In doing so, He removed the ability for sin to condemn and control us. The implication of this is that for the Law to be fulfilled in us is not merely satisfaction for our disobedience in Christ, but an empowered outworking and walking in obedience to the Law that we by our sins break.

Paul explains earlier in Romans 7 that this transformation is an ongoing process which he wrestles through:

> For we know that *the law is spiritual, but I am of the flesh, sold under sin*. For I do not understand my own actions. For I do not do what I want, but I do the very thing I hate. Now *if I do what I do not want, I agree with the law, that it is good*. So now it is no longer I who do it, but sin that dwells within me.[434]

Here, Paul is explaining that his new nature wants him to conform to the Law's instructions because his renewed mind sees it as good. However, the remaining sinful nature still fights against this. For Paul, it is this struggle that reveals not only the genuineness of his regeneration, but also his agreement with the Law. Therefore, it is this new heart that wishes to obey, and a new spirit that empowers this obedience, that makes the New Covenant 'new.' But how are we to understand 'new?'

---

[434] Rom 7:14-17

Based on the citation of Jeremiah 31 in Hebrews, the author's use of the Greek *kainos*, reveals that it's not new in the sense of 'recently formed'[435] (i.e. it's not some second thought, disconnected, ex nihilo Plan B). But rather new with regards to its quality. There are two, and possibly equal ways to understand this. One is that it is 'novel, or different.' Based on Jeremiah's historical context of Israel's national disobedience, makes this understanding quite reasonable, considering how it would be novel and new to have a covenant where all its members are continually obedient. The author of Hebrews reflects this idea of the New Covenant addressing inadequacies with the people rather than the Law when they write: "For he finds fault with *them*..."[436], referring to the imperfect High Priests of the earthly tent, over which Christ has a superior ministry.[437] This links into the second understanding, namely that it is of a superior quality, which is quite evident in the way it promises to internalise the Law, rather than keeping it as a mere externalisation. Thus, based on passages like Jeremiah 31 and Ezekiel 36, it becomes apparent that the Law was intended to be an integral part of the New Covenant. Moreover, the declarations in the Mosaic Covenant, especially in Deuteronomy, that the Lord will circumcise His people's hearts,[438] which is another way to describe the internalising of the Law, reveals that the New Covenant is also a fulfilment and continuation of the Mosaic Covenant and its expectations as well. How then, are we to define the New Covenant? Based on the passages we have considered, we can say that the New Covenant is the promise that in response to an individual's faith in the person and work of Jesus, Yahweh declares that the superior sacrifice of Christ atones for all of their sins, achieving forgiveness

435 Gk: neos.

436 Heb 8:8

437 Heb 8:3,5

438 See '*Comparing the Covenants*'

of sins and justification of the believer, and the creation of a new heart so that by the empowerment by the Holy Spirit, they may live out the righteous demands of God's law.[439]

So, what about the Old Covenant?

This leads us to a second question: if there is a New Covenant, there must be an Old Covenant. If so, what exactly is that? I think this question is important for two reasons. One is that by understanding the Old, we can better understand the nature of the New. The other is that those wanting to separate the New Covenant from the Law, an idea that Jeremiah 31 and Romans 7-8 makes impossible, will use references to *Old Covenant* in the Apostolic Scriptures to do so. In order to respond to this, we need to be able to understand what it is.

The general understanding of many preachers, teachers and some scholars is that the Old Covenant *is* the Mosaic Covenant, of which the Law is a significant component, and therefore Old Covenant becomes interchangeable with Law. But is this an accurate chain of thought? Does this reflect what Scripture teaches? To answer this, we need to consider two common and central key verses that dispensationalists will use. The first is found in Hebrews 8, which is written as follows:

> Christ has obtained a ministry that is as much more excellent than the old as the covenant he mediates is better, since it is enacted on better promises. For if that first covenant had been faultless, there would have been no occasion to look for a second. For he finds fault with them when he says:

[439] Grudem, W. *Systematic Theology.* p.1249; Ladd, G. *New Testament Theology.* p.629

> "Behold, the days are coming, declares the Lord, when I will establish a new covenant with the house of Israel and with the house of Judah [citation of Jer 31:31-34]...
>
> In speaking of a new covenant, he makes the first one obsolete. And what is becoming obsolete and growing old is ready to vanish away.[440]

The reasoning here is that the New Covenant makes the Old Covenant obsolete. Andy Stanley elaborates on this passage in Hebrews in his book, *Irresistible*:

> Comparing Jesus' capacity as a priest to the priest down the street, [the author of Hebrews] writes: But, in fact, the ministry Jesus has received is as superior to theirs as the covenant of which he is mediator is superior to the old one, since the new covenant is established on better promises. Note the compare-and-contrast terminology: 'superior,' old,' 'new,' 'better.'... There's no mention of blending, mixing, or combining... He continues: For if there had been nothing wrong with that first covenant, no place would have been sought for another. This is an extraordinary and unsettling statement. Apparently there was something wrong with the *old covenant*. If he's correct, the Bible says there's something wrong with part of the Bible... He goes on to quote the prophet Jeremiah who predicted the old covenant would eventually be replaced by a new one... The author of Hebrews says the new

440 Heb 8:6-8, 13

> covenant rendered *the old* and everything associated with it obsolete.[441]

It is apparent that for Andy Stanley, as it is with many others, that the 'first covenant' in verse 7 is a reference to the 'Old Covenant.' Thus, if 'the first is done away with', then the Mosaic Covenant and the Law, ended with the coming of Christ and the institution of the New. Here is the primary problem with saying the end of the Mosaic Covenant is the end of the Law: they are not dependant on each other. As discussed in my first book '*Why then the Law*?', the Law existed externally to the Mosaic Covenant. There, I explained that "the Law expressed in the Mosaic covenant was not a brand-new revelation at Mt Sinai"[442] since it is a revelation of the moral character of God that defines sin through all ages. Therefore, if one could show that the Mosaic Covenant was completely abrogated, the Law would continue as it did even before the days of Moses.

But what about the Mosaic Covenant itself? Does Hebrews 8 say it and everything associated with it is done away with? Based on the rendering of the text in the NIV, which many people read, and Andy preaches from since he considers it "THE translation for our generation"[443], as well as the ESV, it is easy to come to that conclusion. But what is interesting is that the phrase 'the old' is not in the original Greek or any textual variants. The original text for verse six can be best rendered as: "But now He has obtained a more excellent ministry, by as much as He is also the mediator of a better covenant."[444] Thus, the translators have added 'old' to the translated text. So, to say that this passage is even talking about 'the old covenant' is

---

441 Stanley. A. *Irresistable.* p.151-153

442 Watson. R. *Why then the Law?* p.7

443 https://www.biblica.com/niv-bible/niv-bible-endorsements/ Emphasis in original

444 Heb 8:6 (NASB)

inaccurate. In fact, the word covenant in both verses 7 and 13 have been added by English translators as well. And when we read these verses, in context, without the added words, it becomes apparent the author of Hebrews wasn't even trying to compare the totality of the Mosaic Covenant with the New Covenant. Consider verses 6-7 as it appears in the Greek translated into English:

> [Christ] has obtained a more excellent ministry, by as much as He is also the mediator of a better covenant, which has been enacted on better promises. For if that first had been faultless there would have been no occasion to look for a second.

Here, after discussing the superiority of Christ's High Priestly ministry into the Heavenly Places over those who minister in the Temple in verses 1-5, the author has said that Christ has a greater *ministry*. This is the context. What this means is that when the author continues, he is saying that because of the faultiness of the first *ministry*, a second and superior *ministry* (Christ's) was needed. The ministry of the priests who served in the Tabernacle and Temple was sufficient for its earthly and temporal purpose, however, it did nothing for humanity's sinful condition. Indeed, it was never intended to do so.

While the above passage does say that Christ mediates a better covenant, it is a comparative description. The idea there is that Jesus' ministry is superior because His covenant is superior, and because it is a parenthetical statement, the focus of this comparison is on the ministry. Thus, here in Hebrew 8, 'first' refers to the Levitical ministry of the priesthood and the Aaronic High Priestly line, and not the Mosaic Covenant. This understanding that it was the priesthood and not the law, nor the whole Mosaic covenant, that is in view is quite evident when one realises the wider context for this portion of Scripture is a comparison of Jesus' ministry with that of the High Priests'. From the end of chapter 4, but especially from 7, to 10 is effectively all about comparing Christ to the High Priest. This is why, contrary to the interpretation of Stanley and a number of other commentators, verse 8 declares that the fault is not with *that* (the Mosaic covenant, nor the Law), but rather with *them*; the priests. In fact, the language of 8:7 is a repetition of the previous chapter.

> "For if that first [covenant] had been faultless, there would have been no occasion to look for a second."[445]

> "Now if perfection had been attainable through the Levitical priesthood… what further need would there have been for another priest to arise."[446]

That the author is highlighting in Hebrews 8 the fault with the priesthood and not the Mosaic Covenant and/or the Law is likewise reflected through the way much of Hebrews explains the priest's shortcomings. They sin and thus need atonement for themselves (Heb 5:2, 9:7), are appointed only by bodily descent rather than an indestructible life (Heb 7:16), their ministry was only temporary because they die (Heb 7:23), serve only in the shadow of the true temple (Heb 8:5), and they cannot offer the sacrifice that can cleanse the conscience (Heb 9:9, 10:11).

We come to a similar conclusion when we read Hebrews 8:13 without the insertion of the word covenant which is absent in the Greek text: "When He said, 'new' He has made the first obsolete. But whatever is becoming obsolete and growing old is ready to disappear."

---

445 Heb 8:7

446 Heb 7:11

Now, this insertion of 'covenant' is not completely dishonest since the context of quoting Jeremiah 31 means it was a reference to the New Covenant. But why was it left out here? It seems that by leaving it out, the author of Hebrews was reinforcing that what was in view here was a comparison of ministries, not covenants. Thus, here, as in verse 7, 'the first' that was faulty and becoming obsolete is the earthly priestly ministry, and not the Law, nor the Mosaic Covenant, with the destruction of the Temple in 70AD.

However, we need to rightly understand 'he has made obsolete'. The word behind this phrase'[447] in Hebrews 8:13 doesn't mean to abolish or do away with but carries the idea of wearing out and no longer being able to work as it was designed to. The word is also used in Hebrews 1:11 where it says, "they will all *wear out* like a garment." With the temple gone, the priesthood would not be able to function as God had commanded. And this makes sense whether one dates the letter before or after 70AD since both Josephus after 90AD,[448] and the Mishnah and Talmud describe some sacrifices still taking place after the Temple's destruction.[449]

So no, Jeremiah did not predict the end of the Torah, nor did the author of Hebrews say that the Law and everything related to the Mosaic covenant was abolished with the coming New Covenant. Thus, to understand what the Old Covenant is, we need to look at the one and only genuine mention of 'old covenant' in the Bible, and that is in 2 Corinthians.

The bulk of the Second letter to Corinth (Chapters 1-7) is considered to be Paul defending the legitimacy of his Apostolic ministry against his opponents and false apostles. One significant argument that Paul uses,

[447] *Pepalaiōken*

[448] Josephus. *Contra Apion.* 2.6.23

[449] Guttmann, A. "The End of the Jewish Sacrificial Cult." *HUCA.* p.138-139

found in chapter three, is the genuine work of the Spirit in the lives of those who have been recipients of his Apostolic Ministry. As he wrote:

> You yourselves are our letter of recommendation, written on our hearts, to be known and read by all. And you show that you are a letter from Christ delivered by us, written not with ink but with the Spirit of the living God, not on tablets of stone but on tablets of human hearts.[450]

Here, Paul is saying that as per the promises of Jeremiah 31 and Ezekiel 36 that God would write His Law on the hearts of His people, the Spirit's work in transforming the believers in Corinth[451] is proof that Paul is a genuine minister of the New Covenant. From here, Paul begins to discuss the difference between the New and the Old Covenants. The first contrast is that the Old Covenant is a ministry of death "For the letter kills, but the Spirit gives life."[452] It appears most likely that Paul has the Law in mind, rather than the Mosaic Covenant as a whole, since verse three contrasts the writing of the Law on hearts rather than stone, which was accomplished by Moses in Exodus 34. Many will stop here and say 'See. The letter kills. Therefore, avoid the Law; the Law is bad. Just follow the Spirit.' But the reason Paul has said the letter kills is that on its own, all the written law can do is define righteousness, identify sin, and condemn sinners. There is nothing inherent in the written Law that allows and empowers people to obey it. So, it is not as though the Law is bad for many passages of Scripture talk of the goodness and rightness of the Law. In fact, Paul in this very passage goes on to describe the Law being given with glory. The problem is with the stiff-necked and sinful

---

450 2Cor 3:2-3

451 See 1Cor 6:11 for example

452 2Cor 3:6

covenant members who need the ministry of the Spirit to transform their hearts and minds and bring life. This is the focus and context that we need to keep in mind as we read on.

Paul continues his appeal to Exodus 34 2 Corinthians 3 to further identify the difference between the Old and New Covenants:

> Now if the ministry of death, carved in letters on stone, came with such glory that the Israelites could not gaze at Moses' face because of its glory, which was being brought to an end, will not the ministry of the Spirit have even more glory? For if there was glory in the ministry of condemnation, the ministry of righteousness must far exceed it in glory. Indeed, in this case, what once had glory has come to have no glory at all, because of the glory that surpasses it. For if what was being brought to an end came with glory, much more will what is permanent have glory.
>
> Since we have such a hope, we are very bold, not like Moses, who would put a veil over his face so that the Israelites might not gaze at the outcome of what was being brought to an end. But their minds were hardened. For to this day, when they read *the old covenant*, that same veil remains unlifted, because only through Christ is it taken away. Yes, to this day whenever Moses is read a veil lies over their hearts. But when one turns to the Lord, the veil is removed. Now the Lord is the Spirit, and where the Spirit of the Lord is, there is freedom. And we all, with unveiled face, beholding the glory of the Lord, are being transformed into the same

> image from one degree of glory to another. For this comes from the Lord who is the Spirit.[453]

This is another passage used by those who want to distance Moses from Jesus. And this is because, through the use of parallelism in verses 14 and 15, the reading of the old covenant is equated with the reading of Moses. Dispensationalists, such as William MacDonald, will say that here Paul is contrasting the Law with the Gospel and, by emphasising the repeated phrase 'brought to an end', conclude that the temporary law has served its purpose and now replaced with Christ who is the fulfilment of the Law.[454] Others will say that in this passage, *old* means obsolete and outdated, like an old iPhone, concluding that "Paul could not be clearer. God's covenant with Israel was made obsolete the moment Jesus ratified the new covenant."[455] But as we consider the key details of this passage, we will see that Paul is not talking about the Gospel and Jesus making Moses, the Law, and God's promises to the descendants of Abraham obsolete.

The first aspect that we need to consider is Paul's purpose. As we have considered over the previous pages, the Apostle is seeking to compare and contrast the glory of the *ministry*[456] *of Moses with that of the Holy Spirit. This is most evident when we look at verses 7-9 when we are given a two-fold comparison of the two ministries:*

> Now if the *ministry* of death… came with such glory…
> will not the *ministry* of the Spirit have even more glory?

453 2Cor 3:7-18

454 MacDonald, W. *Believer's Bible Commentary – Second Ed.* p.1847

455 Stanley. *Irresistible.* p.139

456 *Diakonia* – service, ministry. From diakonos, lit. 'to kick up dust' as one running an errand. Cf. Acts 6:1-2, 12:25; 2Cor 11:8

> For if there was glory in the *ministry* of condemnation, the *ministry* of righteousness must far exceed it in glory.

Thus, the apostle's focus is not on the difference between the Old and New Covenant, nor does he take issue with the content of the Old Covenant (i.e. the Law), rather, especially in light of verse 3, he is contrasting the external (old) and internal (new) ministries.

The second aspect involves the nature of the internal ministry. Using Exodus 34 as an illustration, Paul describes the spiritual condition of people outside of faith in Christ. The account in Exodus says that when Moses descended from the mountain with the stone tables of the Law, his face glowed with the reflected glory of God. In fact, it would glow after every time he was in the Lord's presence. But Moses would wear a veil over his face apart from when he entered the tent or shared revelation from God with the people. Paul explains that just as the veil meant that the people of Israel were unable to see the glory on Moses' face, the veil over people's hearts means they are unable to see the glory of God 'whenever Moses is read.' Thus, Moses' veil is a typological symbol of the hardness of heart that creates a spiritual barrier to faith in Christ. What this means is that, as George Guthrie explains, "Paul is concerned with a person's ability to 'hear' the truth of the gospel in the Scriptures."[457] Even MacDonald recognises that when "...the veil is taken away [by Christ], the obscurity is gone. Then the truth dawns that all the types and shadows of the law find their fulfilment in God's beloved Son..."[458] This is hinted at in verse 13 when Paul writes: "Moses... would put a veil over his face so that the Israelites might not gaze at the outcome of what was being brought to an end." The deeper significance is lost in the translation, but the Greek word for 'end', *telos*, in

---

457 Guthrie, G. *2 Corinthians*. np

458 MacDonald. *Believer's Bible Commentary*. p.1849

this context means, the end goal, outcome, and final purpose. What this is saying is that in the immediate context of Exodus, the Israelites were unable to see the full purpose (telos) of the blessings of God's presence, as reflected in their ongoing rebellion and grumbling which resulted in the Lord withdrawing His presence as the nation left Sinai.[459] But for Paul's purpose in 2 Corinthians, the spiritual blindness means that those whose hearts are veiled are unable to behold Christ, who is the ultimate goal and purpose of the Law.[460] Thus, to recognise the glory of Christ in the Law requires healing from spiritual blindness.

This healing and awakening is a significant part of the wider context of the passage, as explained in the following chapter of 2 Corinthians:

> ...the god of this world has *blinded the minds of the unbelievers, to keep them from seeing the light of the gospel of the glory of Christ,* who is the image of God. For what we proclaim is not ourselves, but Jesus Christ as Lord, with ourselves as your servants for Jesus' sake. For God, who said, "Let light shine out of darkness," has shone in our hearts to give the light of the knowledge of the glory of God in the face of Jesus Christ.[461]

This blindness is what Jesus challenged the Pharisees about, as recorded in the John's Gospel:

> Do not think that I will accuse you to the Father. There is one who accuses you: Moses, on whom you have set your

[459] Ex 33:3, 15-16

[460] "Christ is the *telos* of the law for righteousness to everyone who believes" (Rom 10:4) c.f. Rom 8:1-4

[461] 2Cor 4:4-6

> hope. For if you believed Moses, you would believe me; for he wrote of me. But if you do not believe his writings, how will you believe my words?"[462]

> Jesus said [to the man born blind], "For judgment I came into this world, that those who do not see may see, and those who see may become blind." Some of the Pharisees near him heard these things, and said to him, "Are we also blind?" Jesus said to them, "If you were blind, you would have no guilt; but now that you say, 'We see,' your guilt remains.[463]

Therefore, what Paul is emphasising in this passage is the surpassing ability of the New Covenant ministry given to him and the other apostles to open the eyes of the spiritually blind over and against Moses' ministry that was unable to achieve that goal.[464]

But there is a final element that we need to consider, and it is related to the motive of why Moses covered his face with a veil. Throughout the passage quoted from 2 Corinthians 3, we find that the glory that came with Moses is described three times as coming to an end. For instance:

> Now if the ministry of death, carved in letters on stone, came with such glory that the Israelites could not gaze at Moses' face because of its glory, *which was being brought to*

---

462 Jn 5:45-47

463 Jn 9:39-41

464 The passage's context and use of the veil imagery keeping people from recognising the glory of Christ in the Mosaic Covenant means that although *telos* can mean the end or conclusion of something, that is not the definition being used in this passage.

> *an end*, will not the ministry of the Spirit have even more glory?[465]

Other translations describe the glory as fading (NASB) and 'passing away' (NIV). And based on this description, a number of commentators reason that Moses covered his face to prevent "the Israelites from seeing the end of the glory on his face."[466] This fading glory, according to preachers such as John MacArthur, "symbolized the impermanence of the old covenant..."[467] And because of the wide understanding that Old Covenant equals Moses and the Law, they conclude that this passage is teaching that Moses and the Law have no relevance in the New Covenant. This for them is what makes the old different from the new — obeying the commandments versus following the Spirit. How then, do we reconcile this with passages such as Jeremiah 31 that plainly describe the place of the Law in the New Covenant?

The solution is simple: the original Greek of this passage does not say fading or abolishing. The highly debated word behind 'being brought to an end', *katageo*, never means 'to fade' or 'fading.' Guthrie explains that based on the word's usage in classical writings and the Septuagint, its normal use carries the meaning of rendering powerless and ineffective.[468] For example, it is used in Romans when Paul writes:

> "For if it is the adherents of the law who are to be the heirs, faith is null (*katergatai*) and the promise is void."[469]

---

[465] 2 Cor 3:7-8

[466] Barnett, P. *The Second Epistle to the Corinthians.* p.192

[467] MacArthur, J. *2 Corinthians.* p.103

[468] Guthrie, G. *2 Corinthians.* np.

[469] Rom 4:14

And it is used by the Greek playwright Euripides in the following context:

> "But I will go, that my hands may no longer hang idle (*katargomen*) And may I find my brother face to face, meet him in battle and kill him with my spear…"[470]

Therefore, Paul is not in 2 Corinthians 3 describing a radiant glory fading like a dying fire, an image Exodus 34 says nothing about. Rather, he is describing a glory that was rendered powerless and ineffective by it being veiled.

Admittedly, *katargeo*, can mean to destroy and bring to an end and is applied to different themes such as death in 1 Corinthians 15:24-26, the offence of the Gospel in Galatians 5:11, and the 'man of lawlessness' in 2 Thessalonians 2:8. This is the favoured translation in this passage by commentators such as Moyer Hubbard.[471] However, when the word is used with this meaning, it is always in the context of being overcome and disempowered by a greater power. So, the ESV is not entirely incorrect here in 2 Corinthians, but linguistically and contextually, it's not the best choice for two reasons.

One is because, in Greek, it is the word *kataluo* that is used to describe the annulment and termination of laws and institutions. For instance, Gamaliel the Pharisee said "but if it is of God, you will not be able to overthrow (*katalusai*) them…"[472]Extra-biblically, Xenophon also makes use of the term when describing "those who obey the laws on the ground that the laws may be annulled (*katalutheien*)…"[473] Yet Jesus in Matthew 5:17 said

---

[470] Eur. *Phoen.* 753

[471] Hubbard, M. *2 Corinthians – Teach the Text.* np.

[472] Acts 5:39

[473] Xen. *Mem.* 4.4.14

he did not come to abolish (*katalusai*) the law and the prophets. Moreover, even when Paul uses the previous term in Romans 3:31 when he asks whether justification by faith nullifies (*katargoumen*) the Law, the answer was a strong 'by no means.' Thus, Paul could not have intended to describe the Law as being brought to an end here in 2 Corinthians. The closest the passage could come to this use of *kataluo* is by the way the surpassing glory of the Spirit's ministry makes Moses' look like nothing in comparison.

The second is that the meaning of *katageo* as 'make ineffective' fits the wider context and purpose. With the veil covering Moses' face, the ability of the glory to be perceived by the people of Israel is hindered. Thus, rather than Israel being blinded by the brilliance of the eventually fading glory shining from Moses' face, as suggested by our translation of verse 7, the people were kept from *continuing to look* at the glory[474] because Moses put the veil on his face after talking to the people. Although this sounds like a description of the initial occurrence in Exodus 34:30, the grammar of the verb[475] 'to gaze' means that the whole, general story of Moses and the veil through to verse 35 is in view, not just the one segmented part. Therefore, because of the veil over Moses' face, the shining glory of the Lord was hindered from transforming the people, as is also the case for the veil over people's hearts. Or to put it another way, Paul is saying that the glory of Christ that the Law reveals and foreshadows[476] is 'rendered powerless' because of its inability to penetrate the veil over people's hearts.

In light of these understandings, we might paraphrase verses 12-14, which Paul Balla considers the "key to the whole chapter",[477] as follows:

---

[474] As seen in the grammatical aorist conjugation of the verb

[475] Perfective aspect

[476] The *telios*

[477] Balla, P. "2 Corinthians." *CNTUOT.* p.759

> Since we have such a hope, we are very bold, not like Moses, who would put a veil over his face so that, *consequently*, the Israelites *could not continue gazing at the glory of Christ, which is the goal of the Law, because it was made ineffective* since their minds were hardened. For to this day, when they read the old covenant, that same veil remains unlifted, because only through Christ is it taken away.

The imagery of Christ removing the veil, as elaborated on in verse 16, can be linked typologically to the statement in Exodus 34:34; "Whenever Moses went in before the Lord to speak with him, he would remove the veil, until he came out." According to Hafemann, Paul has alluded to this event to describe "Moses' experience in the tent of meeting as a type of one whose heart has been changed by the power of the Spirit under the ministry of the New Covenant."[478] Thus, it is the removal of the veil that is a significant goal of the New Covenant, not the erasure of all that Moses proclaimed, the success of which giving credibility to Paul's ministry.

Therefore, rather than a proclamation that the Mosaic Covenant and its contents are done away with, 2 Corinthians 3's description of the glory on Moses' face provides the reader with Paul's answer as to what hinders people, in particular Jews, to come to faith when hearing the Gospel in the Law.[479] This makes much more sense of not only the passage's context and purpose, but also the wider canon of Scripture's description of the hardening of Israel[480] and the repeated description of the Law's inclusion in the New Covenant. In fact, verse 18 harkens back to passages like Jeremiah 31 in the way that it explains how those with their veil removed, "beholding

---

478 Hafemann, S. "Paul, Moses and the History of Israel." *WUNT.* p.388

479 As was Paul's M.O. See Acts 17:2

480 E.g. Matt 13:14-15, Rom 11:8,25

the glory of the Lord, are being transformed into the same image from one degree of glory to another. For this comes from the Lord who is the Spirit."[481] Paul's point, therefore, is that apart from the Spirit's work in people's heart, no one can experience the blessings of the New Covenant promises.

In light of the passages we have looked at: Jeremiah 31, Ezekiel 36, Romans 7-8, and here in 2 Corinthians 3, how then are we to define the Old Covenant and New Covenant? Based on these passage's explanations and descriptions, we may conclude that rather than being the whole Mosaic covenant, the 'Old Covenant' is the cold words of revelation 'written on stone', without any spiritual empowerment or enlightenment. The hearers, therefore, are unable to not only be transformed by or respond appropriately to those words with reverence, worship and obedience, but also unable to believe the Gospel hidden within because it is heard with a veiled heart or an un-regenerated heart of stone. That Paul had this aspect in mind rather than just simply the Mosaic Covenant can be seen in how the designator Old Covenant is used only once, whereas the authors of the Apostolic Scriptures when talking about the Mosaic Covenant often referred to it as 'Moses' or 'The Law.' And although 'the Old Covenant' is implied with mentions of 'The New Covenant', the emphasis of difference, as we have repeatedly seen in this chapter, is the administration and not the content.

So, contra to Andy Stanley's claims, 'old' does not mean obsolete. The Greek word for old, *palaios*, can mean either worn out or simply not new. John in his first letter describes walking in love as an old (*palaios*) commandment[482], which means it has been around for a long time. Are we

---

481 2 Cor 3:18

482 1Jn 2:7

to think of 'love one another' and 'love the Lord your God' as obsolete commandments? I surely think not. Rather, the designator 'old' merely serves to describe both the ancient nature of what was revealed at Sinai[483] and to contrast its 'worn out' and ineffective nature with the effective realities of the 'new covenant.' The New Covenant, therefore, where one experiences transformation, forgiveness, reconciliation with God, and restoration of being a divine image-bearer, is what one enters when the Holy Spirit empowers the hearer to believe and respond to God's revelation. This distinction reflects Paul's categories of the 'old[484] man' with their sinful and fallen nature, and the 'new[485] man' with their changed desires and transformed heart that pursues righteousness by loving God and loving neighbour.[486]

The difference, therefore, between the Old and the New Covenant, is not the role or relevance of the law. Rather, it's the difference in the work of the Spirit. This contrast between the Spirit and the Letter, according to Guthrie,

> sets forth the two covenants as a continuum and the contrast… as… between those who attempted to keep the law apart from the work of the Spirit, and new-covenant people who have the ability to fulfil the law because of the Spirit.[487]

This understanding of the nature of the New Covenant, as we will see, makes clear the continuity from Abraham, to Moses, and to Christ.

---

483 c. 2000 years prior to the writing of the Apostolic Scriptures

484 *palaios*

485 *kainon.* Cf. 2Cor 3:6 and Heb 8:8

486 Eph 4:22-32

487 Guthrie. *2 Corinthians.* np.

The Promise and the New Covenant

Since, as discussed in the previous section of this book, the Mosaic Covenant was a fulfilled development of the Abrahamic Covenant, and the New Covenant is a development of the Mosaic Covenant whereby God's people are empowered to keep His Law, we should begin to see a deepening continuity between the covenants, rather than a fragmented progression.

The question was asked at the beginning of the chapter, 'how exactly are we to understand the relationship between the Abrahamic and New Covenant?' The answer, simply put, is that the New Covenant embodies and empowers the fullness of everything the Abrahamic Covenant anticipated. As we have seen through this book, the Abrahamic outlines and describes God's intentions, the Mosaic describes what it looks like, and the New makes it possible. We will consider the promise of land and nation in the next chapter, but the promise of blessing is certainly a New Covenant reality. The restoration of the relationship lost in the fall made possible through the forgiveness of sins, having peace with God, and having a transformed heart that reflects God's original purpose for humanity, are all made possible through the atoning sacrifice of Christ which inaugurated the New Covenant.

Before we end this chapter, we still need to consider the question I raised towards the beginning of the chapter: did *anyone* before Christ's appearance on Earth experience what was anticipated in the Abrahamic Covenant promise of blessing? Did *anyone* know the benefits of the New Covenant? Because if the New Covenant did not begin until Christ's death in 33AD, then how could anyone be saved or experience anything of God's plan to rescue and restore creation before then? What we will find, as we look at the record of the Tanakh, is that there were those who did have the Law written on their heart, and experienced forgiveness and salvation.

When it comes to delighting in the Law, no character from the Tanakh stands out more than David. David used many positive terms to illustrate the Law, the Torah of God. In Psalm 19 he describes it as perfect, reliable, pure, more desirable than gold, sweeter than honey. And in the final verses, we find this longing to obey it:

> Keep back your servant also from presumptuous sins; let them not have dominion over me! Then I shall be blameless, and innocent of great transgression. Let the words of my mouth and the meditation of my heart be acceptable in your sight...[488]

He expresses something similar in Psalm 119 when he writes,

> With my whole heart I seek you; let me not wander from your commandments! I have stored up your word in my heart, that I might not sin against you... Give me understanding, that I may keep your law and observe it with my whole heart. Lead me in the path of your commandments, for I delight in it.[489]

The use of 'meditation of my heart' reveals that David's desire is not simply external conformity, a type of obedience that is falsely attributed to the requirements of the Mosaic Covenant. Rather, this is a prayer for the empowerment to obey Yahweh from even the deepest parts of his thoughts and emotions. What's more is that David explains that he longs to obey, not out of fear of negative consequences, but because the Law is something he delights in and loves. This passion for the Torah is a significant part of

---

488 Ps 19:13-14a

489 Ps 119: 10-11, 34-35

why David was called 'a man after God's own heart.' In the account of the Lord's rejection of Saul when he broke the Law regarding sacrifices, we find these words from Samuel: "The Lord has sought out a man *after his own heart*, and the Lord has commanded him to be prince over his people, *because* you have not *kept what the Lord commanded you*."[490] In short, this man after God's own heart will, unlike Saul, seek to obey the Lord's commandments.[491] This is why David's imperfect record, especially the incident with Uriah, burdened him so much. In Psalm 51, widely considered to be inspired by the events of 2 Samuel 11, David describes feeling like the Lord had crushed his bones and expresses a recognition that ultimately it was against God that he had sinned.

Psalm 32 goes into more detail about his conviction over sin. David describes how he felt before confessing sin as follows: "For when I kept silent, my bones wasted away through my groaning all day long. For day and night your hand was heavy upon me; my strength was dried up as by the heat of summer."[492] To be burdened by sin like this reveals a heart that has been inscribed with and transformed by God's Law. In fact, Psalm 51 contains a request for the Lord to continue this work of sanctification: "Create in me a clean heart, O God, and renew a right spirit within me."[493]

When I consider David's attitude towards the Law, and the response of his heart when he fails to keep it, I cannot help but think that David could just as easily have written Romans 7:

---

490 1Sam 13:14. cf. Acts 13:22

491 Interestingly, Paul makes mention of this when in the synagogue in Pisida Antioch, preaching to those he calls 'Brothers, sons of the family of Abraham.' According to Marshall (2007, 584), Paul's "commendation of David may be meant to set up a typology with David's descendant, Christ…"

492 Ps 32:3-4

493 Ps 51:10

> For I do not do what I want, but I do the very thing I hate. Now if I do what I do not want, I agree with the law, that it is good. So now it is no longer I who do it, but sin that dwells within me… For I delight in the law of God, in my inner being, but I see in my members another law waging war against the law of my mind and making me captive to the law of sin that dwells in my members. Wretched man that I am! Who will deliver me from this body of death? Thanks be to God through Jesus Christ our Lord! So then, I myself serve the law of God with my mind, but with my flesh I serve the law of sin.[494]

David, however, is not alone in this. Daniel[495] grieved Israel's national failure to keep the Law; Ezra, like David, "set his heart to study the Law of the Lord, and to do it and to teach his statutes and rules in Israel."[496] And, as mentioned in the chapter *The Promise,* God told Isaac that his father, Abraham, "obeyed my voice and kept my charge, my commandments, my statutes, and my laws."[497] How could these and many other people living in the period before Christ have such a transformed character that seeks after God, and a heart for and ability to submit to the Law[498] apart from that New Covenant work of the Spirit? As we saw earlier in this chapter, Romans 8 tells us that "the mind that is set on the flesh [i.e. not the Spirit] is hostile to God, for it *does not* submit to God's law; indeed, *it cannot.*" It is the work and ministry of the Holy Spirit as described in Jeremiah 31 and Ezekiel 36, describing New Covenant realities, that makes this possible for the like of David and Abraham.

---

494 Rom 7:15-17, 22-25

495 Dan 9:3-19

496 Ezr 7:10

497 Gen 26:5

498 Cf. Rom 3:11, 7:22,25, 8:7

What about the blessings of forgiveness, salvation and eternal life? Well, as touched on in the chapter, *Cutting a Covenant*, we find these words in Genesis 15:6, "Abraham believed God, and it was counted to him as righteousness." This passage that shows it was Abraham's faith and confidence in God's promises that put him into a right relationship with the Lord is a significant theological foundation for Paul. In the book of Romans and Galatians, Abraham is used as the ultimate case study for justification by faith alone by quoting this verse in both letters. According to Douglas Moo, Paul utilises Abraham not only to dismantle the pervading idea that Abraham was considered righteous because he adhered to the Law, but also because "Abraham is a key figure in God's plan of salvation as revealed in the Old Testament. One of Paul's purposes… is to demonstrate that the gospel is in continuity with the Old Testament… Proving that the story of Abraham fits into Paul's conception of salvation history is an important step toward this goal."[499] What this means is that by referring back to Abraham, Paul was not simply using him as some kind of moral example such as, 'Abraham had faith, you should have faith too.' Nor was he a mere typological precursor to justification by faith as though Abraham's faith was of the right kind for salvation, or of a different type to Christians. Rather, Abraham's experience is the same as those who are followers of Christ.

We see firstly in Romans 4 that it is the same because he was credited as righteous because of faith and not because of works. Paul explains how Genesis 15:6 teaches us that:

> the one who does not work but believes in him who justifies the ungodly, his faith is counted as righteousness, just as David also speaks of the blessing of the one to whom God counts righteousness apart from works: 'Blessed are

499 Moo, D. *Romans - NIV.* p.144

> those whose lawless deeds are forgiven, and whose sins are covered; blessed is the man against whom the Lord will not count his sin.'[500]

By repeating the term 'counted'[501], which is used in the passage in Genesis, Paul is reinforcing that people like Abraham and David who had faith in God have a status of righteousness that is not inherently theirs or something they have earned that could 'counted' to them.[502] More than that, their sins have been forgiven and are 'no longer' credited to them. This formula is repeated in 2 Corinthians 5:21, and referred to by Martin Luther as 'the great exchange.' In short, their standing with God is based purely on God's grace in response to their faith. By quoting Psalm 32 in verse 8, Paul is saying that the experience of justification — being given the status of righteous and the reality of forgiveness, as something unearned or deserved — is a blessing. And including this in the context of Abraham means that Paul, as we will see shortly in this chapter, is including this benefit in the promise of blessing from the Abrahamic covenant. We see also that Paul intends to explain that the experience of Abraham and David is the same as the Christian when he explains later in the chapter:

> But the words 'it was counted to him' were not written for his sake alone, but for ours also. It will be counted to us who believe in him who raised from the dead Jesus our Lord.[503]

---

500 Rom 4:5-8

501 *Logizomai* – to credit, enumerate, regard. E.g. "There is danger not only that this trade of ours will fall into disrepute, but also that the temple of the great goddess Artemis is in danger of being regarded (*logisthēnai*) as worthless" (Acts 19:27)

502 Moo. *Romans - NIV*. p.145

503 Rom 4:23-24

The question that follows is whether the object and promises of Abraham's faith were the same as New Covenant members (i.e. the death and resurrection of Jesus for sin), or is it just the general principle of faith that we share? Firstly, we see that in this passage, Paul makes God himself the object of the Christian's faith. Douglas Moo explains that Paul:

> [u]ndoubtedly… does so here to bring the Christian faith into the closest possible relationship to Abraham's faith. Not only is our faith of the same nature as Abraham's: it ultimately has as its object the same God, "who gives life to the dead" (cf. v. 17b). And the connection is even closer. For Abraham's faith in God has to do not just with the miraculous creation of life… but with the fulfilment of God's promise to bless the world through him.[504]

In other words, the object and promise of our faith are the same as Abraham's. Granted, with the nature of progressive revelation, we have more detail, but nevertheless, both Abraham and Joe Christian's faith is in Christ. Paul's treatment of Genesis 15:6 in the letter to the Galatians elaborates on this further.

The Promise and the Gospel

In rebuking those Galatians who have bought into the lie that Christians are saved by observing works of the law,[505] Paul again uses Abraham as the foundation of his teaching:

504 Moo. D. *Romans.* p.287-288

505 A term that will be defined in the following chapter

O foolish Galatians! Who has bewitched you? It was before your eyes that Jesus Christ was publicly portrayed as crucified. Let me ask you only this: Did you receive the Spirit by works of the law or by hearing with faith? Are you so foolish? Having begun by the Spirit, are you now being perfected by the flesh? Did you suffer so many things in vain—if indeed it was in vain? Does he who supplies the Spirit to you and works miracles among you do so by works of the law, or by hearing with faith—*just as Abraham "believed God, and it was counted to him as righteousness"?* Know then that it is those of faith who are the sons of Abraham. And the Scripture, *foreseeing that God would justify the Gentiles by faith, preached the gospel beforehand to Abraham, saying, "In you shall all the nations be blessed." So then, those who are of faith are blessed along with Abraham, the man of faith.* For all who rely on works of the law are under a curse; for it is written, "Cursed be everyone who does not abide by all things written in the Book of the Law, and do them." Now it is evident that no one is justified before God by the law, for "The righteous shall live by faith." But the law is not of faith, rather "The one who does them shall live by them." Christ redeemed us from the curse of the law by becoming a curse for us—for it is written, "Cursed is everyone who is hanged on a tree"— *so that in Christ Jesus the blessing of Abraham might come to the Gentiles, so that we might receive the promised Spirit through faith.*[506]

---

506 Gal 3:1-14

These fourteen verses help us to see the Gospel clearly within the Tanakh. Here, Paul seeks to explain that the Christian's experience of the Spirit and New Covenant blessings are not limited to this letter's recipients in Galatia, or any other post-incarnation follower of Christ for that matter. Rather, that justification and the giving of the Spirit in response to faith was Abraham's experience too. This is evident from the use of the conjunction *kathos* in verse 6, translated 'just as', which effectively means in the same manner. This connective is used, for example, in John 15 when Jesus said: "This is my commandment: Love one another, as [in the same way] (*kathos*) I have loved you." To say that Abraham experienced justification by faith 'in the same way' the believers in Galatia did shows not only that Abraham's faith is the same that the Gospel requires, but also shows that Paul considers the continuity in God's covenant economy as a given.[507] What this means is that rather than functioning as some mere illustration, Abraham is functioning as the foundation of Paul's argument in Galatians 3-4. As Silva explains, "...the apostle's point is not simply that we should believe as Abraham believed... but those who believe become recipients of the redemptive blessings associated with the patriarch."[508]

This connection between Abraham, the Abrahamic covenant and its promises, and the Gospel is drawn at its closest in verse 8 when Paul writes: "the Scripture, foreseeing that God would justify the Gentiles by faith, *preached the gospel beforehand to Abraham*, saying, 'In you shall all the nations be blessed.'" Not many think of Abraham as even knowing the Gospel, although they will acknowledge he had varying levels of awareness of elements of it, but here it says that God in his establishing of the covenant promises God gave Abraham the Gospel. The phrase "preached

[507] Fung, R. *The Epistle to the Galatians.* p.136

[508] Silva, M. "Galatians." *CNTUOT.* p.793

the gospel beforehand" is based on a unique Greek word, *proeuangelisato,* which can be translated more literally as 'pre-declaring the gospel.' Thus, Genesis 12:3 isn't some kind of preliminary gospel to tide him over, but rather, it is an advanced preaching of *The* Gospel. The fact that Jesus could say in John's Gospel that 'Abraham saw His day and rejoiced'[509] means that this wasn't some obscure promise given in seed form that would be later unveiled. Rather, Abraham was somehow quite aware of the depths of this significant promise, and with the eyes of faith 'saw' and believed the work of Gospel completed by the Messiah to come through his line. Indeed, as Martin Luther in his commentary on Galatians explains, "The faith of the fathers in the Old Testament era, and our faith in the New Testament are one and the same faith in Christ Jesus."[510] This declaration that the Gospel was preached to Abraham reveals how integral the Abrahamic covenant is to the Gospel for Paul. As Moses Silva highlights, this verse and the use of *proeuangelisata* reveals "the fundamental continuity between the Hebrew Scriptures and the gospel."[511]

Likewise, James Dunn explains:

> Not only was Abraham himself the beginning of the gospel and archetypal example of one 'justified by faith', but the gospel itself could only be adequately understood by Paul as the outworking of the promises to Abraham. Indeed, the line of continuity and fulfilment was so central to the gospel that Paul would have judged the gospel itself to have failed had that line been decisively breached.[512]

---

509 Jn 8:56

510 Luther. *Galatians.* p.71

511 Silva. *CNTUOT.* p. 795

512 Dunn, J. "How New was Paul's Gospel?" *The New Perspective on Paul.* p.252-253

In light of this, we cannot separate the Gospel from the Abrahamic covenant. And not in a typological sense either. This passage makes evident the reality that the Abrahamic Covenant contains the Gospel. What Paul is demonstrating here is that the Gospel, the declaration of justification and restoration of relationship with our creator by faith, is the blessing promised to Abraham for all the families of the earth. This relationship becomes even more evident in the verses that follow.

In verses 10-14, Paul is seeking to drive home to the Galatians that obedience to the Law cannot help us escape the curse of sin; we need the work of Christ on the cross. In verse 14, Paul gives us two purposes as to why "Christ redeemed us from the curse by becoming a curse for us." The first is "*so that* in Christ Jesus the *blessing of Abraham* might come to the Gentiles." The second is "*so that* we might receive the promised Spirit through faith." The exact relationship between these two is somewhat debated, however, it is probably best to consider the blessing of justification and the promised Spirit "as related but separate gifts of the new covenant…"[513] As Fung aptly explains:

> In the original promise to Abraham there was no mention of the Spirit but only the blessing of justification by faith, and yet here Paul conceives of the fulfilment of that promise as constituted above all in the bestowal of the Spirit upon those who have faith. It is thus manifest that in Paul's thinking the blessing of justification is almost synonymous (it is certainly contemporaneous) with the reception of the Spirit.[514]

---

513 Moo. *Galatians – Baker*. np.
514 Fung. *Galatians*. p.152

Thus, here in verse 14, we are given two parts of the one blessing of restoration since, as Luther puts it, the "Spirit spells freedom from… sin, death, the curse, hell, and the judgement of God."[515] By using the emphatic conjunction *hina*[516] ('so that') in this verse to connect the cross to Abraham, Paul is highlighting that Christ's death which brings deliverance from the curse was not some isolated or disconnected idea from the Tanakh, but rather the means by which the promise of blessing in Genesis 12:3 was made possible. Although Paul does single out Gentiles in this passage, he does so because of the wider context of the letter, which the next chapter of this book will address. He is certainly not saying that the Jews experience justification by some other means; salvation is only ever in Christ. Thus, when Jesus went to the cross, he was not merely seeking to undo the curse of sin and death introduced in the fall, as though Scripture from Genesis 3 to Matthew 1 was just historical filler. Nor was He executing Plan B because 'the law didn't work'. But rather, He was bringing about the blessing promised to Abraham. Thus, it is in this verse that what I have been describing throughout this book becomes most explicit: the promise of blessing made to Abraham was a declaration that in him, all the families of the Earth would be able to experience the restoration and redemption from the corrupted creation, as initially promised in Genesis 3. And as we have seen thus far, this blessing involves justification[517] and the giving of the Spirit to restore our nature as image-bearers of God by giving us a new heart and desires. Therefore, what we experience in our union with Jesus, belongs to the Abrahamic promises.

---

515 Luther. *Galatians.* p.85. cf. 2Cor 3:17

516 Webb and Kysar. *Greek for Preachers.* p.86

517 This could be considered a summary term for the forgiveness of sins and peace with God.

However, as I explained in the previous section on Romans 4, not only did the Abrahamic Covenant promise these things for those of us post-incarnation who have their faith in Jesus, but Abraham experienced this blessing as well. This is highlighted in verse 9 when Paul says that "those of faith are blessed *along* with Abraham, the man of faith." This unifying Greek preposition *sun* — from which we get our prefix for the English word *synergy* — emphatically expresses a sense of togetherness and accompaniment of an experience, condition or action.[518] For instance, Matthew uses it to explain that "two robbers were crucified with (*sun*) [Jesus], one on his right and one on his left."[519] And Paul uses it in Romans to describe our unity 'with (*sun*) Christ' in His death.[520] Thus, if we are blessed together with, and share in the same experience as Abraham, then logically, Abraham was blessed in the same way we are. When, as verse 8 tells us, God preached the Gospel to Abraham, the quote of Genesis 15:6 two verses earlier tells us that he believed and put his faith in the Gospel, which resulted in his justification.

This justification is what gave him a place in the world to come. This is why Jesus said, as a fulfilment of the Abrahamic promises: "many will come from east and west and recline at table *with Abraham*, Isaac, and Jacob in the kingdom of heaven."[521] Here we are told that Abraham will be with those who belong to Christ at the eschatological "messianic banquet which was a popular way of thinking of the ultimate blessedness of the true people of God."[522] This means that Abraham being 'counted as righteous' was no mere pat on the head as a commendation for the righteous nature of his

518 Webb and Kysar. *Greek for Preachers.* p.78

519 Matt 27:38

520 Rom 6:8

521 Matt 8:11

522 France. *Matthew.* p.316

faith, nor was it a temporary state of good pleasure. Rather, it was an eternal justification made possible by his faith in the death and resurrection of the Christ to come, just as it is with us.

Abraham in the New Covenant

When we consider how the Old and New Covenants are defined not by chronology but by the nature, quality and effectiveness of their ministry, and how Abraham received the blessings of the New Covenant, which were anticipated in the Abrahamic promises, then we must conclude that Abraham was a part of the New Covenant. This may sound like a radical idea to many, but as we have seen, the biblical evidence supports it.

Abraham's experience matches Grudem's definition, that in the New Covenant, "Christ's atoning death covers all of the believer's sins and the Holy Spirit empowers the believer to fulfil the righteous demands of the law."[523] Abraham was declared righteous by his faith in the future ministry of his ultimate descendant, Jesus, and given a place in the world to come, and was declared by God to have satisfied His charge, commandments, statutes, and laws.

This raises the question, how is this possible? How could someone be a part of the New Covenant, which was instituted by the cross of Christ, prior to the crucifixion and resurrection of Jesus? The answer can be found in the book of Revelation. It was revealed to John that "all who dwell on earth will worship [the beast], everyone whose name has not been *written before the foundation of the world* in the book of life of the Lamb who was slain."[524] There is debate regarding the placement of 'before the foundation

523 Grudem. *Systematic Theology.* p.1249
524 Rev 13:8

of the world.' While translations such as the ESV and NASB connects this time to the writing of the names, the NIV associates it with the slaying of the lamb. When one looks at the order of the Greek, we find that it reads '...have been written the names of them in the book of life of the Lamb having been slain from the founding of the world.' According to Mounce, the reason the ESV et al. have opted with their translation is based on the parallel passage in Revelation 17:8 whereby "the faithful are guarded by their election"[525] which occurred before the foundation of the earth. However, he argues that

> [t]here is no particular reason why [John] should be denied the freedom to use a given phrase in several ways. It is better in this case to follow the order of the Greek syntax and read, "the Lamb that was slain from the creation of the world."[526]

While commentators generally agree that the Lamb being slain before the foundation of the world refers to the establishment of God's redemptive plan according to His foreknowledge of the fall,[527] there is still a very real and active sense to it. For if the election of the saints was settled at the same time[528], and obviously on the basis of the death of Christ, then there must be a sense in which the death of Christ transcends chronological limitations. This is especially so since, as we have seen, Abraham's name must be included in the Lamb's book of Life. Even dispensationalist Lewis Chafer agrees that

---

525 Mounce, R. *The Book of Revelation.* p.252

526 Ibid.

527 E.g. Osborne. *Revelation.* p.503-504

528 Rev 17:8, Eph 1:4

> God never saved any one person or group of persons on any other ground to so which the Cross of Christ secured. There is, therefore, but one way to be saved and that is by the power of God made possible through the sacrifice of Christ.[529]

It is this timeless application of the blood of Christ by the God who transcends time to those of faith, whether it be in the Messiah who came or in the Messiah to come, that makes the salvation of the 'Old Testament Saints' possible. And since, as Luke recorded in his gospel, it was Jesus' blood that inaugurated the New Covenant,[530] then those sealed in His blood in the Tanakh must be a part of that covenant too.

Within the Lord's Supper, Jesus makes a reference to Exodus 24:8, a verse discussed in the previous section,[531] by explaining that the cup and its contents are symbolic of the New Covenant established in His blood. As we saw, the ritual of Exodus 24 did not create the vocational covenant God had with Israel since it began in chapter 19. The ceremony was merely the ratification, as was the ceremony of Genesis 15. In the same way, it is not as though the crucifixion began the New Covenant, rather, it was the revelation in material history that ratified and sealed what God had determined in eternity past. We, therefore, cannot limit the New Covenant to a period of time. Justification, salvation, Spirit-empowered regeneration and sanctification, all of which are blessings of the New Covenant, and have always been experienced by all those who have faith in Christ and the Gospel, even Abraham.

---

529 Chafer, L. "Inventing Heretics Through Misunderstanding" *BS.* p.1

530 Lk 22:20

531 See *Comparing the Covenants.*

As we have considered the intertwining of the Abrahamic Covenant and its promises with the blessings of the New Covenant throughout this chapter, we should begin to see how inseparable they are. As discussed in Part II, '*What is the Mosaic Covenant*', Galatians 3 reveals a building and layering of covenants through Scripture, meaning we should not think of them as independent or replacement covenants, but rather one expanding and evolving covenant with different parts. Not only is the Gospel an extension of the Abrahamic Covenant, but Abraham is a fellow member of the New Covenant with all followers of Christ. He belongs to this covenant because of His faith in the Gospel, expressed in the promise of blessing to him and all the families of the earth. In a sense, when we believe the Gospel and put our faith in the ministry of Jesus, we become heirs and members of the Abrahamic Covenant as well.

Our previous chapter sought to explain the fulfilment of the promise of offspring, while this chapter has been primarily focused on the third promise of blessing. But what about the promise of nationhood? Our next chapter, *Abraham and the Church*, will address this question.

ABRAHAM AND THE CHURCH

Know then that it is those of faith who are the sons of Abraham[532]

"This isn't history, this is English." This phrase is one that I have heard many times from my High School students at the beginning of a new unit of study. Whenever I have taught novels like *The Outsiders*, *Macbeth*, and *Parvana* (a story of a young girl living under Taliban rule in Afghanistan), I begin by explaining the historical context of these books. I do this so that when they read of the problems the characters face, the ways the protagonist approaches them, as well as their motivations and fears, we who read these texts in the 21st Century Western society can understand why. And because many of the cultural and historical influences in the novel are hidden behind the text and often assumed, it is important to highlight it so that we can make better sense of the text. After I explain this, they usually get it.

532 Gal 3:7

I encountered this experience when undertaking a historical research project while studying at University. As part of the Centenary of World War 1, students in that course were asked to conduct some kind of research into something related to the war. My project was on the use of the phrase 'unequal sacrifice' and the way it influenced many contemporary discussions of the war. This phrase became part of how the war was memorialised, played a big role in the debate around conscription, and was a significant influence on how some perceived others. It almost became the equivalent of how some might throw the word 'bigot' around today. But what I found was that the attitude behind this complaint of unequal sacrifice is different to how some might discuss inequality today. When people talk about it now, many would complain 'they didn't give, so why should I?' But for those in 1916, because of many of the cultural values reflected in the elaborations made in various news articles etc..., it is a complaint of 'I gave, so why aren't they?' Without this understanding, it would be easy to miss what was going on.

When we read the Apostolic Scriptures, we can do the same thing. We can read it through our own particular cultural-historical lens, and miss what is going on in the background of the text because the authors and their audience knew exactly what was meant. They didn't need to elaborate on everything because for them, as it is for many things today, their cultural, historical, theological and linguistic norms were assumed. And while many theologians across history have done well in the study of Scripture, some nuances can be missed which can affect interpretation. In a podcast I was listening to, James White gave a rather apt explanation about how the

> second and third generation reformers are dealing with the counter-reformation, and so, Rome is pressing them on particular issues. Can you see evidence of that in their

> exegesis? Yes, you can. … [And what we learn from this is that] when you are in the midst of a battle, a pitched battle with the world or with false religious systems or whatever else it might be, the tendency is to start seeing those things in passages of Scripture that might actually not be there… Obviously, …what the goal should be is to always strive to handle the text in such a way that if the original author was standing there, they'd go 'yeah, that's what I meant to communicate.'[533]

And so, it is important that when we study Scripture, we are aware of the historical influences that have shaped its writing. There is, however, an issue and question that is often overlooked and ignored because it is a concept that we take for granted. But for the first-century authors and audience, it was a major one. And as a result, some parts of Scripture have been somewhat misunderstood. The first-century question that this chapter will be unpacking, which is key to the remainder of the Abrahamic promises, is the question about the inclusion of the Gentiles into the people of God. By highlighting and understanding how this question shaped a number of parts of the Apostolic Scriptures, I believe we will not only have a deeper appreciation for what is going on in and behind these passages, but also have a richer understanding of our identity as New Covenant members in Christ. But more important for our purposes, we will understand how Abraham relates to the church.

---

533 White, J. "Acts 2:39 in Context, Interpreted, Applied." *AOMin.* Podcast Audio.

Blessing for all Nations

As I touched on in Part I, when God made His promises to Abraham, its fulfilment had a global intention. When He promised blessing, it was for all the families of the earth. When He promised land, the Messiah would inherit all of creation. When He promised descendants, Abraham was to become the 'Father of many nations.'[534] This was certainly a plan that expanded beyond bloodlines. And as we see in Part II, these promises were partially fulfilled with the creation of a nation, which was joined by a number of Gentiles, whose vocation was to be a light to the nations, Then, when we come to the prophets like Isaiah, we see the anticipation that the scale of Gentiles to be included into God's covenant people would expand greatly. Although there was a great expectation of the inclusion of the nations, there was a mystery as to 'how' this would happen.

Unfortunately, by Jesus' day, many people had forgotten and lost sight of this goal. After centuries of occupation and oppression by the Gentiles, namely the Greek Seleucids and the Romans, Jewish nationalism and identity became entrenched and shifted to a point of prominence. As a result, their answer to the mystery of the inclusion of the Gentiles became distorted. This comes through, often in subtle ways, in the Apostolic Scriptures as a number of figures challenge their hereditary presumptions.

A clear example can be found in Matthew 3:9 when John the Baptist said to the Pharisees: "do not presume to say to yourselves, 'We have Abraham as our father,' for I tell you, God is able from these stones to raise up children for Abraham." What we see here is that the Jews of Jesus' day, and no doubt in the centuries leading up to it too, believed that because they were the flesh and blood descendants of Abraham, they were guaranteed a

---

534 Gen 17:4-5

place in the world to come and exempt from judgement. Although a later document, the Mishna preserves this belief by declaring:

> All of the Jewish people, even sinners and those who are liable to be executed with a court-imposed death penalty, have a share in the World-to-Come, as it is stated: "And your people also shall be all righteous, they shall inherit the land forever; the branch of My planting, the work of My hands, for My name to be glorified" (Isaiah 60:21).[535]

John's response, however, is that God's judgement is coming, and that "one could not simply appeal to one's ethnic character or descent from Abraham to be exempted from it."[536] Moreover, as France suggests, it is almost as though John is attacking their pride by saying "even stones have more chance of being God's true people than they have."[537] And this choice of stones isn't arbitrary. Firstly, he is using a Hebrew pun as the word for stone *abanim*, which sounds like the word for children: *banim*. Secondly, Scripture often uses stones as a covenantal symbol of both God's people and as signs for covenants such as those between Jacob and Laban,[538] God and Israel,[539] and after Joshua crossed the Jordan.[540] And thirdly, he is using their appeal to Abraham against them. Tim Hegg in his commentary on Matthew makes this insightful comment:

> In a very real sense, Abraham and Sarah were as 'rocks' when it came to having children: Sarah had ceased having

535 M. *Sanh.* 10:1
536 Keener. C. *The Gospel of Matthew: A Socio-Rhetorical Commentary.* p.123
537 France. *Matthew.* p.112
538 Gen 31:44-46
539 Ex 24:4
540 Josh 4:20-24

> her monthly cycle, and thus was physically incapable of conceiving children. Yet the miraculous birth of Isaac was forever to stand as a witness that God's covenant children were the result of his mighty hand. [John] therefore cuts the ground out from under the Pharisees and Sadducees who claimed to stand on the basis of their own flesh (i.e., physical lineage) rather than upon God's miraculous and gracious favour.[541]

John the Apostle also seeks to correct their ethnocentric attitude in the prologue of his Gospel when he writes, "But to all who did receive him, who believed in his name, he gave the right to become children of God, who were born, not of blood nor of the will of the flesh nor of the will of man, but of God."[542] Here, it is explained that rebirth and regeneration are the product of God's grace in response to faith and not any heritage. As Dr. D.A Carson explains in his commentary, those who demonstrate their reception of Christ by their faith "enjoy the privilege of becoming the covenant people of God… heritage and race, even the Jewish race, are irrelevant to spiritual birth… New birth is… nothing other than an act of God."[543]

Jesus, likewise, challenges the presumptions of the Jewish people that their bloodline somehow gives them special privilege when it comes to a relationship with Yahweh. In John's Gospel we find that after Jesus offered freedom through faith in him, a group of Jews became insulted at the implication that they were slaves to sin. They replied, "We are offspring of Abraham and have never been enslaved to anyone. How is it

---

541 Hegg. *Matthew*. p.102

542 Jn 1:12-13

543 Carson. *John*. p.126

that you say, 'You will become free'?"[544] Those who know their history should realise that the Jews have indeed been in subjection to a long line of political powers including Egypt, Babylon, Greece and now Rome. It is therefore most likely that they are referring to spiritual freedom, especially considering Jesus' description of being a 'slave to sin' in the next verse. By asserting that they are Abraham's children in response to this, they are claiming that because of their lineage they measure up to God's moral and ethical demands. This attitude is preserved in Rabbi Akiba's teaching that the descendants of Abraham, Isaac and Jacob are sons, or princes, of the Kingdom.[545][546] In response, Jesus points out that their rejection of Him and His truth undermines this claim since, as Jesus points out, Abraham believed in Him and anticipated His coming.[547] Thus, "unlike Abraham, [these Jews] have no real heart for God, no sensitivity to his voice. Their 'father' must therefore be someone else",[548] i.e. the Devil. Thus, the point here is the same as in John's prologue; unless one's faith is genuine — since these Jews claimed to have believed, yet demonstrate the fickleness of their faith by rejecting Jesus' teaching — a connection to Abraham means nothing. This is a lesson that Paul would later make more explicit in his epistles.

As well as challenging the presumption that lineage from Abraham carried a special privilege when it came to a covenant relationship with Yahweh, Jesus and the Apostles had to challenge the Jewish exclusivism that came with this attitude. In the previous chapter, we looked at the portion of Scripture that described people dining with Abraham, Isaac and Jacob in

544 Jn 8:33

545 M. *Shabbath.* 128a.7

546 This attitude is challenged in passages such as Matt. 8:11-12, Mk 2:17 and Jn 9:40-41

547 Jn 8:56

548 Carson. *John.* p.352

the world to come. We will now consider the wider context of that passage. Prior to this teaching, Jesus had just encountered a gentile with great faith:

> When he had entered Capernaum, a centurion came forward to him, appealing to him, "Lord, my servant is lying paralyzed at home, suffering terribly." And he said to him, "I will come and heal him." But the centurion replied, "Lord, I am not worthy to have you come under my roof, but only say the word, and my servant will be healed. For I too am a man under authority, with soldiers under me. And I say to one, 'Go,' and he goes, and to another, 'Come,' and he comes, and to my servant, 'Do this,' and he does it." When Jesus heard this, he marveled and said to those who followed him, "Truly, I tell you, with no one in Israel have I found such faith. I tell you, many will come from east and west and recline at table with Abraham, Isaac, and Jacob in the kingdom of heaven, while the sons of the kingdom will be thrown into the outer darkness.[549]

In this story, a centurion, a gentile, demonstrates great faith in Christ's ability to heal. In response, Jesus *marvels*[550] at and commends his faith as greater than that of the Jews. He then goes on to talk about a great banquet where Gentiles would come and dine with Abraham, suggesting that "Jesus regards this exceptional Gentile as the promise of more Gentiles to come."[551] This story not only challenges the Jewish assumption that is the Messianic banquet a Jewish event, but also implies that those Jews who do

---

549 Matt 8:5-12

550 The same reaction (*thumazo*) the disciples would later have to Jesus calming the storm (Matt 8:27)

551 Keener. *Matthew.* p.268

not follow the Gentile's example will be excluded. As France explains, by including many people from 'east and west' (i.e. foreigners) and excluding those who assumed that they belonged (those hoping in their lineage from Abraham), Jesus flips their assumptions on the head. This is because one's 'invite to the banquet', a symbol of citizenship in God's Kingdom, "is found to depend not on ancestry but on faith."[552]

As the Apostles and early church sought to fulfil the Great Commission, which is the fulfilment of the Abrahamic blessing to all nations, they had to deal with this deeply entrenched, distorted, and nationalistic view of covenant membership. It was believed that entrance into the Covenant of Grace with God (justification), and inheritance in the world to come (salvation), was a Jewish affair. But, just as John the Baptist and Jesus challenged and deconstructed this belief, the apostles (Paul in particular) would also spend a lot of time challenging this Judaised Gospel. But before we unpack how this comes through in the Book of Acts and Paul's letters, it would be helpful to explain how this theology sought to answer the mystery of the inclusion of the Gentiles.

Works of the Law

The phrase 'works of the law' appears a number of times in Paul's letters, especially in Romans and Galatians. It is commonly understood to mean obedience to the Mosaic Law, which is true, but there's more to it than that. The Works of the Law is actually a part of a concept that belongs to a theology known as Covenantal Nomism.

Covenantal Nomism is the term coined by E.P. Sanders that describes a soteriology that was founded on the idea that salvation was dependant on

---

[552] France. *Matthew.* p.316

whether one was in the national covenant between God and Israel (Mosaic Covenant) or not. It is commonly argued that the salvation of the Jews was a 'works' or 'merit-based' soteriology, however, that's not quite accurate. Yes, the end result is similar, but the nuance is different since getting in and staying in was somewhat more complicated than mere obedience. The Jews believed that they are graciously elected into God's covenant people, as Christians do today, but the difference is that it was based on being descendants of Abraham, Isaac and Jacob. And indeed, Israel was a special nation and, as descendants of Abraham, they did hold a unique status. However, that did not mean they could presume on their connection to Abraham. Faith was always essential, and that genuine faith was to be demonstrated with obedience. Staying in, however, is where the works come into it. It was believed that in order to keep their covenant status, they must maintain obedience to 'works of the law.' And it was those who maintained their status in this way to the end that would avoid God's judgement and inherit a place in the world to come i.e. salvation.

These works of the law that had to be maintained were not simply Torah commandments. It was a sectarian term to describe the specific ways laws were to be applied and obeyed according to a particular group. It wasn't enough to keep the Sabbath, it was to be obeyed in the way that group defined it. What's more, is that each of the different groups of Jews in the first century believed that their interpretation of the Law was the right and proper interpretation. Failure to follow their teachings meant they were effectively disobeying Yahweh and excluding themselves from the covenant. Thus, by maintaining their 'works of the law', they maintained their group's status.

We find this concept reflected in one of the Dead Sea Scroll documents referred to as 4QMMT. The 4Q refers to the location of the scroll, and MMT is short for *Miqsat Ma'ase ha-Torah*, which is Hebrew for 'Some

Precepts of the Torah.' The document outlines a lot of sacrificial and ceremonial procedures, which are introduced by the author as "works of the law which we have determined... and all of them concern defiling mixtures and the purity of the sanctuary."[553] One such procedure was the banning of people who are deaf and blind from the temple proper, Because of their inability to see what they're doing or hear the instructions correctly could result in an error in their sacrifices and consequently defile the sacrifices.

What is interesting is that the group at Qumran who is behind this letter took a strong stance against Gentiles, forbidding the use of grain bought from Gentiles, stored in gentile vessels, and even Gentiles offering sacrifices. At the close of the letter is a reminder of God's coming judgement and a warning that disobedience to 'the Law' (as interpreted by them) will bring judgement. The author concludes the letter by exhorting its recipient with the following:

> Now we have written to you some of *the works of the Law*... Understand all these things and beseech Him to set your counsel straight and so keep you away from evil thoughts and the counsel of Belial. Then you shall rejoice at the end time when you find the essence of our words to be true. And it will be reckoned to you as righteousness, in that you have done what is right and good before Him...[554]

Thus, we see that this is what is meant by salvation by works of the law: belief that obedience in the correct way would maintain covenant status and bring justification and salvation.

---

553 4Q394. Frags 3-7 Cols 1-2 in Wise, Abegg, and Cook. The Dead Sea Scrolls. p.455

554 Ibid. p.462

The document's anti-Gentile attitude is reflective of the nature of Covenantal Nomism, works of the Law, and forgetting God's global purposes and vision. The works of the law that were emphasised most, as reflected in Paul's teaching in his letters, was on the sabbath, food laws and circumcision. This focus began during the Seleucid occupation of Israel in the Hellenic period between 332BC and 142BC when the Maccabees regained independence. The harsh persecution during the reign of Antiochus Epiphanes, targeted these elements of the Law, as well as Temple sacrifices, in an effort to make his empire of 'one people'. For example:

> Now the five and twentieth day of the month they [the Greeks] did sacrifice upon the idol altar, which was upon the altar of God. At which time according to the commandment they put to death certain women, that had caused their children to be circumcised. And they hanged the infants about their necks, and rifled their houses, and slew them that had circumcised them. Howbeit many in Israel were fully resolved and confirmed in themselves not to eat any unclean thing. Wherefore the rather to die, that they might not be defiled with meats, and that they might not profane the holy covenant: so then they died.[555]

In response, although a number are said to have given into the Greek pressure,[556] others, possibly inspired by the likes of Daniel, Shadrach Meshach and Abednego in Babylon, sought to solidify their identity as Israelites and God's covenant people. They did this both positively through obedience to Torah, and negatively by separating themselves from the

555 1Macc 1:59-63
556 1Macc 1:11-15

Gentiles. According to James Dunn, it is during this time that 'Judaism' first appears "as a protest against hellenizing pressure... that is, as a way of marking off the entity of Jewish self-identity from a Hellenism that had swamped and threatened to obliterate such national distinctives."[557] Thus, because the Jews were the only ones doing them, the food laws, circumcision and the Sabbath *became* an ethnic boundary marker for the Jews.

This is a belief and understanding that has remained to this day. I've heard many Christians claim that within the Law of God, "the moral Law" is for everyone, but the "ceremonial laws" were just for 'the Jews' to set them apart from the Gentiles. But this was never intended from the beginning. In fact, the Torah itself says the opposite. In the book of Numbers, after the Lord told Moses to teach the people what is required for each of the sacrifices, He goes on to say:

> And if a stranger is sojourning with you, or anyone is living permanently among you, and he wishes to offer a food offering, with a pleasing aroma to the Lord, *he shall do as you do*. For the assembly, there shall be one statute for you and for the stranger who sojourns with you, a statute forever throughout your generations. *You and the sojourner shall be alike before the Lord. One law and one rule shall be for you and for the stranger who sojourns with you.*"[558]

This passage reveals three key principles when it comes to the relationship of the Gentile to the Torah. The first is that it was anticipated that 'the stranger' (non-native born), would participate in the ceremonial practices that the people of Israel would. This is especially evident when the

[557] Dunn. "The Theology of Galatians." *The New Perspective on Paul.* p.174

[558] Num 15:14-16

Lord explains how "for the *assembly*, there is one law..." Implicit in the statement is the revelation that the assembly[559] would be consist of both strangers and the native-born, just as those who were standing at Sinai were made up of the descendants of Israel and the mixed multitude. Moreover, in Isaiah, we find the Lord explicitly inviting and encouraging Gentiles to participate in the Temple practices. Many Christians would be familiar with some of these words because Jesus quoted them when clearing out the money-changers at the temple:

> And the foreigners who join themselves to the Lord,
> to minister to him, to love the name of the Lord,
> and to be his servants...
> these I will bring to my holy mountain,
> and make them joyful in my house of prayer;
> their burnt offerings and their sacrifices
> will be accepted on my altar;
> for my house shall be called a house of prayer
> for all peoples.[560]

Some may try and say that this is spiritual, and try and allegorise it as a metaphor of Gentiles worshipping God. But the fact that Jesus applied this passage to condemn the money changers who were either exploiting or keeping the foreigners away from the sacrifices at the temple, shows a real invitation to participate. Likewise, the promise of the acceptance of their sacrifice tells us that these passages from Numbers and Isaiah had a concrete application while the Tabernacle and Temple were operating. Of

559 Heb: *qahal* – congregation, worshipping community
560 Isa 56:6-7

course, it reveals a deeper truth that Yahweh is not just for the Jews, but not at the cost of application to those for whom these words were written.

This also supports the second point, that the native-born were not of some special, distinct class. Why would only the literal descendants of one person be able to participate in the ceremonial aspects of God's covenant with humanity? This is why Yahweh said that 'the stranger and the native-born shall be alike before the Lord', and again in Isaiah, the Lord said: "Let not the foreigner who has joined himself to the Lord say, 'The Lord will surely separate me from his people.'" Both the native-born and the foreigner who calls on the name of the Lord have equal status, even during the Mosaic phase of salvation history.

And the third is that there were no Jewish laws and Gentile laws, rather, there is one Law for both. Repeatedly, the Torah explains that His commandments apply to both the stranger and the native-born.[561] In fact, that passage in Isaiah includes the Lord saying that He expects the foreigner to keep the Sabbath,[562] and Leviticus includes them in the observation of The Day of Atonement.[563] If the Torah is the standard for God's covenant people, and those people were made up of both the stranger and native-born, it makes no sense to create a racial division lest that body is divided.

I have heard some people make the rebuttal, especially in response to Isaiah 56, that 'those Gentiles became Jewish, so of course they were expected to keep the Sabbath.' If that were the case, why would these passages maintain the distinction between the stranger and the native-born? If they had lost their 'Gentileness' and become 'Jewish', then this wording is not only unnecessary but also inaccurate. Thus, it becomes quite obvious that no part of God's Law was ever intended to function as an ethnic

561 E.g. Ex 12:49; Lev 17:10, 18:26, 20:2; Num 19:10 See also Josh 20:9; Ez 14:7
562 Isa 56:4
563 Lev 16:29

boundary, but rather, a covenantal boundary to distinguish God's *qahal*, made of the native-born and the stranger, and the nations (those outside of His covenant).

This heresy of covenantal nomism that sees the eschatological inheritance only for those who 'become Jewish' and live out the 'works of the law' by observing 'Jewish distinctives' in Jewish ways is what Paul is battling in his letters. In particular, his letter to the Galatians. When we find Paul speaking negatively about the Law, it is important to understand that he was talking in the context of salvation. As Craig Keener explains: when Paul says we are not justified by Works of the Law, he of course meant "any [part] of the law, but the issues at hand were especially those issues that particularly defined one as having become Jewish – in Galatians, most prominently circumcision."[564]

The Judaizers

Because of the strong ethnic boundaries that were created by the Second Temple period Jews, and the belief that salvation was only for those within God's covenant with Israel, the answer for many Jews to the inclusion of the Gentiles was to change their ethnic status and make them Jewish through circumcision. What this means, therefore, is that when we read about circumcision in the Apostolic Scriptures, Paul isn't talking about the mere practice in and of itself. Rather, circumcision is a kind of synecdoche that refers to becoming a Jew and embracing the Works of the Law of one of the Judaisms of their day. One particular group that promoted this practice are the Judaisers we encounter in the Apostolic Scriptures.

[564] Keener. *Galatians: A Commentary.* np.

This term comes from the verb, 'to Judaise', which refers to "those Gentiles who chose to live their lives in accord with the ancestral customs and practices distinctive of the Jewish nation."[565] We find this concept used in Josephus' *Wars of the Jews*. He talks of one Metilius, a defeated Roman General, who, after "he entreated for mercy, and promised that he would turn Jew [*judaisein*], and be circumcised", had his life spared by Eleazer's men. Thus, Judaising is not the mere teaching that one needs to observe the Law, but the full embracing of a Jewish identity. Since, as discussed above, the Sabbath, Food Laws and Circumcision had *become* significant Jewish boundary markers by the first century, these practices were significantly emphasised.

It was this view of the relationship between salvation and ethnic identity that sparked the events of Acts 15. Because of their soteriology, these Jewish Christians were teaching: "It is necessary to circumcise them [bring them into the covenant so that Christ's work can save them] and to order them to keep the law of Moses [so that they can stay in]."[566] Because of their traditions, they genuinely believed that is what they needed to do for the Gentile converts eternal good. But, as Peter, Paul and Barnabas shared in their missionary testimonies of how they experienced the Gentiles receiving the Holy Spirit, they concluded that Gentiles are 'saved [i.e. brought into the covenant and experience its blessings] through the grace of the Lord Jesus' just as the native-born is. They also questioned why they would 'place a "yoke that neither our fathers nor we have been able to bear" upon them.'[567] Now, many believe that the Apostles are talking about the Torah here, and therefore conclude that it has no relevance for the Gentiles.

565 Dunn, J. *The New Perspective on Paul.* p.174

566 Acts 15:5

567 Acts 15:10

However, as we have already seen, this does not fit the Biblical text for three reasons:

1. The Law was not a division between 'Jews and Gentiles.'
2. Passages like Deuteronomy 30:11-14 and Psalm 19 show that the Torah was not seen as an unbearable yoke, and,
3. The very next verse says: "*But* we believe that we will be *saved* through the grace of the Lord Jesus, *just as they will.*" By contrasting the unbearable yoke with God's global salvation, it is evident that this yoke is the strict 'works of the Law' that the Judaizers believed they needed to keep for salvation. Peter was saying that the yoke of burden that they shouldn't place on them is the works of the law to 'make them Jewish' because Gentiles will be saved through Christ just as the Jews are.

As successful as the Jerusalem Council was at reaching a consensus that the New Covenant ratified by Christ was not just for the native-born, but available for both Jew and Gentiles, as evidenced by the experiences of the apostles and Scripture,[568] this was not the end of the matter. As hinted at above, several of Paul's letters deal with this ongoing conflict between Jew and Gentile and their place in the New Covenant; especially in Romans, Galatians and Ephesians. While an exhaustive commentary would be way beyond the scope of this book, I believe a consideration of two prominent passages of Paul's letters will be beneficial.

568 Acts 15:12-17

Case Study 1: Ephesians 2:11-19

The book of Ephesians is a letter that has the unity of the church as one of its major themes. In Chapter Two, Paul begins by describing how through the cross, Christ has achieved not only dominion over all creation, but also united the church in Himself as its head[569] after redeeming them by grace through faith from Satan, sin and death.[570] Following this, Paul then goes on to explain that one of the significant implications of this universal[571] salvation is unity. This transition and connection between the individual and corporate realities of salvation is a valuable reminder that Christ's work is bigger than getting individuals into heaven. Rather, by His blood, Jesus was bringing individuals from all the families of the earth, as promised to Abraham, into a united body.

As Paul writes:

> Therefore remember that at one time you Gentiles in the flesh, called "the uncircumcision" by what is called the circumcision, which is made in the flesh by hands—remember that you were at that time separated from Christ, alienated from the commonwealth of Israel and strangers to the covenants of promise, having no hope and without God in the world. But now in Christ Jesus you who once were far off have been brought near by the blood of Christ. For he himself is our peace, who has made us both one and has broken down in his flesh the dividing wall of hostility by abolishing the law of commandments expressed in

569 Eph 1:20-23

570 Eph 2:1-10

571 Universal in the sense that it involves all aspects of creation and people from all nations. Not universal in the sense of each and every person.

> ordinances, that he might create in himself one new man in place of the two, so making peace, and might reconcile us both to God in one body through the cross, thereby killing the hostility. And he came and preached peace to you who were far off and peace to those who were near. For through him we both have access in one Spirit to the Father. So then you are no longer strangers and aliens, but you are fellow citizens with the saints and members of the household of God...[572]

This passage of Scripture gives a comparison of Gentiles before and after faith in Christ. Speaking to Gentile followers of Christ, both those at Ephesus and even us today, he tells them to 'remember' their former status, to remember what life was like before God reached out and reconciled them back to himself. Perhaps the Gentiles, like those in Rome,[573] were boasting against the Jews about their inclusion and needed humbling. Or maybe, as the beginning of this passage suggests, the Jews regarded the Gentiles as inferior, second-class members of the body because they were uncircumcised. This is certainly a carryover from their history of occupation. Jonathan Klawans in his article on Gentiles in Ancient Judaism explains that during the Greco-Roman period there was an emerging attitude of the need to separate from Gentiles due to their moral impurity and a belief that they have a "lower, and more profane status."[574] Thus, Paul is encouraging the Gentiles by reminding them of their new status. However, it is quite possible that arrogance on both sides was present.

---

572 Eph 2:11-19

573 Rom 11:18

574 Klawans, J. "Notions of Gentile Impurity in Ancient Judaism." *AJS*. p.293

Although Paul depicts the Gentile's prior state through a variety of imagery and descriptions, they can all be summarised as alienation and separation. But in the interest of space and the scope of this book, I want to focus on just one aspect. And that is how the Gentiles at Ephesus, and all non-Israelites who follow Christ, were once *alienated from the commonwealth of Israel.* But what exactly does this mean?

To understand this, we need to focus on the Greek word for commonwealth, *politeia*, which is one of those difficult to translate words. Especially since our historical and cultural distance means that there is no true equivalent today. The term is used historically in four primary ways: a constitution,[575] an empire,[576] citizenship,[577] and an organised state and political entity.[578] Francis Wolff, however, gives a comprehensive definition of *politeia.* According to him, a *politeia* is the "overall project of common life, including programs of education, the organization of labor and leisure, moral rules, etc…"[579] Thus, *politeia* carries with it a strong sense of identity and culture that is not bound by geography. It was, in fact, the way that the Jews defined themselves throughout the Greek and Roman Empires. According to professor and author Aryeh Kasher, the Jews living in Alexandria sought "equal status between their own… politeia, and the politeia of the 'other Alexandrians'" as a way to maintain their national and religious identity.[580] This is because full citizenship and civil rights required the worship of the

---

575 "…it proceeds against the laws and the *politeias* (constitution) with wanton licence" (Plato, Republic, 4.424)

576 Josephus writes about Vespasian becoming the leader of the *politeia te Romaion* (Roman Empire). (Vit. 76)

577 "the Italian allies of the Romans were making efforts to obtain Roman *politeias* (citizenship). (Plutarch. Cato the Younger. 2.1)

578 Plato described a leader that is "unsuitable to our *politeia* (State). (Plato. Republic 3.397e)

579 Wolff, F. "*politeia*". Dictionary of Untranslatables. p.802

580 Kasher, A. "The Jewish Politeia in Alexandria." *Homelands and Diasporas*. p.120

state deities, which was incompatible for Jews. Despite being accepted as a part of the city, being their own *politeia* meant that they were still considered a distinct group. As historian Evanthia Polyviou explains, the Roman occupation of Alexandria resulted in a greater distinction between those of the Jewish *politeia* and the Alexandrian and Roman citizens than had existed under Greek rule.[581] Moreover, when Emperor Claudius restored the traditional and civic rights of the Jews and their status as a recognised *politea* in 41AD, which were taken away by Emperor Caligula, they were reminded that they were able to share with the Alexandrians a "great abundance of advantages *in a city not their own.*"[582] Thus, to be their own *politiea* makes them a group that is distinct in traditions, morals and religion from the surrounding *politeies*.

For Paul to write this letter with this understanding in the background, saying that the Gentiles were separated from the *politeia of Israel,* means that they had no place in the rights, duties and privileges that were given to Israel as God's covenant nation. A nation made up of the descendants of Abraham, whose King is the creator of the universe, and whose constitution is the Torah and Mosaic Covenant. In other words, the Gentiles collectively were isolated from the revelation of God in Scripture,[583] and more specifically, "the adoption, the glory, the covenants, the giving of the law, the worship, and the promises."[584] God was at work in the world through the descendants of Abraham, and many Gentiles (with some exceptions) were completely unaware.

---

581 Polyviou, E. "The Civic Status of the Alexandria Jewish Community in Ptolemaic and Early Roman Periods." *Anistoriton Journal.* p. 6

582 Letter to Alexandrians. 1. 95

583 Rom 3:2

584 Rom 9:4

After describing the Gentile's pre-Christ condition, he shifts his focus and goes on to explain:

> *But now* in Christ Jesus you who once were far off have been brought near by the blood of Christ... that he might create in himself one new man in place of the two, so making peace, and might reconcile us both to God in one body through the cross, thereby killing the hostility.[585]

Here, we see a reversal of verses eleven and twelve, where now in Christ, the Gentile's alienation has ended. No longer separated from Christ, they now have hope and reconciliation with God. But more than that, they have become a part of the *politeia* of Israel and partakers in the covenants of promise. As Paul explained, the Gentiles in Christ are "no longer strangers and aliens, but... *fellow citizens* with the saints and members of the household of God."[586] But it is too simplistic to merely say that Gentiles are now citizens of Israel. Rather, because of the blood of Christ, Jesus has united both Jew and Gentile to Himself, and consequently to one another as one *politeia* and one new humanity, 'killing the hostility' not only between people and God, but also between Jews and Gentiles.

It has been suggested that because Jesus has made one *new*[587] man, that the group is one that did not previously exist. However, the 'new' refers to not only the extent of intermixing of Jew and Gentile that had not been seen in the Tanakh, but also the restored and redeemed humanity that has become new creations in Christ.[588] This is emphasised in the way Romans 11 shows that the Gentile has been grafted *into* Israel: "But if some of

585 Eph 2:13, 15b-16

586 Eph 2:19

587 *Kainos.* See *Abraham and the Gospel*

588 2Cor 5:17

the branches were broken off, and you, although a wild olive shoot, were grafted in among the others and now share in the nourishing root of the olive tree..."[589] Notice that there is not the creation of a radically new tree, but rather a continuation with the pruning and expanding of the original tree.

There are some who read this portion of Scripture, in particular, verses 14-15, who will add to the way Christ brought the Gentiles in and achieved this unity between the two groups. But I believe that these verses have often been misinterpreted, leading to conclusions that are not consistent with the rest of Scripture.

The first way they add to the mystery is in their interpretation of the declaration that Jesus had "broken down in his flesh the dividing wall of hostility." A number of preachers and commentators when discussing this verse will say that this is a reference to the small wall in the Temple complex, as described by Josephus,[590] which was a fair distance from the Temple courts proper. It was almost like Gentiles being 'welcome at church', but they had to watch from across the street. And on this fence were 'signs' written in Latin and Greek warning the Gentile not to enter the sanctuary. The archaeological discovery of this inscription reveals that the penalty for crossing was death. And so, when applying this to Ephesians 2:14, they will say that this shows how God kept the Gentile separate from the Jew and covenant community, but they're allowed in now. As John MacArthur explains in his commentary,

> God had originally separated Jews from Gentiles... for the purpose of redeeming both groups... He placed the Court of the Gentiles in the Temple for the very purpose

---

589 Rom 11:17

590 Jos. *War.* 5.5.2

> of winning Gentiles to Himself. It was meant to be a place for Jewish evangelism of Gentiles"[591]

But there are some problems with this idea. The main one is geographical distance. It is unlikely the Ephesian Gentile Christian converts would have been familiar with this structure, but even if they were, the Greek term used for the wall is different to the one used by Josephus. It is most likely, as Best explains, not a strict reference to any particular wall, but rather a simple metaphorical symbol of division.[592] Another problem is with MacArthur's dispensational understanding of Jew-Gentile division under the Mosaic Covenant. Firstly, as we saw previously in many passages from the Torah, God did not separate the Gentile from the Jew in his covenant community. They were to be considered equal partakers in the covenant blessings and obligations. The third is that God did not create a distinct court for the Gentiles. There is no mention of it when Solomon constructed the temple according to the plans given through David. It was something added to Herod's Temple extensions because of Jewish hostility against the Gentiles.

So, the strong separation of the two groups was not part of God's design. In fact, it was in the Court of the Gentiles that Jesus cleared the temple and condemned the way Gentiles were being kept away. As he quoted from Isaiah, "my house shall be a house of prayer *for all nations.*"

However, some dispensationalists may read the following chapter of Ephesians and point to where Paul says, "the mystery of Christ, which was not made known to the sons of men in other generations as it has now been revealed to his holy apostles and prophets by the Spirit. This mystery is that the Gentiles are fellow heirs, members of the same body, and partakers of

591 MacArthur. *Ephesians.* p.77

592 Best. *Ephesians.* p.256

the promise in Christ Jesus through the gospel."[593] From this passage, they will claim that 'the equality of the Gentiles was a new revelation and reality, unknown in the Old Testament.' But as we have seen in the Abrahamic promises and the prophets, that is clearly not the case. The mystery is about the means. The mystery is *how* they became equal. As we saw in Ephesians 2:13, the mystery is that they are "partakers of the promise *in Christ Jesus through the Gospel.*" They knew it was coming, but they were wondering how. 'In Christ alone' is the answer.

The other way people add to the Gentile's inclusion is by claiming that another barrier between the Jew and the Gentile was destroyed. And that barrier is the Law, or more specifically for some, 'the ceremonial law.' In verse 15, Paul says that Jesus abolished "the law of commandments expressed in ordinances…" Many read that and say 'the Law kept Gentiles out because it was just for the Jews, but now that it's gone, Gentiles can come in.' Other times, it is claimed that this is a reference to the ceremonial aspects of the Law, such as the food laws, circumcision, and Sabbath… which were there to separate Jews and Gentiles. As we see in the words of John Stott,

> Paul's primary reference here… seems to be the ceremonial law… that is… circumcision (the main physical distinction between Jews and Gentiles…), the material sacrifices, the dietary regulations, and the rules about ritual 'cleanness' and 'uncleanness' which governed social relationships… They erected a serious barrier between Jews and Gentiles, but Jesus set this whole ceremonial aside.[594]

---

593 Eph 3:4-6

594 Stott. *The Message of Ephesians.* p.100

And Stott is not alone in this interpretation and understanding. Foulkes, for example, says that this passage teaches us that the Law, "as a code, 'specific, rigid, and outward, fulfilled in external ordinances'… and so serving to separate… was abolished."[595][596] From my experience, this seems to be an almost universal belief amongst Christians.

But two questions need to be asked and answered regarding this interpretation:

1. Is that an accurate interpretation of the purpose of the ceremonial law; and
2. Is that what the verse is even saying?

For the first question, as we saw earlier when discussing the works of the law, passages like Isaiah 56 show that the 'ceremonial law' was not there to separate Jew from Gentile; it was there to separate covenant and non-covenant members. In fact, there is no explanation of any 'ceremonial law' that says it served as an ethnic barrier. So, we cannot say that these commandments were used to create ethnic boundaries that now needed to disappear.

Regarding the second question, the Greek terms used in this verse strongly suggest that the Torah was not in mind when Paul wrote them. For it says, "abolishing the law of commandments (*entolon*) expressed in ordinances (*dogmasin*)." While *entolon* can refer to the commandments of God,[597] they can also refer to man-made orders and instructions. For example, after Jesus raised Lazarus from the dead, "the Pharisees had given orders (*entolas*)[598] that if anyone knew where [Jesus] was, he should let them know, so that they might arrest him."[599] Or when Paul gave an instruction (*entolen*) for Silas

595 Foulkes. *Ephesians.* p. 91

596 See also MacArthur. *Ephesians.* p.77-78

597 E.g. Matt 15:3, Mark 7:8, John 15:10

598 Singular form of *entolon*

599 Jn 11:57

and Timothy to come to him.[600] But in order to work out which meaning is intended, we need to consider the second word, *dogmasin*. This is the word from which we get our modern word, dogma, and refers to an opinion, or a decree, and is used in Scripture almost exclusively, to describe orders made from earthly rulers and leaders. Here are some examples: Luke 2:1 describes the 'decree (*dogma*) that went out from Caesar'; Acts 16:4 speaks of the 'decrees (*dogmata*) decided on by the apostles'; and Acts 17:7 says that Paul's opponents made a complaint he had disobeyed 'the decrees (*dogmaton*) of Caesar.' Outside of Scripture, Polybius wrote about the decrees (*dogmaton*) of the Roman Senate regarding the public distribution of money.[601] And in the Book of Maccabees, we read about Dositheus, a Jewish apostate who was described as "a renegade from the laws [*nomima*-lawfulness] and observances [*dogmaton*] of his country."[602] In this passage, the traditions and customs (*dogma*) are separated from the laws and commandments of Israel. The exception is found in Colossians 2:14 which uses it in a somewhat metaphorical way to describe how the crucifixion "cancelled our record of debt[603] that stood against us with its *legal demands*[604]."

Thus, in light of the context of the second half of Ephesians 2 about hostility between Jews and Gentiles, the lack of any Torah commandment that separates the stranger from the native-born, the promotion of the Gentile covenant member's equality with the native-born throughout the Tanakh, and the historical setting of first-century Judaisms, verse 15 is describing

---

600 Acts 17:15

601 Plb. 6.13.2

602 3 Macc 1:3

603 The record of debt, *cheirographon*, refers to notes, or receipts, that were written to show money had been loaned and needed to be paid back by a certain time (Tob 5:3).

604 In the Greek text, *dogmasin* (the legal requirements) is attached to the record of debt (*cheirographon tois dogmasin*), suggesting that this term is part of the metaphor of the debt of our sin towards God.

the eradication of extra-biblical, Pharisaic teachings and traditions, and not the Law itself.

These are the edicts and interpretations of the Law, shaped by their ethnic pride as descendants of Abraham, that aimed to keep the Jew separated from the Gentiles. These were no doubt founded on the emerging ideas written, for example, in the Book of Jubilees. There, Abraham is said to have told Jacob to avoid even eating with Gentiles.[605] In another place, the narrator extends the prohibition of intermarriage to all Gentiles.[606] Therefore, when Paul wrote about the ending of the "law of commandments expressed in ordinances", he was talking not only about the Rabbinic teachings and instructions that enforced in varying degrees separation between Jews and Gentiles. These unbiblical attitudes and practices had carried over into the New Covenant communities, including at Ephesus. And by saying they had ended, Paul was saying that such segregation has no place in the church. Hence, it was the Judaistic traditions that Paul was speaking of, not the ceremonial laws.

As we can see, Paul's purpose in this section of Ephesians is to explain the mystery of the inclusion of the Gentiles. This bringing together was achieved not by changing or annulling the Torah, nor was it by creating a whole new body of people after the crucifixion. Rather, it was reconciling both Jew and Gentile by faith in Christ through the Gospel. The theological significance of this is that the Gentile is no second-rate Christian, nor are they some novel new addition. Rather, Paul speaks of their common unity in Christ to end the 'wall of hostility' between Jew and Gentile. This unity was the picture painted in the Abrahamic promise of blessing.

---

605 Jub 22:16

606 Jub 30:7

Case Study 2: Galatians 2:11-21

Like the previous passage, Galatians is another part of the Bible that is often misunderstood because of a lack of awareness regarding the cultural background of this letter. As a result, Christians exegete certain passages with a narrow understanding of Works of the Law. This section of the letter that we will be focusing on is about Paul's confrontation with Peter, whose relationship with the Gentiles was contradictory to the Gospel.

> But when Cephas came to Antioch, I opposed him to his face, because he stood condemned. For before certain men came from James, he was eating with the Gentiles; but when they came he drew back and separated himself, fearing the circumcision party. And the rest of the Jews acted hypocritically along with him, so that even Barnabas was led astray by their hypocrisy. But when I saw that their conduct was not in step with the truth of the gospel, I said to Cephas before them all, "If you, though a Jew, live like a Gentile and not like a Jew, how can you force the Gentiles to live like Jews?" We ourselves are Jews by birth and not Gentile sinners; yet we know that a person is not justified by works of the law but through faith in Jesus Christ, so we also have believed in Christ Jesus, in order to be justified by faith in Christ and not by works of the law, because by works of the law no one will be justified.[607]

Those who reject the words in passages like Jeremiah 31 and many others which were covered in the previous chapter, and say that the Law has

---

[607] Gal 2:11-16

no relevance for the Gentile Christian, will no doubt come to these verses to support their claim. But when we look at what is actually happening in this passage and understand it in light of its historical and wider biblical context, we can see that the issue of Judaising, and pride in Abrahamic lineage as described earlier, is the issue at the heart of Paul's confrontation of Peter in Galatians 2.

What happened in Antioch is that Peter had succumbed to the social pressures forcing him to withdraw from eating with Gentiles. There is some debate as to where this event fits into the chronology of Acts, and whether Peter was personally opposed to eating with Gentiles. But when we look at the wording of Paul's account, we see that prior to this event, Peter was happy to eat with the Gentiles. This suggests a high probability that this took place after the rooftop experience and subsequent encounter with Cornelius in Acts 10. Hence, why Paul accuses Peter of 'play-acting'[608] by describing Peter as engaging in "conduct which masked and belied [his] genuine convictions."[609] Peter's motive, F.F Bruce suspects, was that those who came from James brought a warning that the militant Jews of the time would see his fraternisation with Gentiles as treason.[610] Paul's concern in this matter was that after Peter withdrew from eating with Gentiles, and other Jews followed suit, this separation gave the impression that Gentiles weren't fit for Jewish company, which is a contradiction of the Gospel.[611]

Often, I have found that people read Paul's words: "If you, though a Jew, live like a Gentile and not like a Jew, how can you force the Gentiles to live like Jews?", and interpret them to mean that Peter was telling

---

608 *Hyperkrisis*, from where we get our English word hypocrisy.
609 Fung, R. *The Epistle to the Galatians.* p.109
610 Bruce, F. *Commentary on Galatians.* p.130
611 Gal 2:14

the Gentiles that they have to conform to 'Jewish food laws' and other 'Jewish' customs. But as we have seen, the food laws — or any part of the Torah — were never Jewish, nor did they exclude Gentiles. Moreover, as we saw, Paul tells us that Peter's actions were inconsistent with his convictions, so he couldn't be saying this. In fact, Paul's use of Greek in verse fourteen suggests that instead of trying to get Gentiles to live like a Jew, he was inadvertently forcing them via social and theological pressure[612] to 'become a Jew', or 'to Judaize' (*ioudaizein*). This is the term we saw earlier that was used to describe the Roman General's circumcision to become a Jew. It was also used in the Greek translation of Esther to describe how "many from the peoples of the country *declared themselves Jews* (*iudaizon*), for fear of the Jews had fallen on them."[613] As Craig Keener describes, the Gentiles would perceive that in order to belong to "the in-group, the most committed gentile Christians would adopt circumcision. In the process, they would also alienate less committed gentile inquirers."[614] Thus, Paul's issue was a fear that the highly respected and well-known Apostle's actions gave the appearance of supporting the message of the Judaizers, promoting 'Works of the Law' as a means of salvation. This was no doubt familiar to the Gentiles in Antioch, and the same message the false teachers were spreading in Galatia. This, Paul says, is in contradiction to the Gospel. The Gentiles are not brought into the New Covenant, nor do they experience its blessings as promised to Abraham, by converting to Judaism via circumcision and observing 'Works of the Law'. Therefore, to deny even one of the 'families of the earth' access to the promise of blessing is to deny the Gospel. This is why Paul, as he does in Romans 3, goes on to say:

---

612 Compel: anankazo (Gk). (Keener. *Galatians: A Commentary.* np)

613 Est 8:17

614 Keener. *Galatians: A Commentary.* np

> ...we know that a person is not justified by works of the law [converting to Judaism and observing their interpretations of the law] but through faith in Jesus Christ, so we also have believed in Christ Jesus, in order to be justified by faith in Christ and not by works of the law, because by works of the law no one will be justified.[615]

This is a significant theme and message in the letter to the Galatians. Not to oppose good works or obedience to the law, but rather to dispute them as the "means of justification as opposed to faith in Christ."[616] When Paul denies 'works of the law', as interpreted by its historical context as a means of salvation, he emphasises the true message of the Gospel; that salvation and justification is by faith in Christ alone, not by becoming a Jew. Which, as Ronald Fung elaborates, is "a principle which applied to Jew and Gentile alike and hence was the basis of the Church's unity."[617][618] Being Jewish made no difference since, as we have seen, the testimony of Scripture reveals they are in need of salvation too. Hence, if the Gentile were to undergo circumcision to *Judaise*, it does them no good.

This is why Paul, almost sarcastically, uses the arguments and mind-set of the Judaisers to highlight their foolishness. He says: "But if, in our endeavor to be justified in Christ, we too were found to be sinners, is Christ then a servant of sin? Certainly not!"[619] Here, Paul explains that it is not a sin to eat with the uncircumcised, which Peter knew. The premise behind the accusation is that eating with Gentiles, (who in the Judaiser's mind were the only sinners), made those who are with them sinners too, which

615 Gal 2:16
616 Keener. *Galatians.* np.
617 Fung, R. *The Epistle to the Galatians.* p.126
618 Rom 3:9-10, 20, 27-30
619 Gal 2:17

is just absurd on both counts. By asking rhetorically, 'is Christ a servant of sin?', it seems Paul had two possible purposes. One is to show how this claim accuses Christ, who has united Jews with Gentiles by their common faith in Him, of making those He justified, sinners. The other is to remind Peter of how Jesus was likewise condemned for 'eating with sinners',[620] and is asking, 'will you accuse Jesus of being a sinner too'? The obvious answer being, no. In this event, Peter knew that eating with the Gentiles who had been brought into the Covenant of Promise by Christ, would not corrupt him and contaminate him. He had already learned this; he was just afraid of the consequences of such accusations. But Paul is reminding Peter, and other Jews who were led astray by his actions, of the truth and correcting any wrong ideas their behaviour may have communicated to the Gentiles.

Paul then goes on to explain why he didn't give in to the pressure from the Judaisers and withdraw. "For if I rebuild what I tore down, I prove myself to be a transgressor. For through the law I died to the law, so that I might live to God."[621] What Paul had torn down was not obedience to the Torah, but rather the 'dividing wall' of Ephesians 2; those cultural barriers that Jews put up between themselves and the Gentiles. Were he to reinstate those barriers, then he would be admitting to being a sinner by fellowshipping with Gentiles, as he had in the past, as well as actually disobeying the Law which allowed for the inclusion of the Gentiles.[622]

Paul's Jewish nationalism and faulty eschatology of 'Works of the Law' that he held to prior to his conversion, and was corrupting his understanding of the Gospel and the promise made to Abraham, was a major obstacle that God needed to eradicate in his mind. This He achieved by revealing His true Gospel to him. Moreover, it was also a major, and deeply

620 E.g. Matt 9:10-11

621 Gal 2:18-19

622 Keener, *Galatians.* np.

engrained obstacle in the minds of his ethnic kin, his missionary audience, and the churches he ministered to. Thus, this 're-education' was a significant mission for Paul, which is the goal behind a number of his letters. By understanding the truth of the Abrahamic promises, and recognising their references in the letters of Paul, we get a better insight into the depths of both the true Gospel message Paul proclaimed and the meaning and message of each of his letters. But more than this, we are given a greater appreciation of what that means for us who are beneficiaries of the Gospel which was built on the Abrahamic promises.

The Children of Abraham

What then does the relationship between Abraham and the Gospel mean for those who have believed the Gospel and put their faith in Christ? As we saw earlier in this chapter, those who were the literal descendants of Abraham saw their lineage as a point of pride and boasting, as though it granted them some special privilege with God. But that is not the case at all since, as Paul explained, the Abrahamic promises said that all the families of the earth would be blessed by their faith in Jesus Christ. So, what then is the Gentile's relationship to Abraham? Are we blessed by some trickle-down effect? Do we benefit from the Commonwealth's prosperity the way strangers living in a foreign land do? Or is there something more?

As discussed frequently through this section of the book, Christ is the means by which the nations receive the Abrahamic blessings of forgiveness, justification, reconciliation with God, and salvation. Faith and unity with Him are how individuals participate. And if Abraham experienced these blessings, then what is our relationship to Abraham? The Jews were somewhat correct that the Abrahamic blessings were for Abraham's offspring, but their understanding of what that meant was in error. And it is in the book of Galatians that Paul directly corrects this faulty thinking. Although we have already looked at this passage from the perspective of Abraham, our emphasis will now be on the perspective of believers in Christ. As Paul says:

> Does he who supplies the Spirit to you and works miracles among you do so by works of the law, or by hearing with faith— just as Abraham "believed God, and it was counted to him as righteousness"? Know then that it is those of faith who are the sons of Abraham. And the Scripture, foreseeing that God would justify the Gentiles by faith, preached the gospel beforehand to Abraham, saying, "In you shall all the nations be blessed." So then, those who are of faith are blessed along with Abraham, the man of faith... There is neither Jew nor Greek, there is neither slave nor free, there is no male and female, for you are all one in Christ Jesus. And if you are Christ's, then you are Abraham's offspring, heirs according to promise.[623]

These verses encapsulate the depth of what is meant by the common unity that the Jew and Gentile experience in Christ by His atoning sacrifice. What Paul is explaining here is that not only do the Jew and Gentile experience the same blessings, and that both are equally united in Christ, but that *all* of those who have their faith in Christ are considered sons of Abraham.

As explained previously, the Galatian Gentiles were told by the Judaisers that they could not belong to the Lord's people and experience the Abrahamic blessings apart from becoming a Jew by undergoing circumcision. But

---

[623] Gal 3:5-9, 28-29

here, Paul adds to his refutation of this idea by explaining that it is "those of faith who are sons of Abraham... [and are therefore] blessed along with Abraham..."[624] This is the message that inclusion "within the fold of Abraham's people... can be true only of those who are in corporate union with the seed, Christ"[625] by faith. Therefore, circumcision is not needed to participate in the Abrahamic blessings.

I touched on this idea at the beginning of this chapter when considering John 8. There, Jesus challenged his Jewish audience's claim to be sons of Abraham because their lack of faith in Him suggested otherwise. There, the idea of 'those of faith are the sons of Abraham' was being taught somewhat figuratively, but Jesus was also hinting at the deeper reality that Paul brings out in this passage. Paul's point here is that all those who have their faith in Christ join Abraham's true line of promise and blessing.

Having explained that covenant membership is not by bloodlines but by faith in Christ, Paul goes on in verse 28 to reject ethnic elitism within the covenant community as he did in Ephesians 2 and Romans 11. As Paul explained: "There is neither Jew nor Greek, there is neither slave nor free, there is no male and female, for you are all one in Christ Jesus."[626] This does not mean that our ethnicity or gender or social status somehow disappear, and we are to no longer consider them valid as though there has been an obliteration of our distinctions. But rather, that there is equality across those distinctions since when it comes to justification, those who have faith in Christ have a common standing before Yahweh. As Craig Keener explains, "Gentile believers are grafted into the patriarchal tree to become members of the covenant people, though Paul is still able to dis-

---

624 Gal 3:7,9

625 Silva, "Galatians", *CNTUOT.* p.807

626 Gal 3:28

tinguish them from 'natural' branches."[627] This unity in the one 'tree', as Romans 11 describes, is expressed in the phrase 'you are all one in Christ.' To be considered 'one' reveals that this mixture of men and women, Jews and Gentiles, and slaves and free men, who have their faith in Jesus, form a single, corporate unit. Moreover, according to Fung, "…it is this sense [of unity] which provides the necessary transition from the thought of Christ as the 'issue' (v. 16) to that of believers as the 'issue' (v. 29) of Abraham."[628] As Paul goes on to explain in verse 29: "And if you are Christ's, then you are Abraham's offspring, heirs according to promise." This is the conclusion to the idea that began in verse 7, namely, that being in the covenantal line of Abraham is about faith in Christ and not the literal genealogy that the Judaisers boasted in.

The reason why those who have faith, regardless of ethnicity, can call themselves Abraham's sons is because our faith unites us with Jesus, who Paul described, is the true 'offspring' and 'son' of Abraham.[629][630] As Fung elaborates on his earlier point: "since Christ is the true offspring of Abraham…, those who thus belong to Christ are collectively also Abraham's true 'issue,' and as such individually heirs in fulfillment of God's promise to Abraham."[631] Thus, by our faith in Jesus as the source of our justification, forgiveness, salvation, and reconciliation with God — the essence of the promise of blessing described throughout this book — we join the covenantal line of promise that began in Genesis 12. This is why in Romans, Paul explains that "Abraham… is the father of us all [who share in Abraham's faith in the Promise], as it is written, 'I have made you the father of many

627 Keener, *Galatians.* np.
628 Fung, *Galatians.* p.176
629 Moo, *Galatians.* np.
630 This book has discussed this designator earlier in the chapter, "*Abraham and Christ.*"
631 Fung, *Galatians.* p.176

nations.'"[632] Martin Luther, likewise, reflects this when he explained in his commentary on Galatians, "Through our faith in Christ Abraham gains paternity over us and over the nations of the earth according to the promise: 'In thy seed shall all the nations of the earth be blessed.'"[633]

To be a son of Abraham as described in Romans and Galatians is not being used as some kind of typological or figurative language, this is a literal adoption since the promises were made to Abraham's offspring. Therefore, to claim that one is a son of Abraham is to declare that they are "a bona fide covenant member with all of the privileges and responsibilities enjoined by the covenant...",[634] regardless of whether they are a Jew or not. In light of this, we can consider Abraham as the earthly father of the *ekklesia*.

---

[632] Rom 4:16-17

[633] Luther, M. *Galatians.* p.106

[634] Hegg, C. *Galatians.* p.165

Part IV
THE CONCLUSION

THE SO WHAT

...application is answering two questions: So what? And Now what? The first question asks, "Why is this passage important to me?" The second asks, "What should I do about it today?"[635]

Having read many books on various theological, ecclesiastical, and missiological topics, I have found many that lack a conclusion to bring it all together and clarify what they've been trying to tell me. I didn't want this book to be a part of that list.

Having spent about 100 pages discussing the relevance of Abraham to the Apostolic Scriptures, the person and work of Christ, the New Covenant, and the church, we need to ask the question: so what? Are these just interesting biblical patterns and theological concepts to impress people at Bible studies, or can they make a difference to the believer today? As we have looked at over the last few chapters, there is a lot that connects the modern, Western, follower of Christ, and the ancient Aramean called Abraham. We both have the same faith in the same messiah for the same promise from

[635] Veerman, D. "Sermons: Apply Within." *Leadership*. p.121

the same God, believing the same Gospel, and as Galatians 3 makes clear, belong to the same family and covenant. If this is the case, then the testimony of Scripture speaks against the popular idea that the church began at Pentecost.

Identity and Origins

To recognise that we have the roots of our identity connected to a promise 4000 years old can only deepen our understanding of who we as believers are. But when dispensationalists divide the Tanakh from the Apostolic Scriptures, they are separating us from the one Paul calls 'our Father,' robbing us of that identity. In a time when the church needs to be at its strongest and distinguish itself from the world, this is an identity that needs to be recovered. Not only does our recognition that we are children of Abraham build our sense of belonging to something bigger, but it also shapes and informs what it means to live by faith, and it can give us endurance in the midst of trials. This was the understanding of Paul and the other apostolic authors, and it should be ours too.

This identity can give us confidence in Christ, both in our immediate experiences and trials, but also when it comes to matters of eternity. As the author of Hebrews explains: "For surely it is not angels that he helps, but he helps the offspring of Abraham."[636] The verses that follow elaborate on the kind of help He provides his descendants.

> Therefore, he had to be made like his brothers in every respect, so that he might become a merciful and faithful high priest in the service of God, to make propitiation for the sins of the people. For because he himself has suffered

[636] Heb 2:16

> when tempted, he is able to help those who are being tempted.[637]

By making an indirect reference to Isaiah 41:8-10, the author is encouraging his audience that just as the sovereign Lord was a source of hope for his people in the days of the Babylonian Exile, his readers can find the same comfort in the face of their own difficult circumstances. And we who read these words today can likewise find the same comfort that the original audience experienced because of our ancient identity.

It is by virtue of our common faith in Christ that we are brought in and grafted into the line of Abraham, just as Ruth and Rahab were. It is because of Christ that the promise of descendants can explode into the global scale that the Lord intended when he declared Abraham would be the father of many nations. What this means is that because of our union with Christ, we don't merely belong to Abraham, but as we saw in our analysis of Ephesians 2, we belong to Israel too, especially since Israel are the descendants of Abraham. As Paul wrote in his letter to the Romans:

> But it is not as though the word of God has failed. For not all who are descended from Israel belong to Israel, and not all are children of Abraham because they are his offspring, but "Through Isaac shall your offspring be named." This means that it is not the children of the flesh who are the children of God, but the children of the promise are counted as offspring.[638]

Here, Paul is explaining that the true descendants of Abraham and the true members of Israel are not necessarily those who follow the bloodline.

---

637 Heb 2:17-18

638 Rom 9:6-8

Rather, the children of Abraham and members of Israel are those who, because of their faith, are a part of the faithful remnant and the 'children of promise.' To highlight this, Paul continues in the following verses by explaining through the example of Ishmael and Isaac, how Ishmael was not considered to be a part of the line of blessing, but Isaac was. It was the same with Jacob, later renamed Israel. He was chosen, but Esau was rejected. "As it is written 'Jacob I loved, but Esau I hated.'"[639] In both cases, being a descendant of Abraham did Ishmael and Esau no good. Rather, their share in the blessing was about the promise. Both these figures, and many others, serve as a kind of foreshadowing of all those who would become a part of God's people. As Paul says in Galatians, writing primarily to Gentiles, "Now you, brothers, like Isaac, are children of promise."[640] And it is these children of promise that makes up the true Israel.

The Church: True Israel

When talking about 'true Israel', it is important to clarify what I mean. This is a phrase that gets attached to all kinds of supersessionist, replacement, and 'transfer' theologies. For me, I don't use the term as though the Israel and people of God in the Tanakh were some kind of fake or temporary group until Acts 2 when the real Israel began. No. True Israel is and has always been the faithful remnant[641] of genuine covenant members.

Paul helps us to see the continuity of this group between the Tanakh and the Apostolic Scriptures through his teaching on what it means to be an Israelite in his discussion of the remnant in Romans 9. In verses 27-28, Paul quotes Isaiah as he writes:

639 Rom 9:13, Mal 1:2-3
640 Gal 4:28
641 Ladd. *New Testament Theology.* p.106

> And Isaiah cries out concerning Israel: "Though the number of the sons of Israel be as the sand of the sea, only a remnant of them will be saved, for the Lord will carry out his sentence upon the earth fully and without delay."[642]

Paul's use of this quote helps demonstrate the continuity of true Israel in a number of ways. The first is in his introduction of the quote. By using the present tense declaration that 'Isaiah cries out' to apply the passage to the Israelites of his day, Paul is, by extension, communicating that the 'faithful remnant' of today is part of the same group as in the Tanakh since Isaiah is still 'crying out'.

Secondly, by using this passage for his contemporary purposes, Paul's use of 'only a remnant will be saved' strongly implies that those who experience salvation by faith in Christ are a part of the same remnant and a part of the restoration of Israel.

And thirdly, the inclusion of the nations further supports its continuity. That this remnant is not ethnically bound comes four verses earlier when Paul speaks of God's calling, salvation and restoration. Paul writes:

> …in order to make known the riches of his glory for vessels of mercy… even us whom he has called, not from the Jews only but also from the Gentiles? As indeed he says in Hosea, "Those who were not my people I will call 'my people,' and her who was not beloved I will call 'beloved.'" "And in the very place where it was said to them, 'You are not my people,' there they will be called 'sons of the living God.'" [643]

---

642 Rom 9:27-28. cf. Isa 10:22-23
643 Rom 9:23-26

Here, the quote "Those who were not my people I will call my people..."[644] helps to show the continuity of the remnant of true Israel into the present day as it describes the inclusion of the nations into this remnant of Israel. For even the Gentiles who respond to the Gospel become a part of this remnant, further reinforcing what we have already seen, namely, that true Israel is comprised of both Jew and Gentile, gathered together in Christ into the 'one new man' described in Ephesians 2.

Paul elaborates further on the inclusion of the Gentiles in Romans 11 when he explains,

> I ask, then, has God rejected his people? By no means! For I myself am an Israelite, a descendant of Abraham, a member of the tribe of Benjamin. God has not rejected his people whom he foreknew. Do you not know what the Scripture says of Elijah, how he appeals to God against Israel? "Lord, they have killed your prophets, they have demolished your altars, and I alone am left, and they seek my life." But what is God's reply to him? "I have kept for myself seven thousand men who have not bowed the knee to Baal." So too at the present time there is a remnant, chosen by grace.[645]

Here, Paul is appealing to the Scriptures as evidence of the hope he has in the salvation of the remnant of Israel. This quote from 1 Kings 19 "speaks about this hope in the experience of Elijah: God's way with the prophet in the past reveals his way with Israel in the present. The former pattern is eschatologically repeated."[646] That Paul is using the prophet's experience to

---

644 Hos 2:23

645 Rom 11:1-5

646 Seifrid, "Romans." *CNTUOT*. p.668

explain the present is apparent in the way that he, again, employs the present tense when saying that 'Elijah… appeals.' This emphasises that God is continuing, 'at the present time' to build His remnant of the true and faithful Israel, which, as Paul later in the chapter goes on to explain, will include grafted in Gentiles. Douglas Moo explains this well when he says:

> It is possible that Paul also finds a parallel between Elijah and himself: each is a key salvation-historical figure, is confronted with the apparent downfall of spiritual Israel, but finds new hope in God's preservation of a remnant of true believers. For God's preservation of a remnant is not only evidence of his present faithfulness to Israel; it is also a pledge of hope for the future of the people.[647]

As we have seen in Paul's letter to the Romans, the true Israelites are those who genuinely belong to God by faith as a 'faithful remnant', not only from amongst those who merely have a place in the genealogical lines, but also from amongst the Gentiles. Just as Paul said in Ephesians; if you belong to Christ, then you are partakers in the promise,[648] and as he explains here in Romans 9, this makes you a true offspring of God, of Abraham, and a member of Israel.

As hinted at earlier, there are some who want to separate 'Israel' and 'the Church' saying that the latter is a 'new invention.' According to Charles Ryrie, "The church stands distinct from Israel, and did not begin until the Day of Pentecost, and thus did not exist in the Old Testament period." [649] To support his claim, he offers the following arguments:

647 Moo. *Romans.* p.677

648 Eph 3:6

649 Ryrie. *Basic Theology: A Popular Systematic Guide to Understanding Biblical Truth.* np.

1. There are passages that distinguish between Israel and Gentiles and the church (e.g. Acts 3:12, 4:8,10; 1Cor 10:32),
2. Before the resurrection, according to Ephesians 1:20, Jesus could not have been the head of the church, and therefore it could not have existed,
3. The united body of believing Jews and Gentiles was unknown in the Old Testament and was a mystery revealed only after Christ, and
4. Jesus said, 'I will build my church', not 'I will continue to build.'

How then are we to respond to these claims in light of Scripture?

Firstly, as we saw in the discussion on Ephesians 2 and especially Galatians 3, these distinctions are easily explained since ethic descriptors from birth do not disappear as both Jew and Gentile are brought into the one corporate unit. Moreover, the Apostles in Acts were often talking about 'natural Israel' as opposed to the surrounding nations. This does not contradict the idea that the church is True Israel since Paul describes it as the remnant that began long before the incarnation. As for the passage in 1 Corinthians 10, there Paul is describing two groups: the unbelieving Jews and Greeks from verse 27; and believers, which could be either Jew or Gentile, who make up the church.

Secondly, the pre-incarnate Christ, as the second person of the Trinity did a fine job ruling over Israel, and preserving His remnant well before John the Baptist arrived on the scene.

The third has been thoroughly disproven through this book. It was made known to Abraham that Gentiles would be blessed alongside his natural offspring. We also saw in the Exodus and the ongoing story of Israel, Gentiles and strangers being considered equal members of the 'congregation of Israel', and the prophets prophesying a great inclusion of the nations to come. Again, as discussed earlier in this chapter, the mystery is the how, not the what.

And fourthly, by Jesus saying that He will build his church, we are not to understand this as some exclusively 'New Testament' concept. Rather, as Ladd explains,

> The saying does not speak of the creation of an organization or institution, nor is it to be interpreted in terms of the distinctly Christian *ekklesia*... but in terms of the Old Testament concept of Israel as the people of God. The idea of 'building' a people is an Old Testament one.[650]

To see that Jesus is drawing on concepts from the Tanakh in the Gospels, consider the following verses:

> Then all the people who were at the gate and the elders said, "We are witnesses. May the Lord make the woman, who is coming into your house, like Rachel and Leah, who together *built up the house of Israel.* May you act worthily in Ephrathah and be renowned in Bethlehem,[651]

> I will set my eyes on them [Israel] for good, and I will bring them back to this land. *I will build them up*, and not tear them down; I will plant them, and not pluck them up.[652]

> Again *I will build you*, and *you shall be built*, O virgin Israel![653]

650 Ladd. *NT Theology.* p.107.
651 Ruth 4:11
652 Jer 24:6
653 Jer 31:4

> In that day I will raise up the booth of David that is fallen and repair its breaches, and raise up its ruins and *rebuild it* as in the days of old...[654]

What is interesting about this last verse is that it is an oracle that includes the restoration of Israel, which will include 'the remnant of... the nations,' and was quoted at the Jerusalem Council as such in Acts 15. What Jesus is suggesting is new, is that "...true Israel now finds its specific identify in its relationship to Jesus"[655] as the incarnated, crucified, and resurrected messiah. And that Jesus had the Gentiles in mind with regards to the ongoing building up of the people of Israel can be seen in the use of the word *church*, and the words of Peter about the purpose of the church.

The Greek behind the word church being used in Matthew 16, and elsewhere, is *ekklesia,* meaning literally 'the citizens who have been *called out* of their homes for an assembly.' Although political in its origin, the word is adopted by the Apostolic authors to describe those who have been *called out* from the world by Christ to belong to Him and glorify Him. This is the word used throughout the whole Apostolic Scriptures for 'the church.' But this usage did not begin with Jesus. When the Tanakh was translated into Greek, the word *ekklesia* was used for the word *qahal* meaning assembly or congregation, in particular, the sacred assembly. For example:

> I will tell of your name to my brothers; in the midst of the *congregation* (*qahal/ekklesia*) I will praise you.[656]

> Now therefore in the sight of all Israel, the *assembly* (*qahal/ ekklesia*) of the Lord, and in the hearing of our God,

654 Amos 9:11
655 Ladd. *NT Theology.* p.108
656 Ps 22:22

> observe and seek out all the commandments of the Lord your God.[657]

Thus, it is likely that when Jesus was speaking to the disciples, He said He would build his *qahal*, which the Gospel writers like Matthew later translated into the Greek *ekklesia.* For the disciples to hear this, they would consider it bizarre that Jesus was going to build a new *qahal.* Jesus speaks of this building in John's Gospel when He says:

> I am the good shepherd. The good shepherd lays down his life for the sheep. He who is a hired hand and not a shepherd, who does not own the sheep, sees the wolf coming and leaves the sheep and flees, and the wolf snatches them and scatters them. He flees because he is a hired hand and cares nothing for the sheep. I am the good shepherd. I know my own and my own know me, just as the Father knows me and I know the Father; and I lay down my life for the sheep. And I have other sheep that are not of this fold. I must bring them also, and they will listen to my voice. So there will be one flock, one shepherd.... My sheep hear my voice, and I know them, and they follow me. I give them eternal life, and they will never perish, and no one will snatch them out of my hand.[658]

This teaching of the Good Shepherd is a fulfilment of Ezekiel 34, where the Lord said after condemning the neglectful 'shepherds' over Israel:

---

657 1 Chr 28:8
658 Jn 10:11-16, 27-28

> I will rescue my flock; they shall no longer be a prey. And I will judge between sheep and sheep. And I will set up over them one shepherd, my servant David, and he shall feed them: he shall feed them and be their shepherd. And I, the Lord, will be their God, and my servant David shall be prince among them. I am the Lord; I have spoken.[659]

Thus, here Jesus is declaring Himself to be the good Shepherd over Israel, who will gather sheep from other flocks (Gentiles) and bring them into His fold (the *ekklesia*). The sharing of terminology between the Tanakh and the Apostolic Scriptures, therefore, emphasises the strong continuity between Israel and the church. The author of Hebrews further reinforces this continuity when they write:

> ...consider Jesus, the apostle and high priest of our confession, who was faithful to him who appointed him, just as Moses also was faithful in all God's house. For Jesus has been counted worthy of more glory than Moses—as much more glory as the builder of a house has more honor than the house itself. (For every house is built by someone, but the builder of all things is God.) Now Moses was faithful in all God's house as a servant, to testify to the things that were to be spoken later, but Christ is faithful over God's house as a son. And we are his house, if indeed we hold fast our confidence and our boasting in our hope.[660]

In this passage, we find a continuity from Moses to Jesus. In it, the author explains that Moses was appointed as a servant in 'God's house',

---

659 Ez 34:22-24
660 Heb 3:1-6

while Jesus is a son and heir over God's house. Here, while 'house'[661] can refer to a physical, literal building, it can also be understood as a 'household' or 'family'. The personal, relational language of 'we are his house' supports this understanding. Paul uses the same word in this way to describe the church when writing to Timothy: "you may know how one ought to behave in the household (*oikos*) of God, which is the church of the living God..."[662] Thus, what Moses was serving in his ministry to Israel as a servant, is the same body over which Jesus is the head. Richard Phillips in his commentary on this passage explains:

> This tells us there is a basic continuity between Old Testament Israel and the New Testament church... despite differences based on their redemptive-historical setting, Israel and the church are one. This passage exposes the error of dispensationalism, which sees Israel and the church as fundamentally different peoples in God's economy. The house in which Moses served is the house over which Jesus is Lord.[663]

This continuity can also be seen in the shared description of their role and purpose. Most notably, is Peter's description in his first epistle: "But you are a chosen race, a royal priesthood, a holy nation, a people for his own possession, that you may proclaim the excellencies of him who called you out of darkness into his marvelous light."[664] This is nothing short of a direct reference to Exodus 19, as discussed in the chapter *What is the Mosaic Covenant?,* as well as adding allusions from Isaiah 43, "I give water

661 Gk: *oikos*
662 1Tim 3:15
663 Phillips, R. *Hebrews.* p.86
664 1Pet 2:9

in the wilderness, rivers in the desert, to give drink to my chosen people, the people whom I formed for myself that they might declare my praise." By describing the church with Israelite terminology, Peter is revealing that the church is everything Israel was intended to be. The difference being, because of the empowerment of the Spirit as described in Jeremiah 31, the church collectively is able to fulfil that vocation. As D.A Carson explains, "Peter is... showing how he understands the true line of continuity to run from the people of God under the old covenant to the people of God under the new covenant."[665]

Just like Israel, the church has been redeemed by their saviour and brought out of slavery and exile. They are now priests who represent God to the nations as the light of the world proclaiming His excellencies, set apart from the ways of the world. They also offer spiritual sacrifices to the King, being a constituted people of one common Patriarch, Abraham.[666] Moreover, the church now lives out the vocational description given to Israel, the Torah, having it written on their heart and empowered to live it out.

Abraham, Mission, and The End

Since, as we saw earlier, Abraham's descendants, Israel, were to be God's representatives in the world, and we, the Church, are the true children of Israel, then we need to see ourselves as the fulfilment of all they were expected and intended to be. The church cannot see itself as some chronologically disconnected people. God did not replace Israel, nor did he put them on the shelf for a while; He expanded it. We, the church, are in a

665 Carson. "1 Peter," *CNTUOT* p.1032

666 The use of *genos* in Isa 43:20 (LXX), as used by Peter, is a reference to the children of Abraham (Carson, *CNTUOT*, p. 1030)

long line of God's special people that formally began with the calling of Abraham. And just as Israel was to be a light to the nations, that has not changed since our Lord Jesus was sent into the world to bring in all the families of the Earth.

This purpose is picked up in the Canticle of Simon, found in Luke's Gospel. While visiting the Temple for the sacrificial rites of purification[667] and the firstborn,[668] Mary and Joseph encounter a man by the name of Simon who was awaiting 'the Lord's Christ'. Led by the Holy Spirit into the outer courts, he sees Jesus and blesses God, saying:

> Lord, now you are letting your servant depart in peace, according to your word; for my eyes have seen your salvation that you have prepared in the presence of all peoples, a light for revelation to the Gentiles, and for glory to your people Israel.[669]

Here, Simon completes the Abrahamic expectation by picking up on the metaphoric purpose of Israel as a 'light to the nations', expressed in passages like Isaiah 46:6, fulfilled in this small child of humble, albeit divine, origins. Richard France elaborates on this point, explaining that the "inclusion of all nations in God's purpose of blessing for Israel was declared as early as the call of Abraham."[670] In fact, this fulfilment is a significant theme in the Lukian narrative, as expressed in Acts 1:8. As Christ's representatives, we are to continue that work, empowered by the Spirit from Pentecost, when the great expansion of Israel began. Just as Jesus commissioned the Apostles, he commissioned the church when he declared that, "you will

---

[667] Lev 12:3-4
[668] Ex 13:2
[669] Lk 2:29:32
[670] France, R. *Luke – Teach the Text Commentary Series*. np.

receive power when the Holy Spirit has come upon you, and you will be my witnesses in Jerusalem and in all Judea and Samaria, and to the end of the earth."

Thus, God fulfils His mission by calling Abraham, who was built into a *politea* and an *ekklesia*, united in Christ — whether by faith in the Messiah to come, or the Messiah who came — culminating in His eschatological purposes which began in the Garden and articulated in the Abrahamic covenant: "in you all the families of the earth shall be blessed." John describes this for us as he writes:

> After this I looked, and behold, a great multitude that no one could number, from every nation, from all tribes and peoples and languages, standing before the throne and before the Lamb, clothed in white robes, with palm branches in their hands, and crying out with a loud voice, "Salvation belongs to our God who sits on the throne, and to the Lamb![671]

Regardless of one's interpretational model of Revelation, this is a picture of God's Kingdom, filled with the redeemed sons of Abraham from all the families of the Earth who worship Him as one people. They are living as heirs of the New Heaven and Earth — a promise of land par excellence — experiencing the blessing of God's presence and free from evil, having been fully transformed into Christ's perfect image.

And here, having drawn the biblical narrative to a close, the Lord has fulfilled his narrative promises. The crowds rejoice, the people are free, and the enemy has been conquered. A celebration, on a scale greater than

---

671 Rev 7:9-10

George Lucas could ever portray following the final destruction of the Death Star. With greater joy than those who danced in the street at the end of World War Two. A greater fulfilment than what was accomplished after the destruction of the One Ring in the fires of Mount Doom. The singular narrative, beginning in the garden, the goal articulated in the calling of Abraham and worked out through the ongoing narrative until the end, cannot be clearer. What is the ultimate application of the fact of this singular narrative? It's simple. Remove the barriers that have been placed between Malachi and Matthew. Reject the distinctions that are made between Israel and the Church. Stick your Bible back together and recognise your place in this grand story of God's restoration. May the promises made to Abraham no longer be the Forgotten Covenant.

BIBLIOGRAPHY

Ancient Sources

Clement of Alexandria. *Stromata*. Trans. Roberts-Donaldson.

Euripides. *Phoenissae*. Trans. E. P. Coleridge (1938).

Eusebius. *Ecclesiastical History, Volume I: Books 1-5*. Trans. Kirsopp Lake. Loeb Classical Library 153. Harvard University Press: Cambridge (1926)

Justin. *Dialogue with Trypho the Jew.* Trans. Marcus Dods and George Reith. Christian Literature Publishing Co: NY (1885).

Josephus. *The Life. Against Apion*. Translated by H. St. J. Thackeray. Loeb Classical Library 186. Cambridge, MA: Harvard University Press, (1926).

Philo. *On Moses.* Trans F. Colson. Loeb Classical Library: Cambridge (1935)

The Gospel of Thomas. Trans. Lambdin, Grenfell, Hunt and Layton. https://www.sacred-texts.com/chr/thomas.htm

Select Papyri II [Loeb Classical Library] (ed. A.S.Hunt and G.C. Edgar) (1934), pp. 78-89, adapted

Modern Sources

Alexander, T. "The Composition of the Sinai Narrative in Exodus XIX 1-XXIV 11." *Vetus Testamentum*. XLIX. (1999)

Avalos, H. "Circumcision as a Slave Mark." *Perspectives in Religious Studies*. 1/42 (2015): 259-274.

Balla, P. "2 Corinthians." *Commentary on the New Testament use of the Old Testament*. Ed. G. Beale and D. Carson. Baker: Grand Rapids (2007): 753-784.

Barrick, W. "The Mosaic Covenant." *TMSJ*. 10/2 (1999). p213-232.

Berg, C. "Election Promises are there for the Breaking." a*bc.net.au* http://www.abc.net.au/news/2014-04-22/berg-election-promises-are-there-for-the-breaking/5403160

Barnett, P. *The Second Epistle to the Corinthians – NICNT*. Eerdmans: Grand Rapids (1997).

Best, E. *Ephesians – International Critical Commentary*. T&T Clark: London (2006).

Boice, J. *Joshua*. Baker Books: Grand Rapids (1989).

Bruce, F. *The Epistle to the Galatians*. Eerdmans: Grand Rapids (1982).

Cameron, A. "Learning Lessons from Indiana Jones 4." *andrewcameron.com* 16 Mar 2016.
https://andrewrcameron.com/2016/03/16/learning-lessons-from-indiana-jones-4/

Campbell, J. *The Hero with a Thousand Faces*. New World Library: Novato (2008).

Calvin, J. *The Book of Joshua. The John Calvin Bible Commentaries*. trans. H. Beveridge. Jazzybee Verlag: Altenmunster (2017)

Carson, D. *The Gospel According to John*. IVP: Leicester (1991).

_______ *The Difficult Doctrine of the Love of God*. IVP: Nottingham (2000)

_______ "1 Peter." *Commentary on the New Testament use of the Old Testament*. Ed. G. Beale and D. Carson. Baker: Grand Rapids (2007): 1015-1046.

Chafer, L. "Inventing Heretics through Misunderstanding." *Biblioteca Sacra* 102 (1945). p. 1-5.

_______ *Systematic Theology Vol. IV*. Dallas Seminary Press: Dallas (1947).

Childs, B. *The Book of Exodus*. Westminster John Knox Press: Louisville (2004).

Christensen, D. *Deuteronomy 1:1-21:9, Vol 6A*. Word Biblical Commentary. Zondervan. Kindle Edition (2001).

_______ *Deuteronomy 21:10-34:12, Vol 6B*. Word Biblical Commentary. Zondervan. Kindle Edition (1997).

Craigie, P. *The Book of Deuteronomy – NICOT*. Eerdmans: Grand Rapids (1976).

Davis, J. "Who are the Heirs of the Abrahamic Covenant." *ERT*. 2 (2005): 149-163.

Dumbrell, W. *Covenant and Creation*. Paternoster: Milton Keynes (2013).

Dunn, J. "The New Perspective on Paul (1983)." *The New Perspective on Paul*. Eerdmans: Grand Rapids (2008): 99-120.

_______ "The Theology of Galatians: The Issue of Covenantal Nomism (1991)." *The New Perspective on Paul*. Eerdmans: Grand Rapids (2008): 173-192.

_______ "How New was Paul's Gospel? The Problem of Continuity and Discontinuity (1994)." *The New Perspective on Paul*. Eerdmans: Grand Rapids (2008): 247-264.

Enns, P. *Exodus: The NIV Application Commentary*. Zondervan: Grand Rapids (2000).

Erickson, M. *Christian Theology*. Baker: Grand Rapids (2009).

Essex, K. "The Abrahamic Covenant." *TMSJ*. 10/2 (1999): 191-212.

Foulkes, F. *Ephesians*. IVP: Downers Grove (1984).

Fretheim, T. *Exodus*. Knoxville Press: Louisville (1991).

France, R. *Matthew*. Eerdmans: Grand Rapids (1985).

_______ *Luke – Teach the Text Commentary Series*. Baker: Grand Rapids (2013).

Fuller, D. *Gospel and Law: Contrast or Continuum? The Hermeneutics of Dispensationalism and Covenant Theology*. Eerdmans: Grand Rapids (1980).

Fung, R. *The Epistle to the Galatians – NICNT*. Eerdmans: Grand Rapids (1988).

Goldingay, J. "The Significance of Circumcision." *JSOT*. 88 (2000): 3-18.

Gopnik, A. "Are Liberals on the Wrong Side of History?" *newyorker.com* 20 Mar 2017. https://www.newyorker.com/magazine/2017/03/20/are-liberals-on-the-wrong-side-of-history

Griffiths, P. *Covenant Theology: A Reformed Baptist Perspective*. WIPF: Eugene (2016).

Grudem, W. *Systematic Theology*. IVP: Nottingham (1994).

Guthrie, G. *2 Corinthians*. Baker: Grand Rapids (2015).

Guttmann, A. "The End of the Jewish Sacrificial Cult." *Hebrew Union College Annual* 38 (1967): 137-148

Hafemann, S. "Paul, Moses, and the History of Israel: The Letter/Spirit Contrast and the Argument from Scripture in 2 Corinthians 3." *WUNT* 81 (1995).

Hamilton, V. *Exodus: An Exegetical Commentary*. Baker: Grand Rapids. (2011).

Hanson, R. "Yes, Tax Lax Ideas." *Overcomingbias.com* 14 Mar. 2009. http://www.overcomingbias.com/2009/03/yes-tax-ideas.html

Harrison "Genealogy." *The International Standard Bible Encyclopedia - Vol 2:E-J*. Eerdmans: Grand Rapids (1979): 424-428

Hegg, T. *Balaam – Prophet or Sorcerer?* Torah Resource: Tacoma (2005).

_______ *The Balaam Oracles*. Torah Resource: Tacoma (2005).

_______ *Genesis: Studies in the Torah Vol. 1*. Torah Resource: Tacoma (2010).

_______ *Exodus: Studies in the Torah Vol. 2*. Torah Resource: Tacoma (2014).

_______ *Deuteronomy: Studies in the Torah Vol. 5*. Torah Resource: Tacoma (2016).

House, P. *Old Testament Theology*. IVP: Downers Grove (1998).

Hubbard, M. *2 Corinthians – Teach the Text Commentary Series*. Baker: Grand Rapids (2017).

Hubbard, R. *Joshua: The NIV Application Commentary*. Zondervan: Grand Rapids (2009).

Jeffrey, S, Ovey, M, Sach, A. *Pierced for our Transgressions*. IVP: Nottingham. (2007).

Jones, P. *Quid Pro Quo: What the Romans Really gave the English Language*. Atlantic: London (2016).

Kaiser, W. *Toward an Old Testament Theology*. Zondervan: Grand Rapids (1978).

_______ "God's Promise Plan and his Gracious Law." *Journal of the Evangelical Theological Society* 33 (Sept 1990): 294.

_______ *The Promise Plan of God*. Zondervan: Grand Rapids (2008).

Kasher, Aryeh. "The Jewish Politeuma in Alexandria: A Pattern of Jewish Communal Life in the Greco-Roman Diaspora." *Homelands and Diasporas: Greeks, Jews and their Migrations*. Ed. M. Rozen. Bloomsbury: New York (2008). p. 109-125

Keener, C. *The Gospel of Matthew - A Socio-Rhetorical Commentary.* Eerdmans: Grand Rapids (2009).

_______ *Galatians: A Commentary*. Baker: Grand Rapids (2019).

Keller, T. "Abraham and the Torch." Redeemer Presbyterian Church, 3 Nov 1996.

_______ "Dr. Timothy Keller at the March 2013 Faith Angle Forum." EPPC: https://eppc.org/publications/dr-timothy-keller-at-the-march-2013-faith-angle-forum/

Klawans, J. "Notions of Gentile Impurity in Ancient Judaism." *AJS* 2(1995). p285-312

Klooster, F. "The Biblical Method of Salvation: A Case for Continuity," *Continuity and Discontinuity*. Ed. John Feinberg. Crossway: Westchester (1988). Accessed on books.google.com.

Kostenberger, A. "John". *Commentary on the New Testament use of the Old Testament.* Baker: Grand Rapids (2007): 415-512.

Ladd, G. *A Theology of the new Testament*. Eerdmans: Grand Rapids (1993).

Lasor, W, Hubbard, D, and Bush, F. *Old Testament Survey*. Eerdmans: Grand Rapids (1996).

Levine, B. "The Deir Alla Plaster Inscriptions." *Journal of the American Oriental Society.* 101/2, (1981): 195-205

Luther, M. *Commentary on the Epistle to the Galatians*. Trans. T. Graebner.

MacArthur, J. *Ephesians*. Moody: Chicago (1986).

_______ *2 Corinthians*. Moody: Chicago (2003).

_______ *The MacArthur Bible Commentary.* Thomas Nelson: Nashville (2005).

MacDonald, W. *Believer's Bible Commentary*. Thomas Nelson: Nashville (2016).

Mathews, K. *Genesis 11:27-50:26 – New American Commentary*. Bradman and Holman: Nashville (2005).

Markovitz, J. "Reel Terror Post 9/11." *Film and Television after 9/11.* Southern Illinois University Press: Carbondale (2004): 201-225.

Marano, Hara. "Our Brain's Negative Bias." *psychologytoday.com* 9 June 2016. https://www.psychologytoday.com/au/articles/200306/our-brains-negative-bias

McComiskey, T. *The Covenants of Promise: A Theology of the Old Testament Covenants.* Grand Rapids: Baker (1985).

Moo, D. *The Epistle to the Romans - NICNT.* Eerdmans: Grand Rapids (1996).

_______ *Galatians - Baker Exegetical Commentary on the New Testament.* Baker: Grand Rapids (2013).

Mounce, R. *The Book of Revelation – NICNT.* Eerdmans: Grand Rapids (1998).

Noth, M. *Numbers.* Westminster Press: Philadelphia (1968).

Olson, D. *Numbers.* Westminster Press: Louisville (2012).

Osborne, G. *Revelation.* Baker: Grand Rapids (2002).

Pau, D & Schnabel, E. "Luke." *Commentary on the New Testament use of the Old Testament.* Ed. G. Beale and D. Carson. Baker: Grand Rapids (2007): 251-414.

Pétry F., C. *Measuring How Political Parties Keep Their Promises: A Positive Perspective from Political Science.* In: Imbeau L. (eds) Do They Walk Like They Talk?. Studies in Public Choice, vol 15. Springer, New York, NY (2009): 65-80.

Phillips, R. *Hebrews – Reformed Expository Commentary.* P&R: Phillipsburg (2006).

Piper, J. "The Covenant of Abraham." *desiringgod.org.* 18 Oct. 1981. https://www.desiringgod.org/messages/the-covenant-of-abraham

Polyviou, E. "The Civic Status of the Alexandria Jewish Community in Ptolemaic and Early Roman Periods." *Anistoriton Journal*, 13 (2013). p1-15.

Ryrie, C. *Dispensationalism Today*. Moody Press: Chicago (1965).

_______ *Basic Theology*. Moody: Chicago (1999)

_______ *Dispensationalism*. Moody Press: Chicago (2007)

Sarna, N. *Exodus*. JPS (1991).

Seltzer, L. "9 Reasons it's so easy to be Misunderstood." p*sychologytoday.com*. 3 Sept 2014. Accessed: https://www.psychologytoday.com/us/blog/evolution-the-self/201409/9-reasons-its-so-easy-be-misunderstood

Seifrid, M. "Romans." *Commentary on the New Testament use of the Old Testament*. Ed. G. Beale and D. Carson. Baker: Grand Rapids (2007): 607-694.

Sherwood, A. "The Mixed Multitude in Exodus 12:38: Glorification, Creation, and Yhwh's Plunder of Israel and the Nations." *HBTH* 34. (2012): 139-154.

Silva, M. "Galatians". *Commentary on the New Testament use of the Old Testament*. Baker: Grand Rapids (2007): 785-812

Sproul, RC. The Covenant. Sermon, St Andrews Chapel in Orlando, Florida, 26 Feb 2017.

Spurgeon, CH. "Commentary on Genesis 15:4". *Spurgeon's Verse Expositions of the Bible*. https://www.studylight.org/commentaries/spe/genesis-15.html. 2011.

Stanley, A. *Irresistable: Reclaiming the New that Jesus Unleashed for the World*. Zondervan: Grand Rapids (2018).

Stott, J. *The Message of Ephesians*. IVP: Nottingham. (2000).

Stuart, D. *Exodus – The New American Commentary*. B&H: Nashville (2006).

Swindoll, C. *Abraham*. Tyndale: Carol Stream (2014).

Thompson, J. "OT Covenant." *The International Standard Bible Encyclopedia - Vol 1:A-D*. Eerdmans: Grand Rapids (1979): 790-793.

Van Harn, R, Strawn, B. *Psalms for Preaching and Worship – A Lectionary Commentary*. Eerdmans: Grand Rapids (2009).

Veerman, D. "Sermons: Apply Within," *Leadership* 11 (1990): 121–122.

Walton, J. *Genesis - The NIV Application Commentary*. Zondervan: Grand Rapids (2001)

Walvoord, John. "Millennial Series: Part 12: The Abrahamic Covenant and Premillennialism." *Walvoord.com*. Accessed 2 Feb 2019: https://walvoord.com/article/49

Warren, R. *All the King's Men*. Harcourt, Inc.: Orlando (2006)

Webb, J and Kysar, R. *Greek for Preachers*. Chalice: St Lewis (2002).

Weinfeld, M. "The Covenant of Grant in the Old Testament and in the Ancient Near East." *Journal of the American Oriental Society*. 90/2, 1970. p184-203.

White, J. "Acts 2:39 in Context, Interpreted, Applied." *Alpha and Omega Ministries*. www.aomin.org/aoblog/uncategorized/acts-239-in-context-interpreted-applied/

Wise, M, Abegg, M, and Cook, E. *The Dead Sea Scrolls – A New Translation*. Harper One: New York. (2005)

Wolff, F. "Polis, Politeia." *Dictionary of Untranslatables: A Philosophical Lexicon*. Ed. B. Cassin. Princeton. Oxford Reference Online. (2017).

Woudstra, M. *The Book of Joshua – NICOT*. Eerdmans: Grand Rapids (1981).

Wright, N.T, *Justification: God's Plan and Paul's Vision*. Kindle, SPCK (2009).

_______ *The Day the Revolution Began*. Harper One: New York (2016).

ABOUT THE AUTHOR

Ryan Watson is passionate about encouraging believers in their faith as well as helping them build good theology from a whole of Scripture understanding of the Bible. He has both a Bachelor of Ministry and a Master of Arts in Theology after studying under the Australian College of Theology at Malyon College in Brisbane, Australia. He has experience in preaching, teaching and has served as a Youth Pastor. At the University of Queensland, he studied a Bachelor of Arts with majors in Ancient and Modern History and English, and completed a Graduate Diploma in Secondary Education.

As well as self-publishing his first book *Why then the Law?*, he has written a number of blog articles and published essays on academia.edu. Ryan lives in Brisbane, Australia with his wife and four boys, and works as a High-School English teacher.

www.ingramcontent.com/pod-product-compliance
Lightning Source LLC
Chambersburg PA
CBHW071405090426
42737CB00011B/1357

* 9 7 8 0 6 4 5 1 4 1 7 9 5 *